D0997594

100
COMPUTER
GAMES TO
PLAY BEFORE
YOU DIE

100
COMPUTER GAMES TO PLAY BEFORE YOU DIE

STEVE BOWDEN

JOHN BLAKE

Published by John Blake Publishing Ltd,
3 Bramber Court, 2 Bramber Road,
London W14 9PB, England

www.johnblakepublishing.co.uk

First published in paperback in 2010

ISBN: 978 184358 309 7

British Library Cataloguing-in-Publication Data:

A catalogue record for this book is available from the British Library.

Design by www.envydesign.co.uk

Printed in Great Britain by CPI Bookmarque, Croydon, CRO 4TD

1 3 5 7 9 10 8 6 4 2

Papers used by John Blake Publishing are natural, recyclable
products made from wood grown in sustainable forests.
The manufacturing processes conform to the environmental
regulations of the country of origin.

INTRODUCTION

ONE HUNDRED IS a very small number. A tiny number, even, in the grand scheme of things. So just how do you go about condensing as wide-reaching an industry as the video-game trade into 100 game examples? With great difficulty.

Trying to narrow down the thousands upon thousands of games throughout the years to just 100 picks to play before you shuffle off this mortal coil depends largely on how you approach your selection. Do you choose the most important games through time – the *firsts*, as it were – or simply the best ones? The most popular titles or the under-appreciated experiences?

Balance is the key. This book is a mixture of all the above because there's no single definition good enough to satisfy all cases. Picking the 100 *best* games from history is going to result in multiple entries from a few long-running series such as the *Mario* titles and *The Legend of Zelda*. That would make for one dull read, which is why the entries that follow conform to a one-per-series rule unless said series has a few radically different gaming experiences living under the naming umbrella.

Listing only the groundbreaking titles, meanwhile, would mean including games which have no place in today's world. The truth is you don't need to play ancient titles like *OXO*, *Tennis for Two* or *Spacewar!* to gain a deeper appreciation for the industry. You can learn all you need to learn by watching them in action on YouTube. By and large, games are getting better every year. Not because of prettier graphics, but because large development teams and increasingly powerful hardware consistently deliver experiences never before possible. The games we play are wholly dependent on the hardware they run on, and, though there are plenty of standout exceptions ahead, better computers and consoles generally make for better games.

With that in mind, I'm delighted to present a list of classics and modern hits, compiled to give any new gamer an exciting peek at the ever-evolving interactive entertainment industry. From the dependable greats to the quirky niche projects, these are the games you *need* to play before you die. And after the last one is finished there are thousands more gaming gems waiting to be discovered and enjoyed. The world of games is wide. It would be a shame to stop at 100.

Luckily, there's never been a better time to jump back into some of the older classics. Unlike movies and music, gaming's dependence on hardware is total. When the hardware is replaced, so too are the games and, outside of illegal emulations, the majority of titles are forever lost to time. But the current generation has seen a retro revival of sorts, and ancient classics are being reworked and re-released on newer consoles. Sadly, there are still a few titles in this collection that will prove tough to track down, but the task would have been doubly hard just a few years ago prior to the launch of the Virtual Console, PlayStation Network and Xbox Live Arcade services.

So, whether you're about to embark on your first gaming adventures or you're a long-time gamer looking to revisit past conquests or discover new experiences, I wish you many happy gaming months ahead. Thank you for taking this journey with me. I hope you find what you're looking for.

Steve Bowden

AUTHOR'S NOTE

Computer games are often ported to different platforms, but these ports can often be a bit iffy. I have endeavoured to suggest the best platform on which to play each game. In the event that the UK release date differed from the worldwide release date, the latter is indicated in brackets.

☗ ☗ ☗

ANIMAL CROSSING: WILD WORLD

**Release date: 2005 (2006) | Platform: Nintendo DS |
Developer: Nintendo**

A TYPICAL DAY in *Animal Crossing* involves reading and replying to the mail, checking the town noticeboard for any new announcements, digging up some dinosaur fossils and donating them to the museum, stockpiling some wild fruit, a spot of fishing, perusing the local store to see what rare items they have in stock, running a few errands for the neighbours and grabbing a coffee from the café for a chinwag with the waiter. A little work, a lot of play and ample opportunities for a quiet stroll: life in *Animal Crossing* sure is relaxing.

Wild World isn't a game about high scores or scoring goals or killing enemies. It's about living a day-to-day life, and in particular it's about companionship. Socialising with others – be they real friends over an internet connection or computer-controlled replacements – takes precedence. There is no aim in *Animal Crossing* other than to have a good time, and if you can make a few friends along the way so much the better.

Earning bigger houses and landscaping your town to turn it into a paradise is a by-product of life in *Animal Crossing*. When you arrive in the hamlet, you have barely a bell (the game's currency) in your pocket, but store owner Tom Nook gives you a home, a job and a uniform, the latter two to pay off the loan for the former. It's not long before you're planting flowers and pulling up weeds and bumping into all the residents.

The game randomly chooses a handful of animals to move into your town from a giant pool of potential neighbours. Sending them gifts, regularly visiting them for talks and contributing to the town's upkeep ensures that they stay happy; ignoring them tends to nark them off. Happy residents usually stay put, unhappy ones soon pack up their bits and move off to another town never to be seen again – especially heartbreaking if it's a resident you get on with and have tried to make feel welcome.

Because everybody's game is a completely different town filled with different animals, you can visit friends' homes over the internet for new sights. The only way to buy certain items and find tropical fruit is by trading with other players, and, while you make those swaps, the game makes some of its own too. Days, weeks or months down the line it's quite feasible that an ex-resident of a friend's town will move to yours and vice versa, and in each instance they'll chat about memories of their life in the other game.

It's a wild world but it also feels like a real one. Clock and calendar synchronisation means life in *Animal Crossing* runs parallel to our own. During the day it's either bright or rainy and the townsfolk are up; at night it grows dark and everybody goes to bed. In spring the town blossoms, in summer it's tropical, in autumn the leaves begin to fall and in winter it snows.

Fishing and bug catching are two fun ways to pass the time, and both are entirely dependent on the clock. Bugs and creatures come out at certain times of the day on specific months. Anybody with aspirations of catching and donating them all to the museum's living exhibitions needs to play the game regularly for at least a year, and even then at all times of the day, to stand a fair chance.

Every Saturday night the singing dog KK Slider visits the café to play a song. Paying a visit unlocks the tune for your home's jukebox. Every Sunday Joan visits the town to sell some turnips. The game has a mini turnip stock market and the price fluctuates on a daily basis. It pays to buy cheap and sell high to make an easy wodge of bells. The veg spoils after a week, so it's imperative to sell at the right time – which could mean visiting a friend's game to do so.

Fishing tournaments, bug hunts, acorn festivals, birthday celebrations, flea markets, firework nights and random visits from a cat with no face (who needs you to draw one on)... *Animal Crossing* delivers something new every single day, and its in-game calendar draws you back in for all its special events. It's pure escapism in a paradise crafted to your liking, and it's a paradise where everybody worships you if you're kind to them. It's funny, it's sweet and at times it can be pretty moving too. As far as living out a fantasy life goes, *Animal Crossing* is the most appealing option out there.

🐙 🐙 🐙

BALDUR'S GATE

Release date: 1998 | Platform: PC | Developer: BioWare

WHEN YOU READ the words *Dungeons & Dragons*, what do you think of? Bearded men in robes gathered around a dusty table rolling dice and dreaming up princesses and orcs? The Marvel cartoon? Warhammer figurines? (For nerdiness sake it had better not be the third – Warhammer is a completely different universe.) Whatever your thoughts of *Dungeons & Dragons*, there's no denying its immense popularity since the mid-seventies. Unsurprisingly, the concept didn't take long to make the leap to video games.

Since 1980, there have been a large number of *Dungeons & Dragons* video games, many of them unfortunately not worthy of the name. Trying to condense a fantasy role-playing game where you can pretty much go anywhere and do anything into a computer format that isn't going to upset the core fans is no easy task. When said game is the first to implement newer rule sets (*Advanced Dungeons & Dragons* 2nd edition rules) into a representation that is practically real-time, it's even tougher. Yet that's precisely what BioWare attempted to do with the first *Baldur's Gate* title: an ambition the developer successfully fulfilled on its first attempt.

The game follows the travels of a lonely orphan investigating the murder of his foster father. The arduous journey along the Sword Coast frontier goes from the town of Candlekeep to the bustling port of Baldur's Gate and back, in and out, around the houses and all over. Soon the lonely orphan is joined by five other characters and the hunt for the killer fast becomes a quest with far-reaching implications for the entire Forgotten Realms universe.

Choice is everything in *Baldur's Gate*. From the places you explore and the quests you accept to which party members you welcome into your group or decline to join forces with, your adventure is as malleable as Silly Putty. Good, neutral and evil characters are there to fight alongside and against, depending on your feelings and the responses you select during conversations.

Starting a new game of *Baldur's Gate* means clearing your gaming calendar of all other entries for at least a few weeks. It's a colossal journey that doesn't benefit from patchy play. Turning your character from an anonymous weakling to a world-beating fighter takes a hell of a lot of effort. Grinding through the missions and the battles is time-consuming work.

A slog it isn't, though, because *Baldur's Gate* rolled a D20 on the humour front and came up with the top score. The worlds of potions and spells aren't deadly serious, so *Baldur's Gate* duly provides more chuckles per square inch than most other games. Misc and his pet Boo, a miniature giant space hamster, are fan favourite icons for both the series and for BioWare, while Biff the Understudy pops up to fill in important dialogue roles for characters who have accidentally been offed on the way to Baldur's Gate. And any game that can get away with the line 'Forsooth, methinks you are no ordinary talking chicken!' has got to be worth playing.

Along with similar-looking (though vastly different) hack 'n' slasher *Diablo*, *Baldur's Gate* rejuvenated the interest in PC role-playing games and reversed traditionally waning sales figures by deservedly becoming a multimillion seller. The game put BioWare on the map and laid the path that took the developer on to projects like *Star Wars: Knights of the Old Republic* (more on that later) and *Mass Effect*. It also began a deluge of *Baldur's Gate* games, spin-offs and imitators. *Baldur's Gate* will forever be the game that brought *Dungeons & Dragons* to the gaming world in a way that did the licence justice – an accomplishment so huge it even overshadows BioWare's handling of the *Star Wars* franchise.

🕹 🕹 🕹

BATMAN: ARKHAM ASYLUM
Release date: 2009 | Platform: PlayStation 3 |
Developer: Rocksteady Studios

NOTHING MAKES GAMERS tremble quite like the news of a new comic book or movie tie-in. In the world of interactive entertainment, the only thing worse than a game-of-a-film is a film-of-a-game. Both are usually rotten. Licensed titles *should* be a match made in heaven, but they rarely end up as anything other than rushed drivel. There's usually a fairly large crossover between gaming audiences and followers of superhero licence X that company Y is peddling, so the appeal actually of being X for a few hours is often enough to safely secure a sale regardless of a game's quality.

Over the generations Batman has been one of the most violated brands of all. The Caped Crusader's treatment through the years has been perverse and the infamous Chinese superhero knock-off toys (check out pictures of Robert Cop, Spader-Man and Silverbat online) are more true to their origins than the Dark Knight's console representations. Boring, buggy or downright broken, it didn't matter: Batman games hit the shelves regardless and sold on the name alone.

When *Arkham Asylum* was announced by a studio with only one previous game to their name, everybody was too concerned about how bad it could be to even contemplate the possibility that it might be good. Given the crime fighter's spectacularly awful past record, an average Batman game would have been welcomed with open arms. Certainly no one foresaw a game that would easily outclass every other title of 2009 and go on to scoop two BAFTA awards for Gameplay and Best Game.

Batman: Arkham Asylum's secret is simple: it lets you play Batman as we all know him. It's amazing to think that of all the hundreds of superhero games throughout time only a handful of them have ever let you be true to the leading character. Past Batman games have forced you to shimmy around on pipes like you're a sloth in a tree, or jump about like a wallaby in moon boots. Tell us something: when was the last time you saw 'proper' Batman jump? Seriously? *Arkham Asylum* ignored all the monkey business and the guns (yes, Batman's shameful gaming history includes packing heat) and zeroed in on the Batman of the comics and films: a stealthy shadow-walker who's at home in the dark and prefers to observe his enemies and pick them off one by one.

It's all set in Arkham Asylum, which should come as no surprise given the subtitle and that it's loosely based on Grant Morrison's peerless Batman graphic novel *Arkham Asylum: A Serious House On Serious Earth*. And, like the disturbing graphic novel, it's one of the darkest versions of Batman ever seen. The asylum oozes choking atmosphere from every pore. When the Joker and his rioting goons capture Arkham Island, they torture and kill their prisoners with glee. More than a few guards are shot or frazzled on-screen, sights made all the more gruesome thanks to a positively chilling Joker performance by Mark 'Luke Skywalker' Hamill.

True to his moral values, Batman doesn't use lethal force. Progression is all about staying quiet, hiding in the rafters and dropping down to floor level to pacify any rioters you've coaxed away from the main pack. Joker's henchmen fear Batman and the game encourages you to play with your prey using decoy gadgets – batarangs, explosive gel and the like. When hostages are brought into the equation, you can't even do that. The second you're detected it's goodnight innocents, and to unbalance the odds even further the goons eventually put on heartbeat monitors to alarm others if they're knocked unconscious. In short, you have to be a ghost.

Batman is also a martial arts expert, so there are moments when you need to break out the fists, elbows and knees for some undignified scrapping (handled imaginatively by Rocksteady Studios with flowing, rhythmic combat). It's the careful balance of the predatory moments, the instances where you must crack out the gadgets to progress and these fighting sections that makes *Batman: Arkham Asylum* a masterpiece.

The real mark of success is this: strip away the Batman-themed exterior and the game is still fundamentally flawless. *Arkham Asylum* is shining proof that, with enough care, licensed games have the potential to rival any original IP (intellectual property) created by the world's so-called greatest developers. Its success means licensed games that are less than extraordinary are no longer acceptable.

BAYONETTA

Release date: 2010 (2009) | Platform: Xbox 360 |
Developer: PlatinumGames

BAYONETTA IS, QUITE simply, a genre perfected. Admittedly, the balletic action slash 'n' shooter first displayed in 2001's *Devil May Cry* is a very niche genre, but even so the accolade of perfection shouldn't be scoffed at. It's difficult to imagine anything celebrating a genre's identity quite like *Bayonetta* celebrates its own. The only flaw is a set of sales figures that doesn't do the accomplishment justice – a fault with the audience, not the game.

Bayonetta is a witch. A bewitching witch caught 'twixt and 'tween a war between heaven and hell, to be more specific and needlessly poetic. A witch who wears a suit made from her own magic hair. A witch who turns her hair into giant angel-squishing Monty Python-esque feet or demon-gobbling dragons at will. A witch whose hair, to the detriment of her modesty, is incapable of performing two tasks at once.

Oh yes, this is a third-person combat-centric action game that plays a sex card so big it's in danger of blotting out the sun. Sassy vixen Bayonetta revels in indecency, tormenting her foes with bullets, swords, bloody torture devices and lurid comments intended to thrill. With a weapon attached to each appendage, she's often seen upside down, gyrating her hips to target the surrounding evil angels with the guns strapped to her feet. And the camera just adores capturing every pelvic flick in all its gory details.

To be fair to Bayonetta and developer PlatinumGames, the sauciness falls short of pornographic. Think of it as a modern-day take on a *Carry On* film: a few fortunately placed strands of hair save Bayonetta from exposing all, and thus the game, from receiving a big ban-hammer from the censors. Which, when you consider the ideas on show, is mighty fortunate for all gamers.

Bayonetta races past the competition in a number of key areas, none more so than the fighting options. There are tons of weapons and power-ups to collect and they can all be mixed and matched in a dizzying number of ways. To complicate things further, you can program and switch between two entirely different arsenals on the fly, instantly swapping Bayonetta's weapons in the middle of an attack and opening up a whole new stream of moves. How many combo opportunities does this create? Nobody knows exactly because the developer genuinely lost count when trying to tally them all up. Freedom has never been this free. You aren't limited to a preset list of moves. You are the orchestrator of Bayonetta's learning, conducting startling strings of strikes even PlatinumGames hadn't thought possible.

Furious fingers are needed to cope with all the options and moves. In the hands of an expert, Bayonetta is an all-spinning, all-necromancing death-bringer with more tricks and spells up her hairy sleeves than Harry Potter could deal with. The simple introduction of a dodge button further sets *Bayonetta* apart from the crowd – a neat work around the clumsy blocking and/or manual avoidance moves the competition relies on.

This type of game isn't for the faint-hearted. Combos need to be memorised and perfected if you want to do well, and purchasing new weapons at every opportunity is the only sure way to defeat the monsters up ahead. There are bosses so huge they don't fit on the screen, and when trounced they're dissected and turn into more powerful weapons. *Bayonetta* needs to be played over and over just to approach a point where you'll be close to seeing it all.

The genre has never been for the incompetent gamer or the 'noob'. *Bayonetta* is the exception. Recognising its bat-dung mental story and off-the-wall characters might alienate a few people, PlatinumGames manages to do the impossible and make the hardest of hardcore games accessible to everybody. It's still the finger-bruising torture for those who want it to be, but a novel approach to difficulty settings ensures *Bayonetta* caters for everyone who picks it up. Even if it's the first time you've ever played a video game, it's easy to enjoy the witching hours from start to finish.

On the easiest setting, Bayonetta can be rinsed with a single button. Tapping that button will make flashy things happen on-screen and dispatch the bad guys too. Grow in confidence and you can adjust the difficulty to give greater control over Bayonetta's moves. It's always gloriously over-the-top no matter what you press, but notching up the difficulty lets you have a bigger say over which ostentatious moves she'll perform.

Veteran gamers also have reasons to rejoice. *Bayonetta* is one big string of gaming in-jokes, often but by no means exclusively aimed towards SEGA, its publisher. Series from *Sonic* to *Space Harrier* to *Resident Evil* are referenced in almost every cutscene. Know your gaming history well enough and *Bayonetta* rises above bizarrely amusing territory into side-splitting hilarity.

It's an entertainer through and through. An adult entertainer, for sure, and one almost too weird for its own good at times. But also one that casts an irresistible spell on anybody who gives is a go. Pure magic.

👾 👾 👾

BEYOND GOOD & EVIL

Release date: 2003 | Platform: PlayStation 2 |
Developer: Ubisoft Montpellier

IT WAS A DARK day for the gaming industry when *Beyond Good & Evil* bombed at retail. Here was a game with it all – great world, lovable characters, funky mechanics, gripping story and a soundtrack to die for – and nobody bought it. Those in the industry wept. Those outside of the industry were blissfully unaware of the masterpiece passing them by unannounced. It can be a cruel world sometimes.

Designed by Michael Ancel, the brains behind limbless platforming hero Rayman, *Beyond Good & Evil* is the saga of journalist and part-time martial artist, Jade, who bags the story of a lifetime. It's a third-person adventure with more than a hint of *Legend of Zelda* about it, set in the distant future on the picturesque mining planet of Hillys. Every day DomZ aliens raid the planet and attack the Hillyans and there seems to be nothing Hillys' defence force, the Alpha Section Intervention, can do about it. But, as Jade soon discovers, there could be a very good reason for Alpha's ineptitude...

Apart from the hugely welcome understated design of Jade (green lipstick aside, she's a strong, intelligent and correctly proportioned woman who manages to remain fully clothed throughout), there's little at first to suggest *Beyond Good & Evil* is anything more than a decent adventure title. Sure, Hillys is a bubbly, vibrant place packed with sights, but the same description could be applied to plenty of other game worlds too.

When Jade isn't out taking photographs for her investigative-reporting assignments, she runs an orphanage in a lighthouse with her 'uncle' Pey'j (a walking, talking, anthropomorphic pig, no less). When Jade's cash supply runs out, she can no longer afford to power the shield generators protecting the little kiddies, so she takes a job taking snapshots of all of Hillys' wildlife species for a local museum. Soon after, she's drafted into a resistance movement and her attentions turn from animals to conspirators – namely Alpha Section Intervention's higher-ups – and she starts to investigate their true motives.

By this point, *Beyond Good & Evil* has already moved past 'good' and into 'comfortably great' territory. Combat sections have proven their worth through meaty and satisfying mêlée-based stand-offs, while hopping in a hoverboat and coasting around the planet surface is an instantly gratifying hair-down experience. The introduction of the conspiracy angle brings stealthy infiltration levels into play too –

acts where you've got to sneak deep into Alpha Section bases and take pictures of any suspicious activity.

Stories are often the weakest links in big games, but *Beyond Good & Evil*'s plot is a startling gaming accomplishment and deserved the industry writing awards it received after launch. Maddeningly it was always designed to be part of a trilogy and so finishes with the mother of all cliffhangers. Poor sales soon axed dreams of a follow-up for years afterwards, and, though at the time of writing Ubisoft has at long last teased a sequel, some rather mixed statements emerging from the French developer throw its status into serious doubt.

Despite the sales fiasco, *Beyond Good & Evil* has an intense cult following among hardened gamers because it offers something genuinely original. It's a melting pot of ideas: exploration, combat, platforming, racing, space flying, stealth, strategy and role-playing elements all combined in one majestic title. And much like Ubisoft's sister project *Prince of Persia: Sands of Time* (a game released within a fortnight of *Beyond Good & Evil*), the game is glazed with pure charisma. As I've recently found out, the only thing better than discovering *Beyond Good & Evil* for the first time is revisiting it after a multi-year absence to do it all over again.

BRAID

Release date: 2008 | Platform: Xbox 360 | Developer: Number None Inc.

WHAT IF THE hands of a ticking clock didn't just move in a metronomic clockwise fashion? What if those hands could be stopped or reversed? What if they could be slowed? What if rewinding the hands' movement caused a second clock to appear from out of nowhere, counting forward for a brief few seconds before disappearing from view?

Braid is a two-dimensional Super Mario game for physics graduates and savants. Educated hero Tim wears a suit and tie instead of overalls, and plot-based cutscenes are traded for verbose books that either talk about Tim's mournful search for a princess (his ex-girlfriend) who has been snatched by a horrible monster, or a scientist's struggle to develop the atomic bomb, depending on your interpretation. Like a magic eye picture, the story appears clear through unfocused eyes but turns fuzzy when scrutinised.

One obvious plot thread is Tim's wish to rewind personal mistakes. It's made clear for a reason: Braid is a game all about manipulating time and capitalising on the consequences. Tim has the power to rewind time back to the beginning of each level, undoing errors and even death. There's no punitive system. No lives to preserve. Put a foot wrong and it's instantly erasable with a touch of the rewind button.

Each room in Tim's house links to a different fantasy world and these worlds, handily broken down into smaller levels, are home to scattered sets of jigsaw pieces. To find his princess, Tim needs to solve environmental puzzles (involving levers, keys, doors and sliding platforms by the dozen), grab the pieces and assemble the jigsaws to open a pathway to the game's sixth and final world. But the worlds differ vastly when it comes to time behaviour. Apart from Tim's constant power of rewind, no two worlds are alike.

One world is home to a ring which, when dropped on the floor, slows all objects in the levels relative to their distance from the ring. Another creates a parallel universe that replays past actions every time Tim uses rewind. In one world, time moves forward when Tim moves right, rewinds when Tim travels left and freezes when he stands still. And the final world is played entirely in reverse. Rewinding in this world, ironically, 'plays' or even fast-forwards time.

Confused yet? Braid is without question the cleverest game you could ever wish to butt heads with. To master the game requires you to think on a whole other level. How else would you ever figure out that the only way on to a certain high platform involves letting a monster drop on your head and bounce upwards, rewinding time to create a parallel world, letting the monster kill 'parallel Tim', and then bouncing on *its* head – now higher thanks to your dead doppelgänger's leg-up – to springboard on to the higher level. Training your mind to think counter-intuitively doesn't come easily, but that just makes solutions all the more rewarding to find. The euphoria at besting just one of *Braid*'s puzzles isn't something many games can match.

There's a secret side to *Braid* too, one that isn't advertised and which goes completely unnoticed by many. The jigsaw puzzles ask you to match *Braid*'s challenges, but eight hidden stars are unlocked by those who outsmart the game. Eight of the most despicably tough puzzles ever written into gaming code force you to break out of levels and think more laterally than a crab on a conveyor belt. Leave the controller untouched for over two hours for one star? Yes indeed – but in a very specific place for a very good reason. Nabbing the final star of the eight requires nothing less than causing a paradox and destroying the game's fundamental laws. No small task.

What makes *Braid* all the more incredible is its source. It is the product of just two men: creator, designer and all-round genius Jonathan Blow and freelance artist David Hellman. Licensed music comes from other sources, admittedly, but Blow makes it his own by linking it directly to *Braid*'s mechanics. Rewind time and the music garbles backwards. Slow time and the tunes grow lethargic.

That a game as groundbreaking as *Braid* could come from a team of two is testament to the staying power of this industry. While big studios come and go and throw millions of pounds at development, two men are capable of putting together a game that stands shoulder to shoulder with anything from the last fifty years.

BURNOUT 3: TAKEDOWN

Release date: 2004 | Platform: PlayStation 2 | Developer: Criterion Games

IMPRESSING A PERSONALITY on to a racing game is one of the toughest tasks a developer can face. Not only are racing titles more common than the cold, car titles don't exactly lend themselves to individualism. To the casual observer, it's hard to tell many apart, and for the purposes of this book it's even harder to single out titles when every sequel and copycat improves upon a game's features by incremental degrees, primarily in the technical department. In its day, for example, PlayStation driving simulator *Gran Turismo* was *the* game of its time. Revisiting it now is like smearing a car windscreen with Vaseline and driving down to the local supermarket on wheel rims.

Burnout 3: Takedown is the racing game that defies this convention. A driving experience harbouring such ferocity under its hood, it's either the most exhilarating racing game you'll ever play, or the most horrific. The sense of speed is second only to chaining yourself to the hood of a Formula 1 car. Its visual splendour is like Guy Fawkes Night at a pyromaniac's retreat.

When it comes to car crashes in games, there are two schools of thought: there's the primal, monster-truck-loving, 'crunching metal is awesome' opinion, and there's those who understandably view over-the-top smashes as distasteful glorifications of real-life horror. *Burnout* plays the 'it's a game' card from the off, teleporting you into a world of racing where your success is directly linked to the most splendiferous car Takedowns-with-a-capital-T you can cause.

In most instances where racers involve some crash- or weapon-based gimmicks, the racing element is often neglected in favour of the kookier part. *Takedown* isn't that shallow. It's underpinned by a core racing engine created for the first *Burnout* and tweaked for *Burnout 2: Point of Impact*, a play-it-straight arcade racer that still deserves revisiting. On top of that, *Burnout 3* adds the notion of these Takedowns. Side-swipe a rival into another vehicle and you'll destroy their ride, scoring a Takedown. Expertly use a ramp to land your car on to a fellow racer and you'll crush them, netting another Takedown. Barge them into a key part of a track, a tunnel entrance for example, and you'll score a signature Takedown along with a virtual postcard of the collision for your scrap book.

Takedowns win you boost, but it works both ways. Get taken out by somebody else and along with the humiliation you'll have to choke down a boost penalty. Yet even then there's room for glory: it's possible gently to steer your wreckage's movement with 'Aftertouch'. Barge your burning shell into a straggler and your penalty will be nullified by the aftertouch Takedown.

That's just the racing. Side mode Road Rage is a straight crash-'em-up: wreck a set number of vehicles while doing laps around a circuit without writing off your car (typically four or five crashes are allowed before your car's overall health is depleted) to win. Of all the modes this is a common favourite and rightly so. New cars are thrown in at every turn, and there's always somebody on screen who's begging to be upended or t-boned into oblivion. Do you veer across oncoming traffic to knock somebody off a cliff edge and run the risk of charging into an articulated lorry (make that a semi-trailer truck – we're in America for the most part) at full pelt? Or do you play it safe and power on to the next car? The thrill of the race doesn't often let you settle for the sensible option.

The carnage continues with crash junctions, a series of scripted roads and junctions where the goal is to become insurance enemy number one by causing as much monetary damage as possible with a single collision. Unleashing the perfect chain reaction takes cunning, guile and plenty of practice sessions, and all the failed runs are worth it the moment you grab a gold medal on one of the 100 courses. Getting all of them takes more time than the average racing career of a rival game.

You shouldn't look to *Takedown* for online thrills nowadays – not unless you've a DeLorean that can clock 88mph in your garage. While team Road Rage races were once a popular online choice, the servers have now been axed, meaning *Burnout 3: Takedown*'s multiplayer online mode is no more. But even half the game is still better than most of the wholes you get with other racing titles. Just make sure you belt up before you play.

CALL OF DUTY 4: MODERN WARFARE

Release date: 2007 | Platform: Xbox 360 | Developer: Infinity Ward

DESPITE A WORLDWIDE average review score of 94 per cent on Metacritic, it's fair to say *Call of Duty 4: Modern Warfare* is an underrated masterpiece. Everybody expected this shooter simply to pull the *Call of Duty* series out of the World War II trenches and into the modern battleground, but it did much, much more besides. It also managed to coax gamers out of nearly every other multiplayer game and keep them locked into *Modern Warfare* for years, even capturing a large chunk of the *Halo 3* audience and converting them for good. Judging by the number of shameless copycats that have followed in its footsteps, the release of *Modern Warfare* is as significant a moment in shooter history as the releases of *Halo* and *GoldenEye 007*.

The campaign is a Hollywood blend of action and suspense of the highest level, pieced together using three rules: surprise, surprise and surprise. No two missions are the same, and, by removing all forms of cutscenes and boxing story elements into playable subsections, *Modern Warfare* manages to advance the plot through doing, not through showing. You're forever swapping between characters to see multiple sides of the same war, a tool used not only to make you care about more people, but also to make you uncertain about the future. The second level is one long sequence that culminates in your unavoidable execution. It's a shocker, and it serves as a warning that no character is safe.

The campaign alone is worthy of the high scores the game received, but, though it marked a step forward for Infinity Ward's pacing and narrative skills, it is questionable whether it would still have earned its place in this list over the original *Call of Duty* – a World War II epic with fewer shocks and wow moments but just as sympathetic and tragic a cast. *Modern Warfare*'s place, however, is secure largely because of the multiplayer game which has made waves – no, tsunamis – in the competitive shooter market.

Modern Warfare's multiplayer mode – still unquestionably better than those of its sequels – revolves around the concept of incremental awards. Every kill is rewarded with experience points that go towards increasing your overall level. Every new level brings about new gear to use. Every piece of gear has challenges assigned to it to unlock further upgrades. Every kill streak you score is immediately rewarded with an instantly deployable bonus move to give you the upper hand in combat – UAV recon drones, helicopter gunships and air strikes, depending on streak length.

Modern Warfare's incremental rewards system does make starting out a chore – new players have significantly weaker equipment than veterans – but when the bonuses start rolling out the fun really begins. Every weapon is finely balanced and it's not long before you start weeding out favourites and singling out weapon-specific challenges to go for in order to unlock more extras. Before *Modern Warfare*, multiplayer matches were all about either winning or losing. Wins are still a nice goal in *Modern Warfare*, but as 'losing' players can still build up their characters' statistics they're, by no means the be all and end all. Nobody walks away from a battle empty-handed.

Though all character models are fundamentally the same person with a different skin, *Modern Warfare*'s perks system births much-copied custom add-ons. Perks allow you to add bonuses to your character's skills, be it faster running speeds, the ability to shoot through walls or the chance to whip out a pistol and fire at your attacker before you die. Like other gear, perks are slowly unlocked over time, and experimenting with different combinations and different gear adds another coating of strategy without bogging the game down in over-complicated statistics.

Call of Duty was a popular franchise from the beginning, but *Modern Warfare* single-handedly turned it into the biggest name in gaming. Once upon a time, *Grand Theft Auto* was the most popular 'cool' brand of them all. Now that honour belongs to *Call of Duty*. And even though all the key Infinity Ward staff now work at Respawn Entertainment, *Modern Warfare*'s legacy and Activision's persistent yearly updates mean the series' dominance is unlikely to change for a very long time.

👾 👾 👾

SID MEIER'S CIVILIZATION

Release date: 1991 | Platform: PC | Developer: MicroProse

SIX THOUSAND ONE hundred years of game: it's a lot by anyone's standards. Six thousand one hundred years to turn one humble caravan unit into a spacefaring civilisation. Six thousand one hundred years to befriend and/or annihilate every other nation on Earth. Six thousand one hundred years to avoid civil unrest by keeping the people happy. Six thousand one hundred years to lose yourself completely.

Civilization is as ambitious a game as you could ever hope to find, and one that doesn't fumble the daunting task it sets itself. It boasts over six millennia of strategy as gripping as superglue. Politics, diplomacy, scientific research, exploration, resource gathering, war...

Civilization lets you micromanage every aspect of a nation's rise from swamps to stars, and it lets you do this on Earth, on any custom planet you care to design or on a random map.

You pick your starting civilisation and begin in an appropriate spot (Greeks begin in Europe, Indians start in south Asia...) with one or two slow-moving settler units. To start with, the world is shrouded by a black veil – otherwise known as the Fog of War – to keep the land and the actions of the people beyond your caravan's visual capabilities a mystery. The settlers are only good for one thing: founding a city. When you're happy with a resource-rich location, it's time to build your capital and move onwards and upwards.

As city-dwellers work the nearby land, they'll gather the resources you specify from neighbouring grid squares. Wheat, fish, wood and minerals are harvested, and you can balance the focus of your outputs as you see fit: do you want to concentrate on researching new technologies or building new units and buildings within the city? New technology means more build options become available, while mammoth Wonders of the World constructions will keep people happy and give your city major bonuses. Your main aim is obviously to ensure there's enough food to feed the population, so you need to strike a balance between the other considerations.

Civilization is a turn-based game, meaning every civilisation moves its units, makes its decision and waits for the others to do the same until everybody's had their turn and the round is over. Every unit your city creates takes a set number of rounds to build, and every science topic your scientists work on takes a certain amount of time to crack, all adjustable by refocusing your city's outputs, of course. You could build more settlers and set up more cities, but they take a while to get ready and it's much better to train some cheap soldiers first and set them off into the world to explore new ground.

Each unit possesses (among other things) speed and strength statistics: the higher the speed level, the more ground they can cover in one turn; the stronger your units, the more likely they are to beat the enemy. Terrain plays a part too: mountains and forests restrict movement (though increase defensive power) tremendously, while open plains and – eventually – roads are easily navigable.

Early days involve discovering abandoned settlements, finding new technologies like pottery or bronze-working and battling barbarians. But soon you'll stumble upon other nations and swap technologies or trade insults and blows as you roll over them. Wipe enough out and you'll become a feared country, one capable of bullying others into submission. If you want.

Civilization really is what you make of it. Peaceful or warmongering, you can choose how your civilisation goes about its existence. Giant and richly detailed tech trees, full of researchable materials, mean there's always new content available just a few turns ahead, and by the time you've morphed into a worldwide empire with interconnecting cities and a democratic population you'll be developing nuclear technology and entering the space race. Not bad for somebody who started off with one family in a caravan.

Best of all, *Civilization* is a doddle to pick up. Its gridded overworld and clear unit stats keep movement and fighting simple to understand. If micromanaging each city's different facets feels like too large a load to bear, advisers can be appointed to help you on your way and shove you in the right direction. Depth exists for more competent players, and it's absolutely impossible to see everything there is to see in one mega multi-hour play-through.

Civilization has everything a strategy game should have, a fitting feature given that it's *about* pretty much everything too. You could spend 6,100 years searching for a better strategy game to play. You wouldn't find one.

👾 👾 👾

HARROW COLLEGE
Learning Centre

COUNTER-STRIKE: SOURCE

Release date: 2004 | Platform: PC | Developer: Valve Corporation

FISH AND CHIPS. Peanut butter and jelly. Jack Daniels and Coke. Some things are just meant to be combined, and in the gaming world no pairing has been as perfectly executed as *Counter-Strike* and Valve Corporation's Source Engine: the most popular online action game of all time (self-proclaimed, but fairly so) and the all-singing, all-dancing, all-wowing game engine that has powered Valve Corporation's best games for well over six years and just never seems to show signs of ageing.

The first of four (and what was very nearly five) Valve Corporation games in this book, *Counter-Strike: Source* is an improved remake of *Counter-Strike* – an online shooter pitting teams of terrorists and counter-terrorist squads against each other in battles centred on bomb plots and hostage capture. Terrorists need to set bombs and ensure they detonate and prevent hostages from being rescued; counter-terrorists, obviously, need to do the exact opposite.

Being online only, newcomers have to jump right into the deep end and cross paths with some rather well-practised opponents. Expertly designed maps are complemented by back-of-the-hand knowledge, and careless wandering is likely to earn you a shot to the skull before you even register anybody from the opposing team. Coupled with the game's individualised mechanics, the going may be tough early on.

Counter-Strike distinguishes itself from other shooters in a number of crucial aspects, starting with a lack of 'respawns'. Die in most shooters and you'll have a few seconds to cool off, collect your thoughts and tinker with kit before diving back into the action. Die in *Counter-Strike* and you're dead until the round is finished, forced to monitor the action as surviving players continue the fight in your absence.

The threat of permanent death adds a caginess rarely felt in other games. One mistake and it's all over. Gung-ho bravado is risky not just for one player but for the welfare of an entire squad. Lone wolves rarely get the better of organised teams. Let the pressure become overwhelming and tetchiness creeps in. *Counter-Strike* is a battle against your nerves as much as it is against the opposition. Of course, those who died in the previous round are monitoring the survivors and watching for patterns. It's not enough to be tactical in *Counter-Strike*; you must be tactical *and* unpredictable.

Each round begins with a short 'freeze time' to buy equipment, which is carried over to future rounds if you manage to stay alive. Buying and knowing when to use or hoard kit is an essential skill to master. Smoke grenades and flashbangs are invaluable items when crossing open ground or clearing rooms. You don't want to blow their advantage early for no reason, but on the flip side grenades are good for nothing if you've croaked. You can find yourself planning two or three rounds ahead. New kit might make you more powerful, but it's likely to make you more cautious too as you try not to lose the advantages it brings.

Gun behaviour plays into the veteran's hands even more. Firing on the move seriously hampers accuracy, and recoil from automatic weapons sends unchecked bullets shooting into the sky if you fail to counteract the kickback. It's important to know your equipment inside-out because the difference between shooting an enemy in the arm and shooting them in the face is often the difference between your own life and death. Injured enemies can still shoot you, and if you fail to make the first shot count there's no guarantee you'll have time for a second.

The *Counter-Strike* community is among the most consistent and well supported of all gaming followings and the game is *the* go-to title for university LAN parties. *Counter-Strike* hasn't fallen out of vogue in well over ten years and new updates ensure it's going to be around for many more years to come. The concept may have started off as a simple modification of *Half-Life*, but it's grown into an irreplaceable part of any self-respecting PC gamer's catalogue. Once you've been bitten by *Counter-Strike: Source*, it'll dominate your gaming library for a very long time.

🐙 🐙 🐙

DANCING STAGE (AKA DANCE DANCE REVOLUTION)

Release date: 1998 | Platform: Arcade | Developer: Konami

NOT FOR THE inhibited, the inebriated or the indolent, *Dancing Stage* is a must for everybody who can bust a move – and most who can't as well. The single-screen, double-platform arcade cabinet with giant speakers and flashing neon lights can be an intimidating structure when you first see it. It's louder than a jumbo jet taking off and as in-your-face as your nose, but its brazen attempt to command attention shouldn't be criticised. *Dancing Stage* is a real showpiece of a game, especially when it's being played by experts.

The 'stage' in the title is a square platform split up into nine squares. The up, down, left and right positions have pressure-sensitive buttons built into them, the four corners and the centre square are filled with metal stoppers. Four columns of arrows scroll vertically up the screen. The goal is to step on the correct button when the relevant arrow crosses the 'step zone', and to hold the note if the on-screen arrow has a long tail.

It isn't a modal pass/miss scenario. Your score depends on precision timing and every note is ranked from Marvellous down to Boo (though this grading system changes with modes and versions) with four ratings in between. Score highly and you'll be allowed to keep playing for a few more songs. Fail to impress the virtual crowd and your daddy dancing will only continue after coughing up more cash.

You pick your difficulty and your song and away you go, dancing to the beat. There's a dance meter which fills up with good dancing and depletes with missteps. Drain it completely and you'll be unceremoniously kicked off before the song's finished. Providing you're able to steer clear of premature ejection, you'll receive a grade for your performance after every routine.

Where it gets impressive is in the highest difficulties encompassing two pads. Rather than accommodating two simultaneous gamers, the double-platform set-up can be used by just one person. Freestyle players often prioritise a real audience over the game's ranking system, and truly gifted players can juggle both targets at once while pulling off some audacious moves – including hand plants and inventive use of the safety rails.

Any *Dancing Stage* arcade machine will do in your quest to play the game. There are, however, major differences between versions – not just in song choices but in whole new scoring systems and modes too. EuroMIX and EuroMIX 2 are by far the easiest machines to track down in the UK. And it's the arcade you should be looking to, not the home console versions. Cheap plastic mats for home use are no substitute for the real thing and can be dangerously slippery to boot. Besides, the cheese of the flashing lights and the ear-bashing speaker volumes are all part of recreating the disco vibe.

As well as being a throwaway slice of gaming fun (though quite how much fun depends on your embarrassment levels), *Dancing Stage* is a jolly good workout too. It's arguably a better exercise machine than Wii Fit and some seasoned enthusiasts have lost weight through repeated play. As a result the game has even worked its way into some American schools as part of their physical education programmes.

Is *Dancing Stage* the 'coolest' game around? No, not by a long shot. In fact, it's a hugely divisive title that has split the gaming community into groups of staunch defenders and hardened critics.

But it's a game, it's a *successful* game and whether you like it or loathe it there's no denying it nails what it wants to achieve. And that deserves at least one chance.

🦑 🦑 🦑

DEFENDER

Release date: 1980 | Platform: Arcade | Developer: Williams Electronics

BEFORE *DEFENDER* BURST on to the scene with its sixteen-colour necromancy and its deafening explosions, the gaming universe usually ended with the four edges that border every monitor. Hitting the edge of one screen – if that was even possible – would normally either stop the character dead like they'd struck a brick wall, or would result in the object in question appearing from the opposite edge as if the monitor were a flat representation of a globe. A few bigger gaming worlds existed (the 1978 game *Adventure* took place over a sprawling kingdom) but they were almost always explored via individual snapshots lined up like dominoes. When one screen finished, the replacement appeared, instantly and jarringly.

Lunar Lander and its trendsetting horizontal scrolling landscapes invented a world that didn't end with the edge of the screen (earlier titles like *Sky Raider* had faux-scrolling worlds that were more like pre-canned rolling backgrounds). When you moved, the camera panned and the ground shifted accordingly. But it wasn't the most riveting of titles, which is why Atari's production soon reverted to piecing together and shipping extra *Asteroids* cabinets to meet arcade demands. Just one year later, however, *Defender* exploded into view, picked up *Lunar Lander*'s ideas and carried the concept into unmapped territory.

You man a spaceship skimming along a planet surface, trying to protect yourself and other humans from alien attacks and abductions.

Not all of these attacks occur on-screen, but a handy map at the top of the arcade cabinet's display points out the areas under threat for you to engage thrusters and zoom across the world to put an end to the alien invasion. The ship is a powerhouse to control: a weighty vessel with a fiery attitude, roaring laser cannons and a sense of inertia that makes it feel tangible. The craft cannot simply change direction on a pinhead – flipping the ship and engaging the engines only reverses your course after you've first cruised backwards while decelerating from the initial velocity.

Defender's concept of winning not only through self-preservation but also through protecting other independent entities on the screen is one of the most common of all recurring gaming themes. *Defender*'s blueprint is essentially one big, long, looping escort mission – saving (helpless) others to save yourself. Any abducted humans not rescued before they're dragged to the top of the screen morph into extra-strong mutants just like men in draughts morph into deadly flying kings once they touch the end zone. Fail to defend mankind and the planet is overrun by mutants or, worse, explodes.

To make things tougher than they already are, aliens come in all shapes, sizes and behaviours, which makes the screen-cleansing smart bomb a godsend in tough situations. *Defender*'s complex arcade set-up doesn't make the task any easier: the joystick handles vertical movement and the rest of the ship's controls sit on no fewer than five buttons (Reverse Thrust, Hyperspace, Smart Bomb, Forward Thrust and Fire).

Defender is one of the top-grossing arcade cabinets of all time and it's not tough to understand why. Beyond the wide-reaching appeal of its pioneering features, it took a heck of a lot of practice to master. People needed to pay through the nose to become defence experts, and the game's alternating two-player modes meant the practice could be conducted socially. Every exploding alien, every crash-landing and every turned mutant is a neuron-firing H-bomb to the senses. Every expert manoeuvre is a fist-pumping moment of glory.

Every fatal hit is a tragic moment of failure. Every game of *Defender* is totally unlike the last, and every alien stand-off is a fight to be remembered. *Defender*'s spot in arcade history is well deserved.

DEMON'S SOULS

Release date: 2010 (2009) | **Platform: PlayStation 3** |
Developer: From Software

THERE ARE FOUR incredibly difficult games listed in this book. *Demon's Souls* is arguably the most punishing of the lot. Normally that's a statement that'll come hand in hand with a warning along the lines of 'Don't try it if you usually play games on the easiest setting' or 'Only for confident gamers', but not here it doesn't. No matter how pants you think you are at games, *Demon's Souls* deserves a go. This book is called *100 Computer Games to Play Before You Die* for a reason, you know…

There are single-player games, there are multiplayer games, there are games with single-player and multiplayer portions, and there is *Demon's Souls*: something completely new. Play *Demon's Souls* while hooked up to the internet and you'll have an integrated online experience that'll change the way you perceive cooperative gaming forever. It's a little too early to tell for sure but it's highly likely we'll all be looking back in a decade's time and tagging *Demon's Souls* as the origin of a new form of inter-player connectivity.

At first glance, it's an exceedingly well-made fantasy yarn, though it's not immediately obvious the game's treading into historic waters. The grim, perma-medieval world of Boletaria is cursed with a rolling fog that harbours demons who thrive on men's souls. When you enter the fog at the beginning of the game, you become just another victim. All is not lost: your soul is taken to the

Nexus, a sort of world-between-worlds, where it's given the chance to return to Boletaria to gather power and eventually battle the main demon tormenting mankind.

If *Demon's Souls'* features ended there, it would still come highly recommended. Pootling about the world as a hero of your choosing, stabbing orcs and dragons and rolling out of the way of danger is immense fun – especially when it's packaged up in as neat and tidy a combat system as *Demon's Souls*. Every slain monster bestows you with precious souls to trade later for equipment and abilities. Die and those souls are dropped where you fell, awaiting retrieval should you manage to make it back to the same spot without dying again. Thankfully you'll have opened up shortcuts along the way to avoid replaying everything. Pressing forward after dying is a smartly balanced form of gambling: you want to rush to take back the lost souls and you already know what's ahead (monsters respawn in the same locations), but if you're too impatient you could fall foul of the brutal difficulty, die and lose the first batch of souls for good.

Then you look at the floor and everything changes, for that's where the gaming landscape-shifting features live. There are two in total and they make up one of the smartest systems of the current console generation.

The first is text. Succinct messages are scrawled all over the place, pointing out things like hidden treasure chests, enemy ambushes, warnings to stay away from areas until you've powered up and good ways to defeat certain monster types. All of it comes from other players, and you can add to the graffiti as well. In truth the message composition's a little clunkier than it should be – you choose from a selection of prefabricated phrases segregated into categories and stitch them together – but with a little practice it's possible to tag locations with a helpful hint in just a few seconds.

If you like messages, you can take a leaf from Facebook's pages and 'like' them in-game. By the same token, other gamers can 'like' your comments, and each time somebody does just that you'll receive an invaluable health boost to aid your cause. This one incentive encourages everybody to club together in their own single-player games and offer tips and advice to other players – also in their own single-player games – through an inter-game Twitter system, without needing to pause the PlayStation 3 and visit online message boards.

The second thing you'll find on the ground is blood. Blood stains are everywhere (it's a really, *really* tough game) and like the messages they all originate from other players. Touch a puddle and you'll summon the ghost of another player to watch their final few seconds. Like the messages, they foreshadow future events, but by carefully studying these replays you can deduce precisely what traps and monsters lie in wait ahead, and where they'll spring from.

You can, if you choose, step fully into the realm of multiplayer and invite others into your game, or visit another player's world to help out. And in a triumphant moment of synergistic multiplayer, you can eventually invade other worlds and fill the role of boss characters for unsuspecting gamers.

Demon's Souls experiments wildly with online gaming and strikes gold with every idea. Even if you ultimately find the going too tough, the startling ingenuity will leave you awestruck.

👾 👾 👾

DEUS EX

Release date: 2000 | Platform: PC | Developer: Ion Storm

DEUS EX IS a game bigger than anybody could truly describe. A title that garnered such a following after its release that word of mouth alone has transformed it into legend. A brand that can now be considered the gaming equivalent of *Donnie Darko* or *The Matrix* (even down to the pitifully rubbish sequels, although the third title is on course to make amends). Just one mention of the name can elicit oohs and aahs from people across the globe – many of them reacting not because they've played it but just because they've heard the stories.

The cyberpunk adventure follows J.C. Denton, a nano-augmented covert operative for the United Nations Anti-Terrorist Coalition. Take a moment to get your breath back there if you need to – we'll stick with UNATCO from now on to make it easier. It's the 2050s and the gulf between the rich and the poor has grown wider than ever. UNATCO is battling the National Secessionist Force (NSF), which claims secret government organisations are deliberately facilitating a worldwide plague called the Gray Death by holding back a cure named Ambrosia. Your elder brother has been an augmented UNATCO agent for a few years and the game begins with your first mission for the same force: the recovery of a hijacked batch of Ambrosia on New York's Liberty Island.

Part role-playing game, part story-driven adventure and part first-person shooter, *Deus Ex* is a genre unto itself. Typically, most 'shooters' prior to *Deus Ex* were fairly linear and didn't give you a whole lot of wriggle room on the options front. *Deus Ex*, however, hands you the keys to the story and urges you to take it wherever you choose. There's no one right way to play the game. If you fancy playing it like a shooter, it allows you to do just that. If you'd rather ditch the weapons entirely and sneak through by hacking security systems, lock-picking and setting up booby traps, that's just as valid an option.

The choices you make have profound impacts on both the story and your progress through the game. Of the eighteen possible cybernetic upgrades available, you can improve just nine, and picking one improvement immediately locks out the alternatives. Do you opt for the faster movement speed to the detriment of silent moving? Do you pick the weapon strength in the knowledge that you'll never be able to lift and pass by heavy objects and find the secrets behind them? Is it more important to choose the regeneration or the aqualung augmentation? One means you'll cope better in combat, but to do so would wipe out almost all hopes of exploring underwater. Cloaks and radar transparencies or ballistic protection and electromagnetic pulse shields? Or a combination of the above?

Then there are the conversation trees. Are you capable of talking somebody into doing something, or will you come across as either too weak or too aggressive and scupper all hopes of persuasion? As the set-up suggests, not everything is as it seems. There's no such thing as a non-shady organisation. Moral grey areas means decision-making is tougher and far more interesting than in titles that are reluctant to dabble in muddy ethics. Who do you side with? Do you want to kill boss characters early on before they can even become bosses in the first place? The choice is entirely yours.

This open-ended approach still shines today over a decade after its release. *Deus Ex* is in this book not because it won the Game of the Year awards in 2000, but because if it was first released yesterday – with a little visual touch-up so it looked the part – it could still win those same awards today. Any choice made in the game locks off alternative routes so no two games are the same. No one person could claim to see it all without multiple completions, which means all those people relying on second-hand information aren't missing out on just one gaming experience, they're missing out on half a dozen. Don't be part of that crowd...

DIABLO

Release date: 1997 | Platform: PC | Developer: Blizzard North

THERE ARE MANY *Diablo* clones but only one *Diablo*. Actually, there are a few *Diablos* and expansions but we're only concerned with the original. That phrase 'one *Diablo*', though... it could cause confusion.

It suggests *Diablo* is a title that appears in one form. In truth, no two games of *Diablo* are ever the same.

Diablo is a hack-and-slash, action Role-playing game (RPG) that mixes random quest selection with random level design, ensuring every adventure is a new journey into the unknown. It's a typical fantasy epic with warriors, rogues, sorcerers and whatnot, set in the medieval town of Tristram and the sixteen floors of dungeons beneath its foundations. There's a battle between heaven and hell under way, and it's down to your fighter/archer/magician to head downstairs, knock on hell's door and give Diablo the Lord of Terror a thorough ticking off. Preferably in a fashion that involves pointed things or dangerous magic.

Though levels and their contents are randomised, the deeper you descend, the tougher it gets. The journey to hell is split into four sections of four levels, and the beginning of each section has a direct path to the surface town of Tristram (though it's only unlocked by opening the passage from inside). To push on down, you'll frequently need to head back up to the top and trade items and gold for stronger weapons, armour and magic buffs. You can yo-yo for as long as you want, gathering new items and becoming stronger indefinitely to improve your chances of surviving hell unscathed.

If different monsters and levels every time aren't enough to pull you back in (what's wrong with you?), the rare drops will be. There are a ridiculous number of items bestowed with unique properties to be found, and harvesting enemies in search of a super secret Mega Sword of Super Stabbing is worth it when you stumble across a genuinely useful piece of kit. Certain weapons are extra powerful against select monster types, and equipment can be traded online with other players if you can find somebody who hasn't cheated their way through the ranks.

Diablo throws traditionally complex role-playing systems out the window. There are numbers and statistics and item modifiers by the dozen, but you needn't have studied as a mathematics postgraduate to put them all into practice. Fans of immediate action will be delighted to know *Diablo* can be played by doing little more than equipping yourself with the latest and greatest equipment, and clicking on monsters individually to hack them into pieces small enough to post through a letterbox. Elixirs, potions and spell books all have their uses, of course, but *Diablo*'s a much simpler project to master than normal role-playing games.

Though *Diablo* isn't the longest of games, there's always something new to see if you hold off charging straight to the end. Multiplayer dungeon-crawling is available via local area networks or through Blizzard's Battle.net web service. As *Diablo* is no exception to the general 'everything's better in co-op' rule that applies to all games, it's worth trying out with partners. Teaming up to take on hell itself is indescribably rewarding if you stick with the same party throughout, and it's great practice for the more refined *Diablo II*, a game really centred round its multiplayer mode.

The series has spawned too many clones to mention, and is still going strong itself thanks to the forthcoming *Diablo III*. But like so many franchises, the first is usually the most important. While it comes in many guises, there's only one true *Diablo*, and that's the one to play.

👾 👾 👾

DONKEY KONG

Release date: 1981 | Platform: Arcade | Developer: Nintendo

IT'S IMPOSSIBLE TO overstate the impact *Donkey Kong* had on the games industry. Even though classics such as *Pong* and *Space Invaders* preceded it, *Donkey Kong* is the most culturally significant game of all time. It was the springboard from which Mario and Donkey Kong (the character) launched; it was the first step in the illustrious career of game designer superstar Shigeru Miyamoto; and, most of all, it was the catalyst that turned Nintendo into the gaming superpower it is today.

Nintendo's story didn't begin with video games. The company started up in 1889 and specialised primarily in card games (though they experimented with other ventures, including taxi firms). It was slow to leap on to the video-game bandwagon, and to begin with the company only enjoyed moderate success at best. It wasn't until a company circular asking its employees to devise new game ideas was written that Nintendo found its true calling. To simplify a long story, Shigeru Miyamoto and his Donkey Kong concept saw to that.

Four levels depicting an angry gorilla kidnapping his owner's girlfriend and the subsequent race to save her was all it took to secure Nintendo's future. It marked the beginning of the princess-rescuing concept and the start of the classic platform genre (Donkey Kong is technically the second 'platformer', after *Space Panic*, but the first to include jumping – the staple move of all spiritual follow-ons).

It was also a game that could be appreciated in two markedly different ways: both as an A-to-B story with a beginning, a middle and an end, and as a score-attack challenge with points awarded for each vaulted object and collected item. The latter is such an iconic feature that Donkey Kong's leaderboard still has a place in today's gaming landscape. World record attempts are held frequently, and the struggle between two famous record holders was immortalised in the 2007 documentary film *The King of Kong: A Fistful of Quarters*.

The sight of Kong climbing to the top of a construction site and stomping girders until they collapse is a true game introduction 101: a sequence that sets up the villain, the level and the obstacles ahead superbly while also coaxing out a few laughs. The art design stems from necessity rather than graphical vision – protagonist Jumpman (who later became Mario) has a cap and a moustache because hair and a mouth were too tricky to replicate, while dungarees are the result of needing multicoloured clothing to replicate running animations – but you wouldn't know it to look at the game. Squint and you can almost imagine the planes circling the top of the Empire State Building and firing at the gorilla to knock him off. Which is presumably why Universal took Nintendo to court over copyright infringement. Nintendo eventually won the case.

Hurdling barrels and fireballs may sound a tad simplistic, but *Donkey Kong* is a deceptively tricky game to master. Jumpman's pursuit of Kong and the 'napped Pauline up a skyscraper spans four unique construction zones littered with more hazards than a Bond villain's chemistry lab. The first 25 metres involve leaping over barrels that roll down diagonal girders, the second 25 introduce horizontal conveyor belts with steaming cement pans and fire-spitting oil drums.

The 50–75-metre-high construct is the trickiest of the lot: an engineering practical joke involving a couple of elevators, a bunch of floating supports and bouncing weights that would cave any worker's head in, construction helmet or not. Above the 75-metre line, you finally get to exact some revenge on Donkey Kong. Knock eight loose rivets out of place and girders and gorilla plummet to the bottom, reuniting the separated lovers once and for all for a few seconds – until the game begins again at higher speeds. A programming bug prevents the challenge passing beyond the 22nd screen, although few people ever make it that far, though not for lack of trying. *Donkey Kong* boasts thirty years of staying power and remains one of the most recognisable titles ever created. Any study conducted on the addictiveness of games would do well to begin the research by looking at this seminal classic...

DOOM

Release date: 1993 | Platform: PC | Developer: id Software

YOU KNOW WHAT you're letting yourself in for when a game's main weapon is called the BFG9000: the Big F*****g Gun. *Doom* isn't exactly subtle. Then again, you'd expect nothing else given the subject matter. After a science experiment on Mars goes awry, you're posted to moon Phobos to prevent the disgruntled forces of hell from piling through a teleporter and invading Earth. To help your line of defence, you're given shotguns, rocket launchers, chainsaws and the monster known as the BFG9000. Yep, subtlety sure isn't *Doom*'s strong point.

Doom was a huge breakthrough for PC gaming. Riding high in the wake of id's own first-person shooter *Wolfenstein 3D* (released one year earlier), *Doom* is the reason for the first-person shooter's meteoric rise to the top of the gaming genre pile. This one free shareware release spearheaded a gaming revolution, offering the entire industry a glimpse at what games were capable of and in which direction they should head.

Doom's emergence on the scene brought with it waves of promise for the future. Grotesque monsters, gloomy levels and lashings of gore made it instantly recognisable. Its visuals were light years ahead of anything seen previously, and its levels were so detailed and so densely packed with features and 'monster closets' (literally small alcoves filled with monsters that open when you step near), every gamer sat up and took notice at what id Software was doing. A revolutionary lighting model transformed the game into a frightfest, and its labyrinthine hallways became the settings for shootouts more intense than any that had come before. *Doom* had a swagger, and that attitude made it stand out from the crowd.

Doom also carries the honour of pioneering network gaming (technically it didn't start the practice, but *Doom* certainly popularised networking). It let gamers link their machines and embark on cooperative campaigns as a pair. More importantly, it also allowed its players to meet up for competitive matches, in games that creator John Romero dubbed deathmatches. *Doom* is the daddy of the deathmatch: the staple multiplayer mode found in every other shooter is traceable right back to 1993 and id's monster masher.

Incredibly, *Doom* still has plenty to offer today's gamers. OK, so it may be as nineties as 'Do The Bartman', but nostalgia isn't the only thing going for this shooting luminary. Its leave-your-brain-at-the-door approach to combat is a welcome break from the current trend of realism. There's a lot to be said for plodding round claustrophobic levels and unleashing everything you've got at anything that moves. Not many games still satisfy that primal thrill.

It's synonymous with carnage, with secret-driven replayability and, most impressive of all, its modding. Modding is the practice of players creating and sharing their own content for an existing game, and *Doom*'s WAD (Where's all the Data?) tools turned the game into one giant Lego playset, letting people take it apart, reassemble it to their liking and even add new pieces of their own if they wanted. Players were able to design and import new monsters, weapons, sounds and entire levels, meaning *Doom* content was limited only by its community's imagination. And given the game's impact on the industry, the community wasn't lacking in either numbers or drive.

Doom is also credited with spawning a so-so movie starring Dwayne 'The Rock' Johnson, a brilliantly awful comic that brought such classic lines as 'Knock Knock. Who's there? Me me me me me me me me me me me' to the world, and driving gaming's sorry obsession with space marine characters. Don't hold it against the game, though. *Doom*'s lasting legacy is responsible for far more good products than bad ones. Deathmatches and modding are the two most talked-about features, but shove them aside and there's still a barrier-shattering game about kicking ass and then kicking some more. Bloody violence and mutilated corpses dominated the headlines on its release, but *Doom* isn't a game that substitutes good content for fan-pleasing gore. It delivers two barrels of each in one explosive blast of sheer awesome.

🐙 🐙 🐙

THE ELDER SCROLLS IV: OBLIVION

Release date: 2006 | Platform: PC | Developer: Bethesda Game Studios

OBLIVION HAS BEEN accused of dumbing down certain role-playing mechanics to cosy up to a less refined console crowd. Its predecessor, *The Elder Scrolls III: Morrowind,* nearly filled this spot (and might well have done if it weren't for the super-annoying flying reptilian stingray gits known as Cliff Racers), but for every person who complains about *Oblivion*'s slight simplification of the genre to appeal to a wider audience, there must be a least a dozen people in said wider audience who are glad *Oblivion* isn't as obtuse a game as its elder *Elder* brethren; otherwise, they might never have been bitten by the *Elder Scrolls* bug.

Oblivion is a prime example of what are known as 'Western' RPGs: role-playing games that scrap the rigidity of a menu-based combat system and shun the idea of strictly linear stories in favour of a go-anywhere, do-anything approach. It takes place in the sprawling province of Cyrodiil (the central part of the Tamriel continent), where wolves and trolls run free. Snow-capped mountains lie to the north of Cyrodiil, boggy marshlands to its south. In between is a mixture of forests, plains and cave systems, not to mention a few hundred villages, towns, cities, getaway shacks, abandoned strongholds and other secret settlements.

Cyrodiil is blighted by so-called Oblivion gates – swirling portals to the Oblivion netherworld plane where blood grass grows out of the blackened bodies of ex-human husks and demonic terrors roam free.

As more and more portals emerge, more and more nightmares spill out of these openings into Cyrodiil's picturesque landscape to infect the surrounding land and raid any nearby habitats.

Oblivion's main storyline involves restoring the royal bloodline to the ruling seats of Cyrodiil and gathering an army to push the forces of Oblivion back into their realm before sealing the doorways once and for all. It's a storyline that drags you all over the province and introduces characters voiced by none other than Patrick Stewart and Sean Bean.

That quest line is really just a formality, though. Compared to the rest of the game, it's a drop in the ocean. There are hundreds of quests in *Oblivion* – far too many to see in under 150 hours, for sure. Fighters', mages', thieves' and assassins' guilds all have lengthy and rewarding stories to uncover (the last two in particular) and every town has dozens of people ready to hand out errands and odd jobs.

These aren't just limited to fetch 'em or slay 'em orders: *Oblivion* can boast of variety like no other game. From being dragged inside a watercolour painting and battling sketched trolls with turpentine to choosing whether to slay a family of vampires or to become one yourself and stalk Cyrodiil at night, regularly feeding on sleeping humans to keep the telltale ashen skin at bay – *Oblivion* deals only in surprises and entertainment.

Not content with letting you go anywhere and do anything, *Oblivion* allows you to become anybody too. Whichever race you wish to be (Cyrodiil is home to cat-like Khajiit and reptilian Argonians among others), whatever skills you yearn to master, you can. Fancy becoming a stealthy Robin Hood character? Build up sneaking, agility and bow and arrow stats to prowl the cities at night and leap from rooftop to rooftop armed with a one-hit-kill bow. If a mix of magic and mêlée combat sounds more appealing, the Spellsword class is probably more to your liking. Picking races, star signs and master skills is an important step in creating your character. *Oblivion* has sold millions upon millions of copies and yet no two people have shared the same experience.

The first-person-perspective epic has so many different characters to meet and items to collect (every item in the game is a tangible object that can be bought or stolen) that no one person could ever realistically hope to discover everything. The library of in-game books alone takes hours to read.

The game is a real water-cooler conversation filler. 'Last night I found the only unicorn in the world and made it my steed.'

'Really? Because *I* hunted it, offered its horn to the Daedric gods and was rewarded with a unique item.'

Swapped stories will uncover new secrets. No traded tales are ever the same.

Is *Oblivion* responsible for simplifying the *Elder Scrolls* series? Yes it is, but for the most part it scraps needlessly obtuse features and replaces them with more elegant systems. *Oblivion* is a game so vast and yet still so polished it shames the *Halos* and co. of this world. Why was *Morrowind* eventually dropped from this book? Because *Oblivion* is in with a good chance of becoming your favourite game ever, and once it's finished there's every chance you'll want to follow it up by getting *Morrowind* anyway, and diving into Cyrodiil's sister province for more of the same greatness.

ELITE

Release date: 1984 | Platform: BBC Micro | Developers: David Braben and Ian Bell

LOAD NEW COMMANDER (Y/N)? The most important question any game has ever fielded first saw the light of day back in 1984.

'Do you want to load a new commander?' it asked. 'Does the sound of exploring an entire universe appeal to you?' it queried. 'Would you like to be sucked into a world with infinite possibilities, and one that makes every other game you've ever played look microscopic in comparison?' it probed.

Among fellow developers, David Braben and Ian Bell certainly can be considered elite. Over a period of two years while at Cambridge University, they designed and coded a piece of software that brings eight galaxies, each with 256 planets, to life. Their game hands you a space ship (the beautiful *Cobra Mark III*), puts 100 credits in your pocket and sends you off into the universe to go make a living for yourself. What living that may be is your decision.

Trading is a good way to start. You can trade legal (textiles, beverages, furs...) or illegal (robot slaves, firearms...) goods, though a bit of both never harmed anybody, right? Asteroid mining? Another viable way to rake in the credits. Scavenging is a simple way to boost cargo – be it picking the bones from a dead ship or turning to full-blown piracy and shooting others out of the sky before looting the debris. One thing's for sure: downing some ships will soon turn your embarrassing 'Harmless' rating into something else (it'll take more than a few knackered trading ships to become an 'Elite' though).

Bounty hunting and Galactic Navy missions are two other avenues for income streams, and they often involve exercising the ship's lasers and missiles a little more than average. Pretty soon it's clear the awesome Cobra-class trading ship isn't nearly awesome enough and upgrades will need to be fitted if you're to stand a fighting chance in space. Pirates are everywhere too, don't forget, so an escape capsule is a smart buy to take you to the nearest space station if the *Cobra* goes down.

Are you feeling the love yet? *Elite* has that effect on people. It's a game with no obvious boundaries, a quality rare enough now let alone back in the mid-eighties. The horror of being dragged into Witch Space and battling Thargoid battlecruisers is very real – especially if you've expanded the hull space to cram more expensive cargo inside your vessel. Hours of upgrading, refitting and exploring makes it hard to remember you're just playing a game on a BBC Micro (or whatever else you use – *Elite* eventually found a home on just about every machine).

It is testament to the level of care Braben and Bell put into their magnum opus that even a nothing task like docking became an event. Latching on to a space station meant aligning ports and matching orbits, something not easily done. The automatic docking computer upgrade soon became a firm favourite for obvious reasons.

Hopping from galaxy to galaxy, refuelling and skimming hydrogen from star surfaces wherever possible, steering clear of the GalCop police if you've been bad and arresting pirates if you're being good: *Elite*'s virtual world captured the imaginations of an entire generation of gamers and started an itch that's never been satisfyingly scratched since.

Load New Commander (Y/N)? Yes, yes, a thousand times yes.

🕹 🕹 🕹

EVE ONLINE

Release date: 2003 | Platform: PC | Developer: CCP Games

IN EARLY 2004, a guns-for-hire group known as the Guiding Hand Social Club received an execution request to satisfy a personal vendetta. Their target: Mirial, Chief Executive Officer of the supremely powerful Ubiqua Seraph corporation. Over the next year, Guiding Hand members joined the Ubiqua Seraph ranks and slowly began working their way up the ladder, spreading themselves across all sub-divisions of the corporation and even worming their way, in one case, into the role of captaining a ridiculously rare and expensive spaceship.

Organising a hit on this grand a scale was like setting up a checkmate on a chessboard 80x80 squares, not 8x8. It took months of planning, and some members of the Guiding Hand became personal confidants of Mirial. One even allegedly reached a position to influence Ubiqua's corporate policy.

When everybody was in place, the order to attack came down, and the Ubiqua Seraph, one of the most dominant forces in *EVE Online* history, was no more.

Seized assets included rare ships, expensive minerals, new technologies and money siphoned straight from the company account. Around 30 billion Interstellar Kredits' worth of damage was inflicted, with the perpetrators netting about 20 billion ISK for their troubles. Mirial was executed, her escape pod nuked and her frozen body recovered and handed to the party who ordered the hit. Calling cards were left in every emptied Ubiqua Seraph hangar so there could be no mistaking what had transpired. The goods were gone and Ubiqua Seraph had been disbanded, never to return. The single greatest video-gaming heist in history had taken place, and nobody could do anything about it.

EVE Online is a world unto itself, a massive multiplayer online (MMO) role-playing sci-fi game set in a giant universe and populated by different races, alliances and professions. Open markets see anything and everything from schematics and books to giant ships trading hands (a giant e-eBay, if you like). Alliance CONCORD acts like a police force, confiscating illegal goods and fining those who break the in-game laws.

CCP Games created this world. Under the guidance of its players, *EVE Online* has flourished into something far greater and more complex than any developer could ever imagine.

Earning a living in *EVE Online* depends on the job you want to do. Material workers can earn good wages by mining rare elements and trading them to areas in short supply. Freelancers can play about taking odd jobs and dabbling with stocks – though like real life there are no financial assurances to fall back on. Ship building is a hugely complex vocation. Piracy, meanwhile, is a very lucrative line of work, albeit risky. Anger the wrong people and you could find yourself hunted by mega-corporations. Then you've got investment management careers to consider: in 2009, user Xabier allegedly embezzled over 100 billion ISK (worth over $2000 at the current exchange rate) through dodgy dealings.

When an MMO lets you create a business, hire employees, commit industrial espionage (by hiring others to infiltrate and wipe out different companies) and cash in on it all, it's not a stretch to claim it's outgrown mere game status. *EVE Online* is a social subset centred around a role-playing game but featuring real ties and contracts between people.

So great is the weight of the world that *EVE Online* even has a council of elected players that acts on behalf of *EVE Online* fans, much like a real government. The Council of Stellar Management meets with developers and producers from CCP Games to suggest improvements and alterations to the game and to discuss issues raised on the official *EVE Online* forums.

It can be a terrifying world to step into, but play it right and it can also be one of the most rewarding of all gaming fictions. Just be aware that, if you find yourself in a position of power, play nice or it won't be long before there's a price on your head too.

👾 👾 👾

F-ZERO GX

**Release date: 2003 | Platform: Nintendo GameCube |
Developer: Amusement Vision (Sega Subsidiary)**

ONCE UPON A TIME, the games industry wasn't a three-way race between Sony, Nintendo and Microsoft. For a long time, there was just SEGA and Nintendo going head to head, and it was a bitter fight that lasted until Sony arrived on the scene and nuked the market with the PlayStation. In those days, people dreamed of a collaboration between

SEGA and Nintendo. A meeting of the minds of the Sonic and Mario creators. Sadly, everybody knew it was fantasy.

But the story didn't end with the predictable outcome. It was a sad day when SEGA eventually exited the hardware business to focus solely on development and production of games. Yet the shift in focus opened new doors for the Japanese publisher, and the world's dream pairing of SEGA and Nintendo finally happened. *F-Zero GX* is the first result of that teamwork.

F-Zero GX has been called one of the greatest racers of all time by some rather respectable industry fellows and you'd be wrong to argue. Thirty micro-plasma-powered antigravity racers, twenty-six tracks that feel like they've fallen out of an Escher painting and speeds of over 2000 km/h make for explosive racing. Did somebody say sonic boom? It's a joining of speed and strategy, and its only faults involve some rather steep difficulty curves – nothing a little practice wouldn't hammer out – and box art so heinous it would send the hunchback of Notre Dame screaming for the hills.

The racer is a cross between the speed and seriousness of *Formula 1* and the dangers of *Total Wipeout*, where all the vehicles have been retrofitted with the little red button from the *Men In Black* car for zany ceiling driving in tunnels. Oh, and that little red button is permanently depressed. Tubular courses wind in every possible direction, and speed boost pads, gravel traps and gigantic jumps add further excitement to already-pulsating levels.

The real beauty of *GX*'s racing comes from its customisation system. Every ship has unique attributes and before each race there's a simple slider to tinker with to rebalance the top speed/acceleration ratio in preparation for each track's personality. If none of the ships is to your liking, custom vehicles can be pieced together from a treasure chest of parts, with better upgrades unlocking the deeper you push into the game.

Ships come fitted with air brakes on either side, which gives rise to a little trick known as snaking. The brakes' primary functions are to lean into turns or to throw a ship into a drift. But leaning also accelerates the ship, and expert players can use the brakes to 'snake' quickly through entire courses and gain artificial boosts through weaving. Snaking isn't for everybody of course, and in certain circles it's even frowned upon, but it's a deliberate inclusion by SEGA and a whole other skill level to try to grasp once the standard racing is over.

While other futuristic racers stray into weapons territory, *F-Zero GX* is refreshingly arms-free. Ships can, however, perform sideways shunts and fast spins to maim other racers or to knock them off the course completely. Knowing when to fight and when to press on is all part of the grand *F-Zero GX* strategy, and it's a strategy mercifully unspoiled by the homing missiles and blue shells of its competitors. Brilliantly there is a boost bar, but it also doubles as a health bar too. It's all well and good boosting forward, but spend all your energy and one collision will knock you out of the race for good.

GX is the first *F-Zero* to feature a single-player story mode, and welcome though it may be, it is merely a sideshow to the Grand Prix tournaments: five cups and twenty-six circuits of eye-bleeding tussles, combat and non-Euclidean geometries. Mastering them takes weeks. Mastering them at the highest difficulties, months.

GX is a racer with it all. It completely reinvigorated a dated franchise without turning its back on *F-Zero*'s heritage, and it did so in a way that hasn't been equalled or bettered by a competitor since.

👾 👾 👾

FINAL FANTASY VII

Release date: 1997 | Platform: PlayStation | Developer: Squaresoft

VII OR VI? Or *IX*? Or possibly *IV* or even *I*? *II, III, V, VIII, X, XI, XIII* and *XIV* can safely be discounted and *XII* is just too much of a departure from the norm to be considered. But the rest? It almost requires a coin toss to set them apart from each other, especially *VI*, *VII* and *IX*.

The issue is *Final Fantasy*, a series of Japanese role-playing games (JRPGs) that is almost universally lauded but extremely divisive. Whether *VII* really is better than *VI* or *IX* is a discussion that could only be tackled in the depth it deserves with a PhD, but as it's the JRPG that conquered the West and one of the biggest games to contribute to the original PlayStation's domination, *VII* is the wisest pick of them all.

With the exception of the original *Final Fantasy*, it's also the most welcoming of the bunch. *Final Fantasy VII*'s explosive beginning (literally – it involves bombing a reactor in the name of freedom) slowly introduces the game's many mechanics, and the drip, drip, drip of new features doesn't let up until well into the thirty-hour-plus journey. Unlike certain other series entries, *Final Fantasy VII*'s mechanics are as intuitive as they come. The JRPG is a monster of a genre with all sorts of difficulties aimed at all sorts of skill levels and so, with its simple-to-grasp mechanics and its unparalleled plot devices, you'd struggle to find a game that's a better ambassador for the genre than *Final Fantasy VII*.

It's the story of Cloud Strife, an ex-soldier turned freedom fighter, who clubs together with a band of misfits to try to prevent a global catastrophe by stopping mega corporation Shinra from sucking all the energy from the planet Gaia (and later a madman from tapping into this energy to rule the world – feel free to insert your best maniacal laugh here). The journey takes the group from continent to continent via submarines and airships, and encompasses everything from shady cities and haunted mansions to abandoned ruins and floating theme parks. It involves breeding and racing ostrich-like birds called chocobos and snowboarding down mountains in the middle of an avalanche. The trip even calls for some treasure-hunting and diplomacy, and what's been described so far is just a fraction of the number of side quests.

Every *Final Fantasy* features, among other things, entirely different worlds, plots, characters and battle mechanics. *VII* boasts the best of everything. The brilliant magic system is based around small collectible orbs called Materia. Different orbs are imbued with different spells and abilities, and whoever has slotted a Materia orb into their weapon or armour has access to its skill. Different equipment has different Materia slots, so choosing the right equipment isn't as simple as looking at which items have the best attack and defence statistics. The more a Materia orb is used, the more powerful it grows, and linking different Materia together with set equipment opens up new strategic doors.

The core action comes from random battles. When exploring hostile territories and moving about the world map, the team will be susceptible to attack. You fight battles by hand-picking a team of three (sometimes fewer in special circumstances) and selecting each individual's actions on a turn-by-turn basis. Needless to say – hence its appearance in this list – the battle system is masterfully designed.

If any game wants to keep you entertained for what will be weeks if not months at a time, it needs to do more than satisfy a few basic criteria. *Final Fantasy VII* is more than a couple of ideas repeated and stretched to cram three discs full of content. Its original score is one of the most evocative soundtracks ever devised for a game, and is rightly held up as a landmark in gaming sound. Likewise, central antagonist Sephiroth is the baddest of all bad guys – a character so despicable it's impossible not to love him. You'll almost find yourself rooting for his success, not because the story is a failure but because he's just too great a character to write off in one game (he's since appeared in a few other titles).

It seems wrong even to attempt to sum up the *Final Fantasy* series, let alone the much, much wider world of JRPGs in general, with just one game. *Skies of Arcadia*, *Chrono Trigger*, *Dragon Quest VIII*, *Lost Odyssey*, *Shining Force*, *Disgaea*, *Tales of Symphonia*, *Fire Emblem* and, of course, *Final Fantasies IV*, *IX* and *VI*... There are more amazing worlds to lose yourself into than one person can fit into a single lifetime. If you want just a tiny glimpse of what you're missing, there's no better place to start than the first *Final Fantasy* of the 3D age, *Final Fantasy VII*.

🐙 🐙 🐙

FORZA MOTORSPORT 3

Release date: 2009 | Platform: Xbox 360 | Developer: Turn 10 Studios

IN THE TIME it took Sony developer Polyphony Digital to make the step across console generations between legendary racing simulator *Gran Turismo*'s fourth and fifth core titles, Microsoft and Turn 10 Studios introduced head-to-head competitor *Forza Motorsport*, released two sequels and had a year spare to sit back and marvel at their surgical strike on Sony's bow. Rush job? Au contraire: *Forza Motorsport 3* is the connoisseur's 'serious' motoring title of choice.

Good looks, pinpoint handling and in-car cockpit cams are all present and accounted for, but, as those features are the absolute bare minimum of what you'd want from a racer that claims to have everything, there's no need to bang on about them. What matters is authenticity. The Ferrari F335 looks, sounds and handles like a Ferrari F335; the Dodge Ram SRT10 looks, sounds and handles like a Dodge Ram SRT10; and the other four-hundred-and-something vehicles (a number that grows with each downloadable content pack) all look, sound and handle like their real counterparts. No expense has been spared in the goal for realism.

Central to everything is a fully customisable assists system you can tweak as your confidence and ability grow. Jump behind the wheel of a Gumpert Apollo in real life and, unless your name's The Stig, you'll barely make it to the end of one lap without introducing the top of its roof to the asphalt and the bonnet to the safety barrier.

In the game you can try it with all assists off, of course, or you can test the waters with auto-braking, ABS, automatic gears and a few other options all tipped to full. Over time the sliding scales – which also include opponent skill – can be lowered and re-raised if necessary across all game modes until you've found the sweet spot you feel you want to race in.

The approach is the first step towards scrapping the traditional notion of a game imposing its will on the player and replacing it with modes that empower the end user. You win more experience for racing with fewer assists on, but as you win plenty for finishing in first place you can decide what's more important: a comfortable victory every time or a nail-biting balance that means every tournament is decided on the last bend. It's your decision. After all, it's your game.

It's a running theme throughout *Forza Motorsport 3*: the game is yours to do with whatever you want. If you mess up you can hit a button to rewind the action back to before it all went askew, or you can carry on and try to claw your way back through the pack to cling on to the badge that says you finished a race cleanly without using the rewind mechanic. As you play the career mode, the game will suggest tournaments tailored precisely to your ability, racing style and favoured vehicles, but you're free to ignore them if you want. You can simply spend all your time in between races accepting the offers it throws in your way and powering through to another, brand-new, event, or the time can be spent picking and choosing your racing calendar carefully. Whatever type of racer you want to be, *Forza Motorsport 3* accommodates your wishes.

Away from the wheel-to-wheel action of the 100-plus tracks, there is more content that underlines your importance as a *Forza Motorsport 3* game owner. While other car games handle their licensed vehicles with great care, *Forza Motorsport 3* gives you the tools to slap whatever paint jobs and decals you like on to your ride and tune under the hood to your heart's content. Custom-tuned cars, skins and plain old vehicles unlocked deeper into the game can be bought and sold in an online marketplace, with each livery job and vehicle going for however much in-game currency the seller wishes to charge. Some *Forza* owners pay their entire way through the campaign with funds raised from expert car painting and selling. Even fully edited replay movies can be uploaded to your personal storefront and sold at a price.

Forza Motorsport 3 is every racer to every racing fan. The *Fast and the Furious* lovers will look for the dedicated drift modes and discover they're part of every single race thanks to a drift-counter button. The driver who wants to take their own real car and put it into a racing situation will be able to do just that and toy with some custom jobs too, just to check them out before investing real money in the car on the driveway outside. Gamers wanting a quick race for instant thrills will find every car and every track accessible from the first second via the exhibition mode. The car enthusiast who wants to work their way up from the Ford Fiesta to the Bugatti Veyron will have months of racing to enjoy. And finally those with a competitive edge will find an online racing world packed with people who are just as passionate about cars as they are. Whatever you could possible want from a 'serious' racer, *Forza 3* delivers it in spades. How could anything else be recommended in its place?

🐙 🐙 🐙

GEOMETRY WARS: RETRO EVOLVED 2

Release date: 2008 | Platform: Xbox 360 | Developer: Bizarre Creations

THE TWIN-STICK shooter is a beautifully simple idea. Plonk one ship/person/animal (delete as appropriate) on to a bordered 2D plane filled with enemies, then assign one stick to the central figure's movement and a second stick to weapon fire, being careful to ensure movement and weapon direction are entirely independent of one another. If an enemy hits you, you die. If you're generous, toss in a get-out-of-jail-free card in the shape of a screen-clearing bomb, and finish by ensuring each wave of enemies is more dangerous than the last. Then sit down, relax and watch people struggle to survive for as long as possible.

Geo Wars 2 (we're all friends here) takes the above formula and runs with it. There have been countless similar titles since *Robotron: 2084* first pioneered this claustrophobic concept in 1982. None has succeeded quite like *Geo Wars 2*, partly because the classic ingredients of the genre make up just one sixth of Bizarre Creations' sequel.

The five other variations are King, Waves, Pacifism, Sequence and Deadline. King hands you one life, places a few short-lived circular safe zones down on the grid and unleashes oodles of baddies all rushing to get at you. The catch? You can only shoot while in the shielded areas and you're stripped of bombs. Waves is another one-life deal that keeps sweeping the entire grid with lines of rockets.

Pacifism is the third mono-life challenge with the added disadvantage of – you've guessed it – no weapons. Thankfully, there are gates that explode when ruptured, wiping out any pursuers in dangerously close proximity. Sequence is just that, a predetermined sequence of twenty thirty-second levels. Finally, Deadline is to all intents and purposes the classic mode from the first *Geometry Wars* (a mini-game tucked away in *Project Gotham Racing 2*), condensed into a three-minute nugget.

Visually it's a corker. *Geo Wars 2*'s colour kaleidoscope lets your television set show off to the best of its capabilities and yet never distracts your eyes from the prize. It would have been easy to bamboozle watchers with multi-coloured fireworks bursting all over the swaying gridlines, but the effects are never overdone. And just to add to the splendour there's a little footnote to the above features: four player co-op and competitive modes. Booyah!

Don't go thinking you're done just yet. There's one other element that fast-tracks *Geo Wars 2* to the top of the pile, and just to confuse matters it's a feature that has been present in games almost from year one. It is – drum roll please – the humble leaderboard.

Leaderboards have traditionally been a passive mainstay of gaming. Primarily used for arcade cabinets when gamers would strive to leave their initials at the top of the scoreboards for all subsequent players to see, leader boards usually appear in two locations: after the Game Over screen and as a sub-section of the main menu.

Not in *Geo Wars 2*. Bizarre Creations saw the potential of the underappreciated high-score system and forced it into the spotlight where it shone like a scorned Scottish singer belting out *Les Misérables* anthems. The move transformed simple post-game statistics into the linchpin of the entire experience and the sole driving force behind its one-more-go factor. When you play *Geo Wars 2*, you can see two important things on the screen: your score and the score of the friend just above you. This info is shown on the main menu and during the game itself. Beat your mate's total and the displayed data reverts to the friend one place higher. It does, of course, all depend on your having gaming friends in the first place, but so do plenty of games nowadays and it's not hard to meet people on the Xbox Live community.

The leaderboard stunt is slowly but surely being adopted by more developers and it's not hard to see why. It taps into the primitive need to measure yourself against your peers, and its instant friend updates are especially pertinent in the days of Twitter, Facebook and other social-networking applications. *Geometry Wars* doesn't just ask you to beat the game, it asks you to beat your friends too. The six modes are different takes on one beautiful concept, and the leader board meta-game holding them all together is the single most addictive gaming bolt-on you'll ever encounter.

GOD HAND

**Release date: 2007 (2006) | Platform: PlayStation 2 |
Developer: Clover Studio**

THE WONDERFUL AND criminally underappreciated Clover Studio only survived for just over two years, but in that time it released three stunning new intellectual properties: *Viewtiful Joe*, *kami* and its final game, *God Hand*. Clover Studio's swansong, a project headed up by legendary *Resident Evil* creator Shinji Mikami, is unquestionably the oddest of the bonkers bunch.

Golden Axe: once good, now terrible. *Streets of Rage II*: once great, now not so hot. *Double Dragon*, *Final Fight* and *Teenage Mutant Ninja Turtles*: once awesome, now flawsome. The beat-'em-up genre has aged terribly, and *God Hand* is the game that single-handedly turns its fortunes around and brings it kicking and screaming through a painful three-dimensional gestation into a bold new world of greatness.

The *God Hand* in question is literally a god's hand, grafted on to the freshly severed arm of martial artist Gene to prevent a powerful demon from rising up and destroying the world. You've probably heard weirder premises, but not many.

God Hand the game is as ridiculous as its plot. The beat-'em-up genre is next to impossible to play straight, and part of what makes *God Hand* so special is that it's a pure parody of its peers. Gene and companion Olivia are caught up in a Wild West adventure where their foes include cosplaying midgets, whip-wielding jester women and gorilla wrestlers, and that's just the saner parts of the quest. Did somebody say something about receiving a lap dance from a woman and then turning into a Chihuahua?

But the game does more than simply plonk the beat-'em-up concept into a 3D world and play the buffoon to untangle the genre's modern-day issues. Clover Studio's last act is a truly groundbreaking release and a glimpse of what the future of beat-'em-ups could be if more development studios follow its lead. Its main hook is to wipe the concept of predefined controls and combos off the table and instead hand you complete freedom in setting up Gene's abilities. Three moves of your choosing are assignable to three spare controller buttons. You can change them at any point, and mix and match attacks to try out new combos.

With over 100 moves in total, there's plenty to experiment with. Whereas old beat-'em-ups tend to give you one or two context-sensitive attacks and a handful of specials, *God Hand* encourages you to take a role in the creation of Gene's combos. On top of that, *God Hand* layers another few mechanics made of pure win: a difficulty meter that rises with good play and inserts tougher enemies and bigger bonuses into levels, but drops when you take damage. Gathering roulette orbs lets you spin a move-filled roulette wheel to unleash a super technique, while taunting and dodging enemies (the right stick lets you dodge in four directions) adds power to the *God Hand* itself and eventually turns Gene into an invincible demon for as long as the charge holds.

God Hand doesn't need to be perfect to pull it all off, and it's not. Frustrations arise from low-health pick-ups (dropped fruit, of course, just like the olden days) and a temperamental lock-on system. Yet all is soon forgiven and forgotten when Gene is bending an enemy over his knee and spanking them so hard they fly head-first into a wall. It's one long string of non sequiturs, a series of bosses and levels that make no sense – weirder, actually, so make that *negative* sense – segregated by trips to a casino to play slots, blackjack and poker.

The reason the industry isn't swimming in beat-'em-ups like *God Hand* is because Clover Studio's closing project vanished from the shelves almost without trace. Nobody's prepared to follow a leader who leads with a disappearing act. The world wasn't ready for *God Hand* or any imitators, and the world is poorer for it. Play *God Hand* and you'll spy a glimpse of what might have been if a few more people had taken the plunge with their wallets. As the box says, there just ain't no justice in the wild, weird West.

🐙 🐙 🐙

GOD OF WAR

Release date: 2005 | Platform: PlayStation 2 |
Developer: Sony Computer Entertainment Santa Monica Studio

IT'S BIG, it's brash, it's brutal. *God of War* is an uberviolent slashathon through Ancient Greek mythology, and it's a strong contender for the crown of Sony's greatest ever exclusive. Read up on your Grecian mythology and you'll discover tales of violence, lust and more violence. *God of War* tells a tale as violent and as saucy as any, and then some.

Cast as hardened warrior Kratos – a beefcake as white as mayonnaise save for some blood-red paint that in all likelihood isn't paint – and armed with two blades attached to long chains, *God of War* throws you into a tumultuous age where armies and gods clash for power. You play a peacekeeper role using the logic that nobody can fight if they're already dead, and set off out to tear man and beast limb from limb, tail from tentacle.

Kratos doesn't discriminate. Gorgons are beheaded, Minotaurs are eviscerated and Hydras are turned into snake sushi. If it moves, Kratos kills it. There is another reason for all the bloodshed, something about Pandora's Box, avenging your family and some other stuff, but don't be suckered into believing any of it: Kratos just loves gore. His trip through Athens, Pandora and Hades itself is just a means to a very bloody end.

God of War makes the PlayStation 2 do things nobody thought it could ever do. Even now, a generation on, it's a feast for the eyes and it's just as exciting to handle. From eye-popping set-pieces to bombastic cutscenes, *God of War* is a stunner. The seamless transition of the opening cinematic into the game fooled more than a few people who couldn't believe anything that looked that good could be playable. Years on and it still has the power to surprise.

It may be built on a bedrock of shock and gore, but *God of War* is no slouch in the other departments. The third-person-perspective action game mixes combat and puzzles to great effect. Its fighting system is as well balanced as any other action game's, and the puzzles are taxing enough without overstaying their welcome. It's an action game after all: there's room for *some* head-scratching, but not much.

Kratos is a slicing machine, a man whose balletic attacks appear only to those in the button-punching groove. At your command, Kratos spins and flails about with chains and blades ripping and shredding all over the shop. He can floor enemy after enemy in seconds, and when up against the more intimidating foes he'll finish them off with a disgusting execution performed by pressing and mashing the correct buttons when prompts appear on-screen. Before Kratos, no character had ever dared sprint up the spine of a Titan and then wrench its head off with his bare hands. Now it seems as though all his imitators are doing it.

God of War is a game about scale. It's a long game, which obviously helps, and it's one that constantly attempts to make your jaw drop. Environments stretch off into the far distance with battles waging as far as the eye can see. Towers climb into the heavens, far higher than you could ever realistically hope to scale (though you'll certainly try). Beasts so huge they could use a blue whale as a toothpick are your foes, and little old Kratos must get his head down, sharpen his blades and push on unperturbed.

The game is the greatest fireworks display ever created: it isn't overly clever but it'll have you cooing right up until the big finish. It's the spectacle of spectacles, and it's the game the *Clash of the Titans* film wishes it could be. All praise the *God of War*.

GOLDENEYE 007

Release date: 1997 | Platform: Nintendo 64 | Developer: Rareware

THE SEVENTEENTH BOND film was a film of firsts. Pierce Brosnan's first portrayal of Bond; Judi Dench's first portrayal of M; the first BMW Bond car; and the first plot to draw inspiration from outside Ian Fleming's stories. It wasn't the first Bond film to have a video-game tie-in, but it was the only film ever to enjoy a game adaptation that captures the hearts and minds of all who play it. *GoldenEye 007* is legendary in gaming circles, and it stands for all that is right in the world of movie licences.

Often imitated, never matched, Rareware's *GoldenEye 007* is the lifeblood of local multiplayer gaming. No title before or since can claim to have brought so many parties of gamers together for game nights. A four-player deathmatch to *that* Bond music and with *those* Bond characters was worth buying a Nintendo 64 for alone. People bled not weeks or months but years into the *GoldenEye 007* multiplayer mode. It was social triumph, and, despite the now-garish graphics (though at the time the game's tech moved virtual mountains), it can still stake that claim.

Revisiting or discovering *GoldenEye 007* for the first time in the current age can be a disappointing experience at first, not least because of a control system rendered obsolete by *Halo* and *Call of Duty*'s newer industry standards. But a couple of practice games are all it takes to flick the switch of the time machine in your mind and warp you back to 1997. Prior to *GoldenEye 007*, multiplayer console shooters were in short supply so it's not hard to see the initial appeal of the shooter. A fortuitous release window was not what kept people hooked, however. That was entirely down to the finely tuned shooting and a selection of memorable levels that would be first in line for nomination were there a video-game equivalent of world heritage sites.

Multiple scenarios and schemes allow you to mix and match game types of your choosing. From the standard deathmatch and a capture-the-flag variant, to 'Man With the Golden Gun' (a one-hit-kill weapon is hidden in each map) and a one-hit-kill galore mode 'Licence to Kill', there is something for everybody, especially when weapon sets including rockets, proximity mines, lasers and just plain slapping are available. Multiplayer gaming just doesn't get better than waiting for an unsuspecting victim by hiding in a secret vent armed with a silenced PP7 pistol.

Four-player split-screen perfection: that's *GoldenEye 007*. Iconic levels that would go on to be remade time and time again ('Facility' might well be the finest map in multiplayer history), iconic characters (anybody picking unfairly short Oddjob would immediately suffer the wrath of the other three players) and iconic mechanics (the radar – a feature from a bygone age – means nobody can hide) make the game, well, *iconic*.

The multiplayer mode forced many people to neglect the single-player offering after the first play through, but that's more to do with the multiplayer's longevity than any dearth of single-player quality. If more of today's shooters were to draw inspiration from *GoldenEye 007* instead of trying to emulate *Call of Duty*, the first-person-shooter landscape would be filled with significantly better titles. *GoldenEye 007*'s revolutionary approach to stealth meant many levels could be cleared through sneaking and silent executions – something completely unheard of at the time.

Precision aiming, and sniping in particular, were also huge advances for the genre. The thrill of performing a successful disarm or a headshot (yes, *GoldenEye 007* started gaming's obsession with the one-hit-kill headshot) was second only to the shock of the game's scale. *GoldenEye 007* is huge, and each level of difficulty is bigger than the last.

There are three difficulties in all, each with an increasing number of objectives. A typical mission on Agent mode might involve simply reaching a level's end, but bump it up to Secret Agent and oo Agent difficulties and, not only will enemies be more deadly, you will also need to steal extra plans or sabotage key equipment along the way – often taking you to previously unexplored areas of the sprawling maps. Why haven't more games borrowed this idea? Some things just belie sense. Complete the objectives within a certain, often tight, time limit and you're rewarded with unlockable cheats to play with, featuring everything from invincibility, invisibility and infinite ammo modes to silly giant-head and paintball-gun options.

Serious or fun, single player or multiplayer: it doesn't matter what you want from a shooter as *GoldenEye 007* has all bases covered. Rareware had planned to resurrect the game with enhanced graphics for the Xbox 360 (this was after EA published an inferior shooter *GoldenEye: Rogue Agent*, related by name only), but despite having an almost complete version ready to go, the release was blocked for licensing reasons. Instead, Activision allowed Eurocom (who played no part in the original) to remake the game for the Wii with Daniel Craig's likeness in place of Pierce Brosnan's. It's *GoldenEye*, to a point, but it's too far gone from the original ever to be considered a replacement. *GoldenEye 007*'s legend rumbles on…

🐙 🐙 🐙

GRAND THEFT AUTO: VICE CITY
Release date: 2002 | Platform: PlayStation 2 | Developer: Rockstar North

GRAND. THEFT. AUTO. If your experience of video games is derived from their portrayal in the mass media, you'll be forgiven for thinking those three little words are the most controversial in the entire industry. *Grand Theft Auto* has been called many things since its inception. Murder simulator. Prostitute bludgeoner. Crime trainer. There's a modicum of truth in all of them. It is a violent game about the seedier side of life, that fact cannot be disputed, but claiming murder is all there is to it would be akin to saying the same about *City of God* or *Goodfellas*. Headline-baiting though it may be, *Grand Theft Auto*, and *Vice City* in particular, are exemplary crime dramas coated in a witty social commentary that's all too aware of its own controversy. Better still, it's one hell of a game.

In *Vice City*, you play as Mafia member Tommy Vercetti, a man recently released from jail who finds himself trapped in the city's criminal underbelly to earn a living. Through shady drug deals and heists, unscrupulous meetings and more than a few shoot-outs and car chases, Tommy climbs the criminal ladder by earning respect and ensuring those about him take on more lead than their bodies can handle.

While other *Grand Theft Autos* focus primarily on the nineties and noughties, *Vice City* flicked the calendar back to 1986. As in every other game in the series, the titular setting is a take-off of a real city, in this case Miami. The setting is an expertly crafted pastiche of films and shows like *Scarface* and *Miami Vice*, with enough explicit nods to each to give anyone a sore neck.

Go anywhere, do anything. That's the raw thrill of *Grand Theft Auto*, and *Vice City* was the first playground where you could really make the most of this promise – more so than in *Grand Theft Auto 3* even, the precursor to *Vice City* and the game that put the series in the limelight. Whether it was stealing a hot rod and charging across the city's beaches, jumping from rooftop to rooftop on a tuned Ducati motorcycle, or hovering in a news helicopter, *Vice City* unlatched the shackles and handed you the keys to the city. The empowerment was unlike anything else on the market, and it was all in a vibrant, colourful world that really embraced its eighties style. The city is so unashamedly pink and fluffy, so focused on framing the bikini-clad roller skaters and the Hawaiian shirts, that it stumbles upon the exaggerated eighties vibe everybody remembers, creating a doorway into the past you step through every time the game is loaded.

The game's sandbox nature applies to everything, right down to hopping into a taxi or a fire engine and partaking in law-abiding missions. Some killing cannot be avoided, but you could just as easily fill your spare time in between missions by working as a freelance policeman or ambulance assistant as you could by making off with night workers and then killing them for your cash back.

The greatest gaming memories are made up of moments, and *Grand Theft Auto: Vice City* is a collection of these moments. A licensed soundtrack far superior to any other in gaming history ensures these moments could occur every time you enter a vehicle. Radio stations cover all genres, from rock and pop to rap, soul, disco, classical and even talk shows, with comical adverts for fictional products (often snipes at real life) between songs and shows. A dusky police chase to the sound of Judas Priest isn't long forgotten. Nor is a slow morning cruise in the Florida sun with 'Billie Jean' pumping out of the car speakers.

Its technological breakthroughs have long since been bettered, but, even though sandbox games seem to be released every other week, nothing has ever come close to recapturing the magic of *Grand Theft Auto: Vice City*'s writing, mechanics, missions and world. Not even the other *Grand Theft Autos*.

🐙 🐙 🐙

HALF-LIFE 2

Release date: 2004 | Platform: PC | Developer: Valve Corporation

HALF-LIFE OR *Half-Life 2*: it's the Sophie's choice of the gaming world. Two groundbreaking heavyweights starring mute scientist Gordon Freeman as a crowbar-brandishing defender of humanity and freedom. Both need to be played, along with their multiple expansions, but *Half-Life 2* is too wonderful and innovative to be kept from these pages.

Some will point towards the zero-point energy field manipulator – otherwise known as the gravity gun – as the reason why *Half-Life 2*'s reviews broke every known scoring system in the galaxy. The weapon can pick up any object within reason and hold it steady to block incoming fire or propel it towards a target at devastating velocities. It can blast obstacles out of the way, or be used to place weights gently on see-saws to open up new paths. Nothing like it had been seen before. Unsurprisingly, plenty like it have been seen since.

Others will want to single out the physics model and the game's Source engine as more general explanations of *Half-Life 2*'s popularity. Level design favours brain over brawn and rewards those with a problem-solving mind. The game is filled with physics puzzles galore, and they all exist because Valve Corporation's Source engine and the Havok physics software is a cut above anything else on the market.

The story is another big favourite when it comes to assigning individual praise. Despite uttering a grand total of zero syllables, Gordon Freeman befriends a few people during *Half-Life 2*, including one Alyx Vance and her pet, a robo-titan called Dog. Alyx is the closest any developer has come to reality when designing a human. Just behind her are *Half-Life 2*'s other characters. They burst through the uncanny valley without taking a scratch, and feel like they could step out of the screen at any moment and carry on their conversations.

Half-Life 2 doesn't just tell its story through characters and dialogue. The world paints hundreds of pictures all at once, revealing struggles and last stands of humans defending their homes long ago without ever showing you anything more than a few directed blood streaks and remnants of failed barricades. Conveying stories in this way is normally a tough skill to master, but Valve Corporation is *the* master of its trade. No inch of the world goes to waste: every brick and every poster is there for a reason, and the world is bursting with untold stories for the inquisitive adventurer to find.

The truth is there's no one reason why *Half-Life 2* is widely believed to be the best PC game of all time. Its greatness comes down to every element working in harmony with one another, from weapons (the gravity gun is just the tip of the iceberg) to level design to music and more. Vehicular sections are commonly the bane of most shooters, but *Half-Life 2*'s off-foot levels contain jaw-dropping sequences still talked about today. Flooring a hoverboat's gas pedal to race underneath a toppling chimney stack or zig-zagging a buggy past homing bombs and pursuit choppers are thrills other games can't come close to matching.

For a title so meticulously pieced together, Valve Corporation's best-loved game – this is the second of four games from the legendary Bellevue-based developer – is frighteningly big. Set-piece after set-piece, chase after chase, the game rumbles on and on through City 17's boroughs and its surrounding countryside. It's a world you've seen fractional glimpses of in films like *Minority Report*, *War of the Worlds* and *Children of Men*: a frightening look at the future and what could come to pass, made all the more horrific by the realism of it all. Freedom fighters versus Big Brother. Backstreet scientists conducting desperate research in secret versus alien technologies and corporations with unlimited resources at their disposal and zero accountabilities.

Half-Life 2 is an epic underdog story created by the industry's best developers using the best technology available. Valve Corporation has never made a bad game. Valve Corporation has never made a good game. Valve Corporation only knows how to make great games, and with *Half-Life 2* they hit the jackpot.

HALO: COMBAT EVOLVED

Release date: 2002 (2001) | Platform: Xbox | Developer: Bungie Studios

CALLING A SHOOTING game *Combat Evolved* is fairly brazen, some might say arrogant. Microsoft didn't wait for the critics to say it in their reviews or the gamers to say it on forums. They wanted to be the first to come right out and proclaim that *Halo* would be the game to change the landscape of shooting games forever. Bold? Unquestionably. Foolhardy? Perhaps. Correct? Without a doubt.

Halo is the first-person shooter from which almost every subsequent first-person shooter – and plenty of other genres too – has taken its cues. It may have missed out on being the first FPS by almost twenty years, but *Halo* dissolved the rules governing the genre since its inception and designed a new blueprint for shooters to follow. The Gregorian Calendar measures time around the traditional incarnation of Jesus; first-person shooters measure time around the release of *Halo.*

The *Halo* in question is a giant ringworld Larry Niven would be proud of, an artificial planetary megastructure with Earth-like landscapes on the inner surface. It's the setting for a futuristic war between humans and an alien race called the Covenant. Fighting the fight for humanity is Spartan fighter Master Chief, a super-soldier who resembles a metallic green Power Ranger.

Before *Halo*, shooters measured progress with weapons. You'd begin with a pistol and you'd end up with a collection of guns so prodigious you'd need to train a pack of invisible mules to follow you behind enemy lines to carry them all. *Halo* recognised even a genetically enhanced super-soldier couldn't store an army's worth of guns on his back and axed the concept immediately. Master Chief can only carry two weapons at once; grenades are assigned to a separate button independent from the guns. Find a better weapon (though you'll struggle to top the godly pistol) and you'll need to sacrifice a current weapon to carry it. The decision to limit weapons to a pair isn't just an effort to remove fiddly inventories: it injects doses of strategy into weapon management, as well as instilling an artificial fear that you might not have the right tools for the unknown jobs up ahead.

Before *Halo*, life was measured with a bar and health was topped up with medipacks. In *Halo*, health is still topped up with medipacks, but the inclusion of a shield eventually brought about the end of clichéd life-giving bandages (along with the conspicuous crates they often came packaged in). Part of Master Chief's cutting-edge gear is the regenerating shield, a piece of kit ensuring the Spartan will never walk into a confrontation with a handicap. It allows the Chief to sprint to better locations and recover after a brief pause. The beep-beep-beep of a depleting shield is a warning to hide behind cover, the sound of the automated recharge a subtle battle cry to stand back up and start shooting again. The regenerating shield redefined gaming health systems across every genre on every platform. Exceptions are few and very far between.

Before *Halo*, death meant reloading old saves, restarting a level or booting up a mid-level quick save if you were playing on a PC. The smart checkpoint system does away with all these frustrations and auto saves in sensible locations as Master Chief works his way deeper into the levels. The checkpoints are essentially an auto quick save for a console game, and have since become a major feature in every major game – action, platform or otherwise.

Before *Halo*, FPS levels were largely corridor based. *Halo* also has its fair share of corridors, including one heinous cut-and-paste monstrosity known as the Library, but other areas feel like multiplayer maps dropped directly into a single-player game. Open areas let the artificial intelligence shine, and you have to figure out the best way to outsmart them. Optional vehicles pile on alternative strategies, obliterating any on-rails sensations that commonly dog other shooters.

The Halo feels like a tangible battleground, not a two-foot-wide strip designed to restrict player movement to either forward or back. And for those instances where Master Chief is confined to corridors, an inspired all-powerful mêlée attack instantly dispatches any alien too close for comfort – another feature cribbed by almost every shooter, first-person or otherwise, since.

From a soundtrack featuring what sounds like chanting monks to a campaign that could be enjoyed both cooperatively and alongside computer-controlled soldiers, *Halo* smashed all conventions. Its sequels expanded the lineage into the online multiplayer space and became the most dominant online shooters of their times, but the original *Halo* remains the best single-player game of them all.

Halo wasn't an evolution, it was a revolution. I once saw somebody with a middling grasp of English nickname the game *Halo: Combat Revolved*. Language barriers scuppered the sentiment somewhat but the comment was in the right place. *Viva la Revolución!*

HEARTS OF IRON II

Release date: 2005 | Platform: PC | Developer: Paradox Interactive

BAFFLING IS ONE word that nicely describes *Hearts of Iron II*. Intimidating is another.

There are more popular, better-received and friendlier strategy games out there, many of which deserve extended praise in another place and time. Yet there are none with the lavish attention to detail of *Hearts of Iron II*. It's a strategy game based on and around the events of World War II, and it's the best form of edutainment ever passed off as a lowly game.

Think board-game behemoth Risk but bigger. Far, far bigger. *Hearts of Iron II* is so huge that it lets you play as all the main ally and axis powers, of course, but it also lets you take control of countries such as Haiti or Ethiopia. You can control 175 nations in all, plus any sovereignty that declared independence (in real life or in the game) between 1936 and 1947, and steer them in a direction of your choosing. And it's not just armies you manage: it's *everything*.

How you fight on the battlefield determines your success in *Hearts of Iron II*. You piece together your land, sea and air forces bit by little bit and send them all over the world to fight the battles that need to be fought. Zoom out and you can act like a puppeteer, sending battalions and squadrons across the globe and telling them to attack and defend provinces on a real-time, hourly basis.

Unlike other strategy games, you don't have a production line of infinite troops you can simply churn out by gathering resources. There's a very small amount of that kind of strategy, but your primary goal in *Hearts of Iron II* is to keep your armies alive and hopefully gain inches of ground at a time as you do so. Zoom into individual battlefields and you can manage everything with frightening accuracy.

Hearts of Iron II is as historically accurate as a game can be. Paradox hit the libraries when researching it and every snippet of information unearthed has made it into the game. Battalions, generals, ministers and other leaders are all named and, in many cases, come with photographs. It's a game, yes, but it's genuinely informative too. Computer behaviour is based largely on truth, and history buffs will feel right at home with its reams of information.

Your staff and squads are all named for a reason. It's because every individual matters. Winning the war is about managing supplies and morale as much as it is about troop movement. Key players must be promoted to where they'll be most effective; recognising and dealing with underperforming branches will nip problems in the bud nice and early.

War isn't just won on the battlefield though. Back home, everything from the economy to scientific research to politics must be handled with absolute precision. Ensuring factories are firing on all cylinders and that clear supply routes thrive keeps the front line armed for the battles ahead, and maintaining diplomatic relations with countries friendly to your cause will let you trade valuable materials.

Diplomatic countries hold elections (you judge the outcome) and sweeping policy changes can be designed and executed to suit your ambitions. If you want to be a turncoat and ambush unsuspecting allies, so be it. It's your war to manage as you see fit.

While other games tend to focus on just big battles, it is *Heart of Iron II*'s treatment of the little skirmishes that really impresses. Two small African nations scrapping it out over a few acres of turf is never going to contribute a bean to the main fronts in Europe or the Pacific, but to those two tiny nations it's everything. *Hearts of Iron II* captures the big picture superbly. It also goes to great lengths to make entire games out of tiny pockets of the world. Its relative obscurity is a sorry tale of a gaming great buried under titles with smaller ideas and bigger budgets.

👾 👾 👾

HITMAN: BLOOD MONEY

Release date: 2006 | Platform: Xbox 360 | Developer: IO Interactive

IF IO INTERACTIVE'S *Hitman* series is to be believed, the life of an assassin is quite the riot. Not only do the grim reapers for hire get to travel the globe and sample some of the world's most exotic locations, they get a fat pay cheque while they do so and can rub shoulders with some of the world's richest and most famous characters. That the hitman would then invariably have to snap the necks of said elite is by the by. There's no such thing as an innocent with a price on their head, so you can rest assured those targets are targets for a good reason. It's a hard job but someone's got to do it. Don't pass up on the pleasure.

Blood Money is neither the biggest *Hitman* game nor the most popular. Its grandparent, *Hitman 2*, is the series' shining star, the game that transformed the brand into an overnight sensation, fondly remembered as a time-sucking masterpiece that let gamers bump off dictators and drug barons in dozens of creative ways. What many don't remember about *Hitman 2*, however, was its descent into a fairly linear and repetitive shooter towards its end.

Hitman: Blood Money, on the contrary, manages to capitalise on the promise glimpsed in earlier games. You play as bald hitman Agent 47 and, if you need to be told what your eventual goal is, it's best to give up on the idea of gaming right now.

Missions begin with briefings and snippets of intel to point you in a few directions. Each contracted kill is a puzzle – an open-ended one with countless correct solutions. Levels aren't A-to-B tales of killing so much as they are murder playgrounds: fully open areas to experiment in and toy with repeatedly. They're created to play over and over again in order to put increasingly complex routines to the test in search of the perfect kill. It's still fundamentally a third-person sneaking game, but at the same time *Blood Money* treads well into quiz-book brainteaser territory with the ability to hide in broad daylight using disguises.

Take the infamous opera-house level. Your targets are an actor, currently rehearsing on stage in front of the show's cast and crew, and a VIP spectator. You could sneak past security and snipe them both from the royal box, but that's fairly simple and just about the dullest thing you could do short of pulling out a book, waiting for rehearsals to finish and tailing them back home for a kill later that evening. OK, that's not actually an option. Suffice to say that the royal-box method is the blandest choice available. Smuggling objects into the theatre is tricky thanks to security checks. Do you ditch equipment and latch on to the tail of a tour group to sneak in, or do you sedate a set worker in the toilets, wear the uniform and then hide your kit in the toolbox? Do you climb to the rafters and place bombs on the lighting rigs and chandeliers, crushing your targets? Do you replace a replica gun with a real one and let a rehearsing actor do your first deadly deed? Do you slip that actor a sedative too, carefully study his routine notes and perform the mock execution scene yourself with the real gun 'accidentally' in your hands, making sure to crush the other victim with that bomb? Then there's the option of shooting your first target from afar with such precision timing that everybody thinks it's the stage gun gone wrong. Target number two can then be bumped off with the old bomb-in-a-toolbox routine outside his door. Decisions, decisions...

And they're just the possibilities if you're keen on playing it to achieve the Silent Assassin rating: a title bestowed on those who finish the jobs with minimal collateral damage in a quick time while arousing no suspicion, preferably by making the hit look like a terrible accident. You could simply throw caution to the wind and stroll in all guns blazing like you're auditioning for *Reservoir Dogs*, but that takes the fun of the *Mousetrap*-style plotting out of the equation.

Injecting birthday cakes with poison, pushing drunken fathers into alligator-infested lakes, exploding bibles during weddings, dousing barbecues with enough petroleum to incinerate the next user, shooting out the base of a glass-bottomed hot-tub overhanging a cliff face. Bad things come to those who are targeted by a hitman who waits, and *Blood Money* lets you scheme like no other game. Do your worst.

ICO

Release date: 2002 (2001) | Platform: PlayStation 2 | Developer: Team Ico

THE CUT-THROAT nature of the gaming business means quality unfortunately doesn't always generate monster sales. In *Ico*'s sad case, there's such a disparity between its gaming achievements and its sales figures, publisher Sony released it more than once to try to earn the figures it so richly deserved.

The few who do play *Ico* are part of an elite and fortunate club. One boy, one girl, one wicked queen, one castle and an infinite supply of evil shadow monsters are the main ingredients of this wonderful precursor to *Shadow of the Colossus*. You are the innocent young boy Ico, sealed and left to die in a deserted castle by a village terrified of the horns that sprouted from your head. An earthquake shatters your crypt and dumps you into a chamber where you soon discover a distressed girl named Yorda, similarly aged and equally lonely.

The goal is immediately obvious: escape the castle and run off together. Best-laid plans aren't always so easy to execute, however. Yorda speaks in an alien tongue and the communication is reduced to pure basics: hopeful calls and beckoning motions to draw Yorda near; anguished yelps in return to signify she's in trouble. The best way to keep the pair together is to link hands. One button does just that, and keeping it held tethers the children together – Ico pulling Yorda through the castle and Yorda every once in a while offering up resistance when she can't run as fast.

Trouble comes in the form of the oily shadow monsters, intent on dragging Yorda into the charcoal depths of conjured wells. Why is a mystery at first, and Ico is all the more harrowing for it. Ico's only riposte is to scoop up a cast-aside stick and bat them away as fast as possible. Fighting isn't his strong point but that's a deliberate feature: you never want to get to a position where you're swinging for the fences to save Yorda in the first place.

Even without clear dialogue between them, the pairing of Ico and Yorda is a heart-warming one. The two come to depend on each other, and not just to pull levers at the right time to open gates and portcullises. If Yorda can't quite jump far enough to bridge a gap in a walkway, Ico will reach down and grab her hand before she falls. She, too, is always on the lookout for Ico's welfare and is quick to call out in worry if he's in danger. And, if the incomprehensible language barrier is just too much to bear, a second play through comes with the option of subtitles to wipe away the mystery of Yorda's speech.

Sprinting through the castle innards with hands and fingers locked tightly together to the sound of nothing but footfalls on stone and wind whipping over the ramparts and whistling through the balustrades is a strangely uplifting sensation. The way the pair tiredly plonk themselves down on a settee and rest their heads on the other's shoulders to save the game is an even more touching moment. The two's escape journey is as beautiful as gaming can be. If Ico had a lonely hearts ad, it would read: 'Enjoys cuddles, long walks on the beach and sunsets. Looking for a companion to pass the time with.'

Ico is as soul-stirring as it gets. Forget about games: *Ico* rivals the very best from all forms of entertainment.

IKARUGA

Release date: 2001 | Platform: Arcade | Developer: Treasure

VERTICAL-SCROLLING shoot-'em-up (or 'shmup' if you're a fan of cheesy gamer slang) *Ikaruga* is a game that has flipped the bird at its humble beginnings and defied time's ravaging hands by growing more and more popular with each passing year. There are so many great scrolling shooters, of both the horizontal and vertical varieties, that it wouldn't be a stretch to fill this book with 100 of them and ignore every other genre, but with space for only one or two there's only room for the best. *Ikaruga* is more than great enough to meet that requirement.

The core elements of all scrolling shooters are the same. You move a ship or another similar vessel about a screen which is itself locked in continuous motion, taking care to dodge through the tiny gaps in between the maelstrom of enemies and bullets. Touch something that disagrees with your ship's hull and you lose a life. Shoot down an enemy fighter and you gain points and, vitally, remove a dangerous source of bullets. And at the end of each level you'll have to battle a shot-happy boss so big it often can't fit on the screen and which is obsessed with pumping more projectiles into the atmosphere than any normal gamer can ever hope to dodge.

Scrolling shooters are among the toughest games known to man but, as the enemies and bullets all follow set patterns, repeated play lets you memorise the best paths through each level. *Ikaruga*'s trial mode is especially friendly to those just beginning their journey through the game: it gives players infinite lives for just one credit, but blocks all content beyond the second end-of-level boss, letting you hone your skills on the early stages before unscrewing the stabilisers and cycling with the big boys.

Trial mode aside, what I've described so far is essentially applicable to every shmup under the sun. What sets one apart from the other is a gimmick. Every shooter has one, and every shooter is instantly recognisable because of its individual gimmick. The reason why *Ikaruga* has now become the figurehead for the genre is a gambit that obliterates all others.

Ikaruga has a unique black 'n' white thing going on. Enemies come in black and white varieties, bullets come in the same colours and at the press of a button your good ship *Ikaruga* and its bullets flip between the polarities as well. *Ikaruga*'s bullets dish out extra damage to enemies of the opposite pigment. Its shields, meanwhile, gobble down enemy slugs of the same colour like Pac-Man wolfing down pills. The resulting power surge fills a screen-clearing homing-missile energy bar. Very handy in a pinch.

It doesn't stop there. 'Chaining' kills involves killing enemies in blocks of three colours at a time, with each additional link ramping up the score multiplier bonus and eventually working towards extra lives. It's even possible to float through most of the game like a pacifist, soaking up the same coloured bullets and waiting for the bosses to get bored and mooch away – although it may take a couple of years' worth of practice to reach the necessary skill level.

The thought-shattering set-up is unapologetically anathema to anybody incapable of keeping a cool head and thinking without pausing. Becoming an expert player is one of the hardest and most gratifying statuses to achieve in gaming. Thankfully you needn't be an expert to appreciate fully what *Ikaruga* has done for the genre's rise in popularity and for gaming in general. Just play it in trial mode if you need to – nobody will think less of you for it.

👾 👾 👾

IL-2 STURMOVIK: BIRDS OF PREY

Release date: 2009 | Platform: Xbox 360 |
Developer: Gaijin Entertainment

WHEN PEOPLE THINK of flight sims, they think of *Microsoft Flight Simulator*, the most comprehensive and detailed series of all time. But *MFS* is a little vanilla for average tastes, so anybody seeking more pulsating ya-yas is better off looking for something less po-faced.

Taxi forward *IL-2 Sturmovik: Birds of Prey*, a flap-perfect World War II flight simulator and arcade shooter all in one package. When the *IL-2* series debuted in 2001, it became an instant PC classic, far outclassing every other combat flyer on the market thanks to a winning combination of handling, visuals and tense missions over the Eastern Front. The console-based *Birds of Prey* takes everything great about its precursors, ups the visuals to ridiculous levels and hands it to a brand-new audience, gifting them entirely different modes of play across fifty key World War II missions. There's the usual array of fighting and bombing runs in missions smartly introduced with real wartime footage, and a smattering of online modes to keep flight sticks waggling long after the war has been won.

Arcade mode is a thrill-seeker's dream. Planes dance about in the air, twisting and turning high above the shores of Dover and the ruins of Stalingrad while entwined in epic dogfights. These are proper aerial battles, not the watered-down version offered by modern-day flight sims thanks to a practically endless supply of fire-and-forget heat-seeking missiles. Machine-gun bullets rip through the air, each one clearly rendered as it leaves the planes' on-board turrets and bursts towards its target. Downed planes spiral out of control and into the detailed environments below, filling the air with smoke and debris from the burning fuel. A handy lock-on targeting reticule tells you precisely where you need to aim in order for bullet trajectories and plane flight paths to collide in a firework finish.

Up the difficulty a notch to Realistic and the bullets behave exactly as they should. On paper, *Birds of Prey*'s damage model sounds too good to be true. Each slug punches its way through the target and inflicts visible, realistic damage. A bullet that misses structural supports will tear through a plane's fabric coating and leave the body or the wing ragged, increasing drag and reducing manoeuvrability. Shots to the ailerons, meanwhile, impair a pilot's ability to turn. And a burst of fire targeted on a wing's framework will shear the wing off entirely and force the pilot to bail.

Shooting the engine will severely damage the plane or make it explode, depending on the exact number and placement of the bullets, while catching the tanks will start fuel and oil leaks, splattering the cockpit of any following plane with opaque liquids and forcing the bleeding bird down if the fuel isn't managed accordingly. For bombers, it's impossible to recover – they descend lower and lower until gravity takes its deathly toll. Finally, a well-aimed bullet to the pilot will drop any plane out of the sky regardless of its structural integrity.

Planes can look tattered and shredded and still fly if nothing too important has been ripped away. But because Realistic models physics realistically – well, *fairly* realistically – a straggly plane can still be upended by bad flying. Recoil from firing guns slows planes down, meaning holey crafts should fire only in short bursts. Limping a wreck back to the landing strip is a nerve-racking sensation – if the dropping fuel levels and the spluttering engines don't get you, there's every chance the increased drag from lowering your landing gear just before touching down will. If you land it, though, you'll feel like a god.

It's Simulation, though, that is *Birds of Prey*'s stunning mode – even if it's something you'll only every try once before returning to Realistic. Each of the three difficulties offers something different: Arcade is for people after a quick burst of satisfying carnage; Realistic is for the strategists who want to fly carefully and be rewarded with some heart-pounding close shaves; and Simulation is for those who want to know precisely what it was like to fly planes during World War II. Almost every feature of every plane has been painstakingly re-created, right down to ammo supplies, petrol levels and handling quirks. In short, they're almost all impossible to fly.

It takes nerves of steel and the hands of an expert to keep a plane in the air, let alone finish a mission and land it again. In World War II, plenty of fighters returned to base without notching up a single downed aircraft, and in Simulation the same thing applies. It's entirely possible to spend all your bullets chasing just one plane. A single hit and a safe landing is considered to be a huge success, especially as there are no icons to tell friend from foe and navigation back to base involves using maps, on-board compass dials and your knowledge of the terrain.

While ill-considered steering frequently leads to stalls in Realistic, almost any wrong move, no matter how slight, will stall a Simulation plane. Certain birds are more forgiving than others, but all need to be coaxed and carried through manoeuvres to stay in one piece. But Simulation isn't really there to be played consistently for anyone other than hardened enthusiasts. It's there for everybody to try, fail and marvel at the bravery and skill of the fighters who fought in the planes for real, and to admire everything they accomplished back in the 1940s. There aren't many games with a lasting impact like that.

👾 👾 👾

KATAMARI DAMACY

Release date: 2004 (no UK release) | Platform: PlayStation 2 |
Developer: Namco

KATAMARI DAMACY IS sheer nonsense gaming at its nonsensest. It's the video-game equivalent of colonic irrigation: a gaming detox that throws everything, sense included, out with the bath water.

Stemming from the childhood art of snowball rolling, *Katamari Damacy* and its equally bonkers sequels ask you to roll around a sticky, knobbly ball – that would be the katamari – to pick up objects. Why? Because the overtly metrosexual, gigantonormic King of all Cosmos enjoyed a few too many drinks and his bender ended up destroying all the stars and planets in the sky. As the king's 10cm-tall son (what a disappointment you must be), you need to roll up as much junk from Earth as possible and blast it into space to replace the celestial masses your dad so carelessly batted into non-existence.

All adept snowball rollers will know this sort of thing needs to be done in stages. Rolling a tiny ball straight into a great big boulder isn't going to embed the rock in the ball's side. At best, it will simply bounce off. A high-speed collision could even shake some material loose from your ball, setting you back a few steps.

The prince's katamari starts off the size of a peach. Not quite good enough to replace Saturn, really. A few paperclips and ants later, it'll grow to the size of a cantaloupe. Some television remotes and shoes will widen the circumference to that of a beach ball and so on and so on. Eventually, the prince will be tearing around a trippy town rolling up bicycles, trees, cows, cars, people and even buildings to hit the target ball size. Oddly, nobody seems to mind the intrusion or the thought of shooting off into the vacuum above. Probably because the stupendously brilliant electro/jazz/J-Pop soundtrack has lulled everybody into a hippy trance.

Your prince is deceptively powerful. The controller's left stick controls his left hand and the right stick his right hand, and no matter how large the katamari grows it always feels under control. Size, weight and surface areas all factor into whether or not an object will join your mobile clump, and this plays a huge part in uncovering the game's secrets.

Most of the time you need to roll up anything and everything as quickly as possible, but there's hidden depth to *Katamari Damacy*. Other levels will require you to forgo the scattershot approach and become choosier about the objects, picking specific groups of items or working towards one single target.

Hidden presents and royal cousins unlock extras when discovered and rolled up – the latter becoming playable characters in the split-screen two-player modes. They all need to be tagged at the precise time: the only way to get a cousin hiding on a shelf, for instance, might be to travel up a ruler acting as a makeshift bridge and barge through the items on the shelf to reach your target. If the ball's too small, it might not be strong enough to pass those items. Too big and it could destroy the bridge altogether by claiming the ruler for itself or, worse, it might not even fit back inside the house.

Unfortunately for UK gamers, *Katamari Damacy* never enjoyed a European release. Luckily its five sequels did, and the only real changes they make to the formula involve plot (the prince and king eventually become aware of their popularity on Earth and play to their fans) and scale (later games see you ripping up entire continents from the Earth's surface as if you were tearing up pieces of felt Velcroed to the floor). If *Katamari Damacy* eludes your grasp, *We Love Katamari* is the next best choice. You certainly will.

🕹 🕹 🕹

LEFT 4 DEAD

Release date: 2008 | Platform: PC | Developer: Valve Corporation

IF HOLLYWOOD'S TAUGHT us one thing, it's that the end of the world's either going to involve mega asteroids, alien attacks or a zombie apocalypse. Or, if we're really unfortunate, a combination of all three. *Left 4 Dead* isn't concerned so much with those first two disaster scenarios, but it takes the zombie-infestation angle and runs with it like a cheetah on a sugar high.

It's Pennsylvania, and a pandemic known as Green Flu has reduced the population to a snarling, flesh-hungry mob of zombies. The only survivors are four immune misfits: IT worker Louis, student Zoey, biker Francis and veteran Bill. Hardly the clean-up crew you'd want to save the world. Being a saviour, though, isn't on the cards. Survival is, and the entire game is spent trekking to extraction points and fleeing the zombie masses.

Left 4 Dead is a four-player game at heart, hence the 4 in the title (the rotten zombie hand with four outstretched fingers on the box only further plays into this pun). It can be played with fewer people, as the computer steps in to control the other characters, but to make the most of the experience *Left 4 Dead* has to be played online. While many other first-person shooters involve one man taking on armies of bad guys and strolling out the other side with a few scratches and plenty of wisecracks, *Left 4 Dead* is all about clubbing together and working as a team.

Selfish play and misplaced heroism will only get you killed and, in turn, your team-mates overrun as well. Zombies attack in scores, and even the greatest marksman in the world would struggle to make a significant dent in an onrushing pack of cannibals before succumbing to the numbers game. Co-op play stems from design as opposed to necessity: there are monsters who attempt to pick off the weakest survivor who cannot be killed by just one person. *Left 4 Dead* isn't a single-player shooter with four times the targets and an end-of-level door that requires four players to open; it's a game that's impossible to play alone.

Another source of fear is the Special Infected, a selection of ultra-powerful mutants who have a variety of moves depending on their species. Some are tank-like, others pounce like an assassin or will single out one survivor and drag them away from the pack. The most disturbing of all is the witch: a gaunt, sobbing woman who is essentially the Blair Witch in all but name. Switching off torches and creeping past while trying not to draw her attention is easily one of the scariest gaming moments ever devised. And just to add to the multiplayer leanings of *Left 4 Dead*, all of them bar the witch can be controlled by other players, bringing the total gamer count for any one game up to eight.

Continuing on with the original theme of four, there are only four levels. At least there *were* only four until a free update – also available on the Xbox 360 at a small price – added a fifth. Even at five, however, the game isn't the longest in the world, and neither is it intended to be. *Left 4 Dead* isn't a traditional beginning-middle-end survival story. There's a plot there, sure, but the real story is the one that unfolds every single time you play. The story of how a separated team member valiantly flanked a horde that had trapped the other three in a corner, or how a last-minute dash to the extraction point was scuppered by a silent pack of zombies hiding in a cornfield.

Left 4 Dead is a game built for replayability, and the key to replayability is the surgical removal of predictability. Play most story-driven shooters a second time through and there will be very few surprises. In almost every case, enemies attack at the same points they did first time round, in the same numbers and the same patterns. That's because many games, shooters in particular, are built first and foremost with one play through in mind and with separate multiplayer modes (where applicable) to boost longevity.

Sitting behind the scenes of *Left 4 Dead* is a figure known as the AI Director – a clever piece of code written into the game that acts like a master puppeteer, pulling the strings of everything the game does. It's the Director's job to ensure that every survival scenario – whether it's your second or your hundredth time through – is unique. Level geometry doesn't alter. The levels are the levels and there's no changing that. But the zombie attacks, item pickups and the mood – the music and sound stings used to signify these attacks or to make you *think* there's an attack coming – can be changed. The Director monitors everybody's playing style and delivers shocks around every bend: attacks where you've never experienced attacks before; moments of calm where you expect to be ambushed. There are only a few choke points where a barrage is certain, most notably when you reach the extraction point and call for help at each campaign's end, but these are daunting showdowns you'll dread every time. The rest of the journey is one giant roulette wheel. Thanks largely to the unpredictability and the masterful timing of the AI Director, *Left 4 Dead* is terrifying – not an easy mood to tap into when there are four people joking around with each other through headsets.

Every game Valve Corporation makes is a lesson in design to other developers. *Left 4 Dead*'s cooperative multiplayer and AI Director breakthroughs are two of Valve Corporation's greatest lessons to date. But that's for the industry to worry about. You don't need to play *Left 4 Dead* to learn how to make better games; you need to play it to enjoy a fantastic title in its own right.

🦑 🦑 🦑

THE LEGEND OF ZELDA: FOUR SWORDS ADVENTURES
Release date: 2005 (2004) | Platform: Nintendo GameCube | Developer: Nintendo

The Legend of Zelda: Four Swords Adventures is the most expensive and complicated game to play in this list, and if it weren't for *Pac-Man Vs.* it would be by some distance. As it stands, to play it in the original format, you have two reasons to invest in a GameCube, up to four Game Boy Advances, four Game Boy-to-GameCube link cables, and to find three like-minded friends/strangers. So, while your bank manager may frown at all the eBay transactions, you'll have single-handedly set up Duracell for the next month, your floor will look like it's covered with tagliatelle and, with more screens lying around than the bridge of the USS *Enterprise*, you'll just have to believe that the effort will all be worth it.

It *will* be worth it.

The Legend of Zelda: Four Swords Adventures is a cooperative Zelda adventure in the mould of the series' classic bird's-eye-view titles. But, while it might look like a retro classic, the GameCube's extra grunt is put to good use, providing visual flair inspired by the system's own *The Legend of Zelda: The Wind Waker* and enemies in numbers that would make a Super Nintendo Entertainment System self-combust (think *Left 4 Dead* with medieval guards). The combat is considerably more intense than anything in the series' other titles, and so it should be for the first meaningful multiplayer *Legend of Zelda* adventure.

Crucially, *Four Swords Adventures* doesn't forget the *Legend of Zelda* part of its name when breaking out of the single-player format. It's still the story of Link (only there are now four of him) and it still features all the trademark items and puzzles. It also forces all four players to discuss and test different potential solutions.

It's a cooperative game that requires real cooperation as opposed to simple companionship through generic scenarios. It makes players visit parallel dark worlds on their individual Game Boy Advance screens to aid players in the light world trapped on the communal television set. And just as it's hammered home how important cooperation truly is, *The Legend of Zelda: Four Swords Adventures* throws a wild card in the form of competition into the mix.

Force gems are scattered all over the levels, and snaffling gems powers up swords and puts you in good stead come the end-of-level ranking system. At each stage's conclusion, the four Links are scored on their gem collections as well as other statistics such as enemies killed and the number of times they fainted. It also asks players to vote for the most and least helpful players, and uses the results to weight the scoring system, bringing some degree of tactical voting into play as well as ensuring the greedy characters don't go unpunished and the helpful players are rewarded.

In the quest to reach first place, some devious tendencies sneak into games. *Four Swords Adventures* lets its players check caves and houses silently on their own Game Boy Advance screens to avoid tipping off other players to hidden gem stashes. Links will 'accidentally' throw fellow Links down holes (bumping the victim an inch closer to losing half of their force gems) and will 'accidentally' shoot others with the fire rod, burning their rears and sending them running in agony away from any nearby gems.

It's the constant see-saw between cooperation and competition that shines through. When the enemies are swarming like girls at a Justin Bieber concert, you'll work to protect each other to the end, and taking on the giant bosses requires clubbing together and unleashing perfectly coordinated attacks. But there's always a Lando Calrissian waiting in the wings, looking for the next opportunity to stab everybody in the back and make off with the prizes.

Unfortunately, the Western release of *The Legend of Zelda: Four Swords Adventures* arrived without the superb treasure-hunting delights of the Japanese *Navi Trackers* adventure. Still, the disturbing-manbeast Tingle (dressed in a onesie with a pair of red underpants pulled over the top) shows up with a selection of ball-bouncing, horse-racing and hammer-tagging mini-games, and the player-versus-player Shadow Battle showdown is the perfect place to air any grievances brought about by the main adventure.

Until Nintendo does the sensible thing and develops a sequel with Wii and Nintendo DS compatibility, *The Legend of Zelda: Four Swords Adventures* is the only *Legend of Zelda* game of its type. That type is a wonderful title held back only by an awkward hardware setup too demanding for many to organise. It's tragic to think that one of the best titles from Nintendo's second most popular franchise is one of the company's abandoned side-quests, and, though it sold modestly in 2004, relatively few Zelda fans have had the opportunity to play it with four players as intended. It's a game worth seeking out, regardless of the effort needed to set it up.

🐙 🐙 🐙

THE LEGEND OF ZELDA: OCARINA OF TIME

Release date: 1998 | Platform: Nintendo 64 | Developer: Nintendo

The Legend of Zelda: Ocarina of Time is the Godfather of games. Not in the sense that it's going to slip a horse's head between your sheets for playing around with other titles, and certainly not in the sense that it's the game of *The Godfather* (that would be, wait for it, wait for it... *The Godfather* by EA from 2006). But much like Francis Ford Coppola's finest film, *The Legend of Zelda: Ocarina of Time* either tops every 'Greatest Game' list published or it runs a close second. This is a feat made even more impressive as games age far more quickly than films because they are completely dependent on the short-lived hardware on which they are first released.

It's often said that many of the sixteen *Zelda* games are similar titles simply repackaged in a different world and re-justified with a tweaked storyline. That it remains Nintendo's second-greatest series, just behind the *Mario* games, speaks volumes for the quality of the underlying template. Like almost every other game in the *Legend of Zelda* series, *Ocarina of Time* features young hero Link and Princess Zelda fighting to stop persistent nemesis Ganondorf from claiming the sacred 'triforce' artefact. And like almost every other game in the series, Link must adventure across the expansive kingdom of Hyrule to forge friendships and gather new abilities and equipment until he's strong enough to slay the king of evil.

At the time of its release in 1998, *The Legend of Zelda: Ocarina of Time* was a jaw-dropping feat of technology. It was a breathtakingly vast quest in a gigantic world gloriously dressed up in three dimensions in the days when true three-dimensional games (that's three dimensions as in the world as we see it every day, not oh-my-gosh-it's-popping-out-of-the-screen-and-would-poke-me-in-the-eye-were-it-not-for-these-clunky-shades stereoscopic 3D) were still in their infancy. Though its splendour and scope have undoubtedly been surpassed over time thanks to newer hardware and more visually arresting software, the game remains as playable and as enthralling today as it did all those years ago.

Ageing graphics textures can't spoil good design, and every minute of the game is stuffed with new content to enjoy. The sheer number and size of the dungeons is enough to keep you occupied for weeks, and if you ever want a break from the pitch-perfect cocktail of combat and puzzles, there are a ton of mini-games (fishing, bowling and archery to name just three) and treasure hunts to enjoy.

The titular ocarina plays a pivotal role in these puzzles, as well as being a tool for those who want to compose a few tunes for fun. Certain songs have the power to change the time of day or to alter the weather – each with major consequences to the game (skeletons rise up from the ground at night, for instance). And to add the finishing touch to a game already big enough to have its own gravitational field, there are two whole timelines at play. Link can hop between his childhood years and his late teens to explore two markedly different worlds. Cue plenty of time conundrums. Only adult Link can ride Epona the horse, but this can't be done until he plays her a song that the young Link first taught the equine seven years previously. Spread these experiences across a thirty-hour game starring unforgettable characters, locations, boss fights and music, and there's no debating *The Legend of Zelda: Ocarina of Time*'s place in history.

The legacy of *The Legend of Zelda: Ocarina of Time* is unmatched in all of gaming. Fans have tried to make films of the adventure, and have attempted to remake the game in the style of the portable *Zelda* titles with bird's-eye-view camera. Two independent projects have even spliced together its enchanting soundtrack – one of gaming's all-time greats – with hip hop for guffawsome bootleg albums called *Ocarina of Rhyme*. The game has captured imaginations in ways no other title has. No wonder Nintendo has remade its finest classic for the Nintendo 3DS.

LEMMINGS

Release date: 1991 | Platform: Commodore Amiga |
Developer: DMA Design

IN THE DAYS before Scottish developer Rockstar North was known as Rockstar North and infamous for creating *Grand Theft Auto*, it was known as DMA Design and famous for a 2D side-scrolling puzzle sensation called *Lemmings*. *Lemmings* buys into the myth of mass lemming suicides and places you into the fur of an omnipotent lemming migration planner to ensure the furry little critters kill themselves as infrequently as possible on their way to pastures new.

Every level begins with a procession of lemmings streaming out of a trapdoor and marching off in one set direction; and every level successfully ends when you direct the target number of lemmings safely through the end doorway. The catch is that lemmings aren't ones for self-preservation and will just walk and walk and walk. They only shift their behaviour when they encounter an impassable obstacle, when you give them individual instructions or when they die. Hopefully, it'll be one of the first two.

They're fragile things: long falls and water kill them instantly, and the perils don't end there. In later levels, the green-haired rodents will encounter lava, nooses, flamethrowers and thumping pistons on their trips through diamond mines and hell, all more than capable of decimating the lemmings' ranks in seconds.

You have a limited number of instructions at your disposal to guide your team past the traps to the exit. Climbers will climb up vertical surfaces; Floaters will parachute down otherwise lethal distances; Bombers explode after a short countdown; Blockers stand still and prevent any other lemmings from passing; Builders lay a rising staircase for a short amount of time; Bashers punch horizontally through rock; Miners use pickaxes to dig down through the floor diagonally; and Diggers dig straight down.

Freely picking and choosing from the above skills would be too easy though. Lemmings gives you enough instructions to make it to a level's end and a few to spare. And, as the Bomber power suggests, not all of your worker lemmings are going to make it to the end zone. Suicide bombing your Blockers (who can't be un-Blocked without removing the floor underneath them) is one of the most painful gaming experiences of all: they're so adorable and do nothing but follow your orders to the letter. Poor guys.

Building over trap buttons and hammering through rock will see you through some levels, but crafty environmental quirks make bypassing the traps and strolling to the exit tougher than it looks. Some surfaces can only be tunnelled through in one direction – indicated by flashing arrows – and metallic deposits are completely impossible to get through full stop. To throw another spanner into the works, levels are timed. You can mercifully pause the action to scope out the area ahead but you'll often need to get a wiggle-on when assigning orders and may even have to speed up the rate of the lemmings' entry through the trapdoor.

A bonus split-screen two-player mode is a neat addition but can safely be ignored in favour of the main selection of 120 gruelling levels. They're the ultimate endurance test; sufficiently puzzly to stump most players and gruesome enough to appeal to a more action-loving audience at the same time. Instrumental renditions of 'She'll Be Coming 'round the Mountain', '(How Much Is) That Doggie in the Window?', 'London Bridge is Falling Down' and 'Ten Green Bottles' prevent the on-screen action from becoming too grim for everybody else.

With its feet firmly planted in the puzzle genre but the ability to make you care about your lemmings as much as you would your troops in any strategy or adventure game, *Lemmings* straddles markedly different classifications with huge success. *Lemmings* might make you laugh but it won't make you cry. It will, however, make you care, and that's the most important and impressive thing of all.

LIMBO

Release date: 2010 | Platform: Xbox 360 | Developer: PlayDead Studios

WHENEVER YOU READ a Top 10, Top 50 or Top 100 anything list, it's only right you should be wary of the entries released within a year of the list's publication. There's always a danger that some flavour-of-the-month title could sneak its way in when really a year's breathing space would have made it abundantly clear it should have never featured. As one of the newest games in this book, *Limbo* could potentially have fallen into this category. Except for one small detail: *Limbo* is exquisite.

Limbo is a downloadable-only title, and to understand the story you need to read the online blurb before loading up the game. 'Concerned for the welfare of his sister, a boy enters Limbo.' Any developments beyond that are up to you. *Limbo*'s story begins and ends with the boy's lonely journey through Limbo. *Your* journey through Limbo.

The game is a black and white, two-dimensional puzzle platformer that is far cleverer than its simple looks suggest. What the monochrome world lacks in colour, it makes up for in mind and soul. The puzzles are designed to stump you for lengthy periods at a time, and the tragic plod through the barren landscape of Limbo successfully tugs on the heartstrings. The boy doesn't speak, but he doesn't need to for you to know he's hurting – mournful eyes and resigned body language convey the message well. *Limbo* is a remarkably poignant adventure, a truth made all the more special considering it hails from a very small development studio nobody had even heard of before the game's release.

The trip through the underworld is fraught with danger and, to make matters worse, the boy in question is completely defenceless. Capable only of jumping and grabbing, the only way through the hell dimension is through timely trap-dodging and leading the evil Limbo denizens into the ambushes originally designed to ensnare you.

Bear traps clank shut and decapitate you before you even realise you've put a foot wrong. Boulders crush you without giving you a chance to jump to safety. Giant tarantulas will hound you constantly, skewering you the moment they get in close. Everything in *Limbo* is hostile, and your frail boy meets some spectacularly sickening ends. The poor guy can't even swim and soon sinks in the drink when you stray into deeper waters.

Mercifully, there's a much-needed gore filter to ensure the younger players and those with a weaker constitution can power on. It's a wise move from PlayDead Studios as *Limbo* deserves to be played by everybody regardless of age. With the filter on, the screen cuts to black every time the boy comes a cropper of a saw blade or a spike pit.

The deaths serve a purpose. They're not just there for violence's sake. Every death is a challenge, the beginning of a puzzle. The game has outsmarted you, now it's your chance to outsmart it. Can you make it through next time without dying?

Die and you'll be instantly placed back to the beginning of the current puzzle, which is usually no more than a couple of seconds in the past. While death is a punishment in other games, *Limbo* has no such punitive system. *Limbo* attempts to kill you every few minutes and so the instant-restart checkpoint system is designed to be as frustration-free as possible.

Getting to the end of *Limbo* is only half the task. The momentum and gravity-based puzzles can be tricky, for sure, but hidden among the game's forests and factories are twenty-one secret eggs. Only by finding them all can you call yourself a true *Limbo* master, but doing so involves besting some Mensa-worthy puzzles and a few leaps of logical faith that will escape most people's grasp.

The remarkable thing about *Limbo*'s puzzles (and not just the tougher egg challenges) is how much mileage PlayDead Studios ekes out of a control scheme so simple it's borderline insulting. Jump and grab is the extent of your powers – and even then the boy will automatically grab on to ropes and ledges to avoid falling. Two buttons are all PlayDead Studios needed to design a mesmerising world filled with terrible traps and exquisite puzzles. In the current days of giant development teams, that kind of intelligent, economic game design is in far too short supply. *Limbo* is a stark wake-up call to all developers.

👾 👾 👾

LITTLE BIG PLANET

Release date: 2008 | Platform: PlayStation 3 | Developer: Media Molecule

LITTLE BIG PLANET is a game forged as much on the promise of a thriving community as it is on the software that ships on the disc. There is a normal platform game tucked away in it somewhere (albeit a slightly wishy-washy one), but the real selling point of *LBP* is an in-game toolbox with infinite level-designing possibilities. If you can dream it, you can build it.

The idea of a level-designer limited solely by the imagination of those designing, not by the tools provided, is something console owners had never experienced before *LBP*. Its Create mode is a blank canvas for you to do with what you want, and then to share online with the rest of the world. The game's motto is 'Play. Create. Share.' Play the game to learn how objects can be used in the world and to gain ideas, create your own *LBP* universes, and share them with others.

Fronted by Sony's knitted mascot Sackboy, *LBP* is development software disguised as a cutesy family game. Sackboy's a lesson in character design for every budding game creator: an instantly recognisable, simple little fellow with personality pouring out between the stitches. He's more than just a game character; he's a vessel for your emotions. You can change his mood from happy to sad to angry and upset in nanoseconds with the press of a button, while twiddling the two controller sticks can move each arm independently, be it to wave at anybody watching or to clout a nearby character round the back of the head.

The big grins of its Sackpersons, the cheerfully chunky artistic design, the forgiving moon physics, the soothing tones of Stephen Fry's delectable narration and the simple pleasure of being able to tag any object with your own custom stickers cleverly conceal a rather complex piece of kit. *LBP* wisely masks its creation suites with what appears to be a normal game – you feel you're simply playing a regular title when in fact you're trying your hand at development. *LBP* takes the daunting world of game design and makes it accessible to everyone – so much so that many won't even twig that they're participating in the creative process of a constantly evolving game.

The Sackpersons can run left and right (and short distances in and out of the screen in the zones where there's a small z-axis at play), they can jump and they can grab. That's all they can do, but in a title where the level items are the real stars of the show those few moves are plenty. You'll pull levers to raise lifts, step on buttons to explode obstacles, jump on giant skateboards to roll them down hills and swing on ropes like Tarzan to bypass holes. Of course, there are no limits to what you can make in *LBP*. Those lifts could very well be space rockets, those obstacles could be buildings, those hills could be the arching back of a tyrannosaurus rex and the holes could be the giant sarlacc pit from *Return of the Jedi*. They're whatever you want them to be.

Playing the main game and collecting the prize bubbles unlocks extra content for the editing modes. Your creations needn't even be traditional A-to-B levels. Some people have made working calculators just with levers, twine and a lot of dials; others have created songs out of nothing but lines of single-note music boxes triggered by a rolling car.

Take *LBP* online and the feature list explodes. Online file sharing opens up a world with more content than is possible to work through in a lifetime. *LBP*'s sharing portal is essentially a YouTube of user-generated levels, only it's one that lets you play the creations instead of simply watching videos of other people's work. Once finished, you can tag them with words and symbols to give thanks and to recommend them to others.

Apart from the few productions yanked for copyright infringements, there are cutesy *LBP* retellings of all your favourite games – from *Space Invaders* to *Pac-Man* – to download and play for nothing. There are literally *millions* of levels, and all are safe for everybody to enjoy thanks to a strict moderation policy that bins anything deemed to be rude or offensive. There have been instances of willy-filled levels in the past. There are no longer.

A year after launch, Media Molecule patched the game to allow co-op creation tools for up to four people to design and build a level simultaneously. The same four people can also play through the game together – part of *LBP*'s community drive is getting people to enjoy the title with friends and families.

To highlight just how breathtaking the tools really are, the facts and figures of Sony's 2008 Electronic Entertainment Expo keynote speech were delivered entirely through the medium of *LBP*. It's been known for people to shun PowerPoint and use *LBP* as the visual half of a presentation, using rising blocks to represent bars and charts, and timing each pertinent bullet point perfectly by writing text on to objects that swing into view at the pull of a bar or the press of a switch. Before the days of *LBP*, the thought of giving an important talk using a game was absurd. Now it's a genuine, albeit quirky, option.

When a game is being used to deliver the most important talk at the most important gaming event in the entire industry, it's a clear indication the game in question is something special. The only thing that's tough to work out is who enjoyed it most of all: the people who made the level, the person who played it or the audience that got to sit back and marvel at the spectacle? In all honesty, everybody was a winner.

LOCOROCO

**Release date: 2006 | Platform: PlayStation Portable |
Developer: Japan Studio**

NOTHING IS CAPABLE of putting a smile on anybody's face quite like the happiest game ever made. *LocoRoco* is that game, a title that involves rolling gelatinous LocoRoco animals around to gather berries, collect friends and stave off an alien invasion by the dreaded Moja Troop clan.

The LocoRoco are little limbless colour splodges with two eyes, a mouth, a tuft of hair and a love of singing. They move only when the ground beneath them tilts, though they can jump perpendicular to their velocity. If they stumble upon red berries, they wolf them down and immediately perform full-body mitosis to create another LocoRoco – a creature that can combine with the original to form a bigger LocoRoco, or can split off and roll about quite happily on its own. The more berries the LocoRoco eat, the more they split and the bigger they grow when they all combine together like a big roll of Blu-Tack.

The goal of *LocoRoco* is to guide these friendly aliens through their vibrant habitats to the end of the forty levels. Squeezing the PSP's left trigger tilts the world left; squeezing the right trigger tilts it right. Pressing and releasing both at the same time makes the LocoRoco jump and the rest is all down to gravity.

The LocoRoco are always chirpy, except for when a Loco-eating Moja is close – at which point they start blubbering in terror (jumping into the Moja soon kills them, though). Otherwise, they're humming as they roll about the levels, and at set points they all separate and burst into song to wake up some sleeping platform (parts of *LocoRoco*'s world are made from living creatures) who will help them along.

Effervescence simply floods out of the PlayStation Portable. *LocoRoco*'s worlds are brightly coloured fields and corrals designed from curves, bubbles, blobs, tunnels and air currents. The spunky accompanying music features children singing buoyant verses in a make-believe language, and it changes dynamically with your progress. The more LocoRoco there are on the screen, the more children take part in the song. There isn't a better pick-me-up in the pharmaceutical world, let alone the game world.

Getting to the end of every level is just the basic goal. In addition to rolling to the finish, there are hundreds of 'pickory dots' to snaffle (analogous to Mario's coins or Sonic's rings) as well as nineteen berries (each one gives you an extra LocoRoco up to a maximum of twenty) and hidden 'friends' called Mui Mui men. Secret areas require adept control skills to access. Sometimes they involve creative use of seesaws and jumps; other times it's as simple as bursting through cracked and hidden walls.

Select zones are even locked away to LocoRoco groups smaller than their greatest potential size at that point in the level: if you've missed a berry earlier on, you won't have enough LocoRoco in a choir to wake up the animal necessary to unlock the secret. On top of all that, fastest completion times and high scores for each collectible category are recorded to encourage repeat completions.

Collected Mui Mui men bestow you with pieces of landscape furniture to decorate a LocoRoco house in a separate editor level. Gathered pickories, meanwhile, can be spent on mini-games outside of the main mode to win even more of these house parts. They're all features designed for one thing and one thing only: to delight and amuse anybody toying with them. *LocoRoco* is an infectious bundle of merriment with catchy tunes and an innovative control twist. Utterly enchanting.

MEGA MAN 2

**Release date: 1990 (1988) | Platform: Nintendo Entertainment System |
Developer: Capcom**

METAL MAN! Quick Man! Heat Man! Wood Man! *Mega Man 2*'s bosses sound like D-list heroes from a rejected children's action show. Instead, they play a part in one of the most brilliantly brutal games known to man. If *Demon's Souls* is the most punishing game mentioned in this book, *Mega Man 2* runs a very close second. Mario for grownups is, well, still Mario. Mario for masochists is *Mega Man 2*.

Mega Man 2 is non-linear platforming at its toughest. Eight hard-as-adamantium-nails bosses lying in wait at the end of eight harder-than-hard levels make up the first half of the game; an even more insane sprint through evil Dr Wily's fortress crammed with traps to test every learned skill makes up the second.

The first *Mega Man* wasn't much of a success for Capcom, but *Mega Man 2* is the game that drove the series' popularity and forged the template for future *Mega Man* games to follow. Eight boss basics aside, a new password system – these were the days before memory cards and hard drives – meant gamers could save their progress and continue another day, while pickups in the form of energy tanks replenished Mega Man's health on request, making the game a teensy, tiny bit fairer than it otherwise would have been. The impact of these features is clear to see: it feels like *Mega Man* games number in their thousands, though in reality 'dozens' is more realistic, and *2*'s influences have never been replaced.

The eight themed levels are *Mega Man 2*'s showpieces. There's no set order, meaning you can pick and choose which levels to tackle and finish first. Flash Man, Air Man, Bubble Man... it doesn't matter who you want to fight first because they're all open from the off.

Only it *does* matter, because those eight levels are saturated in strategy. Every *Mega Man* end-of-level boss has a unique weapon to be collected and used against others. As you'd expect, certain bosses are weaker against specific boss weapons. Quick Man is foiled by the Time Stopper, for instance, and Wood Man doesn't fare so well against Metal Blades. Think rock, paper, scissors plus five, and you don't know what beats what until you experiment.

Mega Man is a simple character. He can run, he can jump and he can fire straight forward. That's all he really needs to do because every themed level brings different sights to the table. Metal Man's cog-filled factory has rotating walkways and slamming spike traps. Air Man's cloud fortress is fraught with danger jumps between hovering clouds. They all reveal secrets when swapping between Mega Man's ulterior guises brought about by the extra boss weapons, so playing a stage through first will be different to playing it when the level's the eighth pick.

Projectile-pumping zones push frustration levels to maximum, but solace comes in the form of soul-stirring MIDI tunes. *Mega Man 2*'s iconic music makes all the heartache worthwhile, and for some it's the reason why experimenting with different level orders never grows tired. Seeing the end credits of *Mega Man 2* is a challenge relatively few people can claim to have completed, but the game's real appeal lies not in seeing those credits but *how* you see them – what route to take and what skills to utilise along the way. Every main *Mega Man* title, even the original, has that appeal, but none is more appealing than the game with the best of everything: *Mega Man 2*.

METAL GEAR SOLID

Release date: 1998 | Platform: PlayStation | Developer: Konami

METAL GEAR SOLID single-handedly rewrote the rules of action games. Prior to its release, the genre was primarily concerned with full-on combat and more explosions than the average Roland Emmerich flick.

Billed as a tactical espionage action game, *Metal Gear Solid* taught you to avoid conflict wherever possible, and turned you into a tip-toeing spy with an unhealthy obsession for cigarettes and small air vents – not a good combination. It changed the landscape forever and triggered a deluge of stealth-based sneak-'em-ups, most notably the *Splinter Cell* series.

Gravelly-voiced leading man Solid Snake is essentially *Escape From New York*'s Snake Plissken. An ex-special-forces agent plucked out of retirement for one last job, Snake's needed to infiltrate his old unit, which has now gone rogue. It all takes place in a supposed nuclear weapons disposal facility on an island just off the coast of Alaska, though you'll eventually discover the base is a secret military research post home to a giant walking tank called Metal Gear REX. Think Megatron with a cockpit in place of a personality and you're not too far wrong.

At the heart of all the success is a simple stealth system and an eclectic mix of bosses to stir the pacing pot occasionally. Guards follow preset patrols unless distracted with a sharp knuckle rap on a nearby wall or if they spot fresh footprints in the snow. They'll enter a seeking mode until the trail runs cold, you're detected or the game of cat and mouse is cut short with a visceral neck snap, as is often the case. Bosses, meanwhile, test other faculties – most notably cunning as one fight can be subverted by hiding in a corner and flying remote-controlled missiles right down the throat of a sniper.

Although the fan-favourite ability to stuff bodies in lockers wasn't introduced until the 2002 sequel (though is present in the slightly inferior GameCube remake), the game is responsible for most of the signature features that have driven the series' popularity. Inordinately long cinematic cutscenes – far lengthier than those in any other games – are a divisive inclusion but an effective vehicle for some convoluted plotlines involving genetic modification and cloning. Far less controversial is creator Hideo Kojima's fixation with taking a hammer to the fourth wall. One freakish boss claims to read your thoughts. Nonsense you think, until he starts talking about games you've played previously and you realise you can't hit him. It turns out the psychic is reading your PlayStation's memory card to see what other save data you have. If you unplug the controller from port one and plug it into the console's second controller slot, it'll throw his psychic connection off and you'll have a much easier time.

Other examples of the fourth-wall breakdown include resting the controller on your arm and letting the internal rumble machine simulate a muscle-replenishment agent after a particularly strenuous button-mashing exercise, and one radio conversation that can only be continued if you check the frequency on the back of the box. Sure enough, you'll rifle through Snake's inventory in vain to find the important item, only to discover the character is talking about the box your game came packaged in. Of course, dirty pirates are rightly left stuck at that point.

The game confidently juggles the roles of both clown and poet. One moment it'll make you laugh by calling you out for trying to interrupt your female sidekick while she's getting changed, or by making you hide under a wee-stained cardboard box to sneak past a den of wolves; the next it'll tug at the heartstrings by severing major character relationships with a few bullets. Even boss deaths are moving, something compounded by a poignant music score that sticks around long after you've moved on to other games (blame the eminently hummable theme tune). Then there's the simplicity of the raw thrill that comes with each and every guard alert – the '!' that appears above the head of a shocked grunt and the accompanying sound cue.

There are games that have to be played because of their impact on the industry, and there are games that need to be sampled because they're among the finest experiences you could ever have with a controller in your hand. The oddity that is *Metal Gear Solid* is one of the elite few to straddle both these groups.

METROID PRIME

Release date: 2003 (2002) | Platform: Nintendo GameCube | Developer: Retro Studios

SCUPPERED BY THE ALPHABET! A quirk in the naming conventions means there's an entry you need to read before this but it's buried waaaaaaay down deep in the 'S's among all the games beginning with Super. Before you carry on, flick forward and take a gander at the *Super Metroid* story. I won't be going anywhere. Or will I?

No, no, I won't. Turns out moving printed text is harder than expected. I had a little game of hide-and-seek planned out and everything. Anyway, now armed with fresh *Super Metroid* info, you're ready to press on with the first instalment of the *Metroid Prime* trilogy.

After *Super Metroid* rocked the critics – if not the game-store shelves – the series went dormant for eight long years. When it finally re-emerged, it did so with two titles: classically styled 2D Game Boy Advance game *Metroid Fusion* (a wonderful little adventure, it has to be said) and GameCube shooter *Metroid Prime*. What makes *Metroid Prime* stand out as an all-time great is that it takes the basic *Metroid* premise, applies it to a three-dimensional environment, adds a first-person viewpoint and leaves the mixture well alone. The shift in perspective changes everything and nothing all at once. *Prime* is unmistakably *Metroid*, only it's one that's been *hurled* into a newer generation of games. *Mario 64* did wonders for the 3D game, but, given the complexity of the *Metroid* games and the unbelievable quality of each and every one, *Metroid Prime* is the best title ever to make the transition from 2D to 3D – so great its name shouldn't be mentioned aloud without listening to *Also sprach Zarathustra*'s 'Sunrise' beforehand.

Whatever you do, don't call it a first-person shooter. That makes the fans very cross. *Metroid Prime* is lovingly referred to as a first-person adventure game and, though it seems like a tomayto-tomahto situation, the finicky naming serves a purpose. Bounty hunter Samus enjoys herself with plenty of shooting, but blasting creatures with a plasma cannon plays second fiddle to exploration.

Probing the darkest recesses of Tallon IV and uncovering the mysteries behind its lost race and its newest antagonists is *Prime*'s main draw, something that could take weeks. As in past *Metroids*, Samus boosts her equipment by uncovering different technologies, but one constant tool is the Scan Visor: a heads-up display that lets her scan the environment for hints and general information. As well as general advice about crumbling obstacles (clue: use missiles) and enemy weaknesses, there's an encyclopaedia's worth of text entries detailing the planet's history to be pulled from hieroglyphs and ancient logs.

When you pick your way through Tallon IV's ruins, you feel like an outcast trespassing on an alien planet. The world is so vast it's scary. *Metroid Prime* wallows in maturity without ever resorting to excessive violence, bad language or sex. It's a tangible place to investigate, and it's filled with so many unknown quantities and secret paths there's too much to take in on the first play through. Between the winding network of caverns and the ancient Chozo lore texts, *Prime* gives the illusion of a world bigger than you can ever hope to explore. You'll keep walking past impassable ice doors and canyons with grappling-hook anchors high above them, filing their location for a return visit when you've gathered new gear. Each collected item opens up a raft of possible ways forward: finding a new beam weapon is a stupendously exciting discovery just for the knowledge of all the new doors it will open, let alone the new combat options.

Taking a much-loved series and morphing it into a different beast can often alienate fans, but *Metroid Prime* pleased absolutely everybody and then some. The 3D transformation respects everything at *Metroid*'s core without being shackled to needless elements. Returning bosses are a nice touch and, if *Super Metroid*'s music is considered to be above and beyond, *Metroid Prime*'s is divine. Taken as a stand-alone game, the soundtrack could blow most other titles out the water, but fans were overjoyed to discover remixed music from *Metroid*'s past.

Finally, there's the matter of a little something called sequence breaking. If you followed the earlier instructions and read *Super Metroid*'s entry, you should be familiar with it. *Prime* is a sequence breaker's paradise, and is one of the most fun titles of the entire series to sink your teeth into and try to rip apart. Like *Super Metroid*, the sequence breaking is just an added bonus to a title that exudes quality from every polygon, every single second.

It could all have gone so terribly wrong – Nintendo entrusted the development of *Metroid Prime* to a start-up studio, and four other titles had to be canned to finish the production. It was worth it. The gamble paid off better than anybody could have dreamed. Take a bow.

👾 👾 👾

MICRO MACHINES

Release date: 1993 | Platform: SEGA Mega Drive | Developer: Codemasters

YOU'D BE HARD-PRESSED to find better toys for growing boys than a set of Matchbox, Micro Machines or Hot Wheels vehicles. For some unknown reasons, miniature cars are the coolest things in the world during the primary-school years. It doesn't matter if you're not even into real cars, because *miniature* cars rock.

The success of the *Micro Machines* games, then, was always a foregone conclusion. The Mega Drive racer dumps tiny cars on pool tables, sandpits and DIY benches, coin-sized boats in the pond and teeny helicopters in the garden. It captures every thrill of the thumbnail childhood cars in game form (apart from loudly humming the 'BRRRRRRRM' noises, perhaps, although the vehicles' mini engine chugs and tyre screeches aren't too far off), and it does so with heaps of charm.

Kitchen races take place on a breakfast-laid table with Cheerios-lined tracks pointing you the right way and puddles of sticky honey slowing you down. Chalked circuits on office tables send you flying over binders, ducking between deadly pencils and hopping on to chairs and back on top of ruler bridges. The pool table is the best of the lot: the solid balls constrict the track, guaranteeing major pile-ups in the bottleneck, and select pockets act as teleportation devices and shoot the cars across the table in an instant. Playing cards take the race up on to the pool table's rim and back down again – a sudden death zone if ever there was one, with a single nudge usually all it takes to career a car off the edge and down to its doom way below.

For the most part, *Micro Machines* takes part in open areas with the racing line etched on to the surface. Obviously this set-up could potentially allow cheaters to chop huge bits of the course out by ignoring the suggested track. *Micro Machines* intelligently counters this by placing invisible checkpoints that wreck any car that ducks past them off-'road'. There's just enough leeway in the system to cut corners still, and there's hours of strategy involved in working out which small parts of any given course are safe to slice off and which track outlines mustn't be ignored.

A single-screen multiplayer mode makes for a unique two-player game: if one character falls back far enough and disappears off the screen, they explode, lose a life and the race resumes with both vehicles neck and neck. Races are much more exciting with two cars at each other's exhaust throughout, and they're often more aggressive too, with argy-bargy often resulting in one person skipping ahead by a screen length. It's not always the attacker who comes off best, though, as a mistimed sideswipe can easily see the aggressor shooting off a table edge.

Sequel *Micro Machines 2: Turbo Tournament* upped the ante with its J-Cart game cartridge that came with two additional controller ports built into the top, allowing four controllers to be in action at any one time. Unfortunately, when consoles grew up, *Micro Machines* struggled to keep up the pace. Its V3 and V4 additions were passable, though the less said about running-character off-shoot *Micro Maniacs* the better... After *Turbo Tournament*, PlayStation racer *Circuit Breakers* picked up the mantle and, although the two PlayStation 2 *Mashed* games put up a good fight, *Circuit Breakers* remains the last great game of its type.

But where *Circuit Breakers'* 3D graphics and swooping camera have aged a little (though not as much as you'd expect, surprisingly), *Micro Machines* hasn't. It's still the classic shrunken-car game with a top-notch two-player mode. All together now: BRRRRRRRM!

MYST

Release date: 1993 | Platform: PC | Developer: Cyan Inc.

FEATURING SERIOUSLY challenging puzzles with buckets of button-prodding, lever-pulling and a tangled plot comprising a family feud, interlinking worlds, beautiful scenery, intrigue, murder, endless journal entries and weird noises, to the uninitiated, *Myst* sounds like *Lost: The Video Game*. If only it were, for the sake of *Lost* fans: the real *Lost* video game is unfiltered drivel you wouldn't wish on your worst enemy.

Myst is a serene point-and-click game with nothing to shoot at, nothing to run from, nothing to drive, nobody to talk to and no clear objective to begin with. Using only the mouse to control a small, unobtrusive hand-shaped cursor to advance from one location to the other, it relies not on your ability to play PC games, but on your logic, puzzle skills and some degree of patience.

Some have criticised the lack of typical gaming skills involved and accused the game of being no more than a series of overly complicated puzzles papered over with picture-perfect postcards. Ignore them. *Myst* is a divisive title for sure, but one that deserves a fair hearing and, most importantly of all, a test run before dismissing it outright. As custodian of the title of 'bestselling PC game of all time' for nine years until *The Sims* arrived on the scene, *Myst* is a game with more fans than haters, and rightly so.

Myst's lore revolves around an art of authoring tomes with worlds inside them. Place your hand inside one of these so-called linking books and you'll be warped into the world described within the pages. The only way out is to touch another book found within that world.

The tale begins to unfold on the mysteriously misty island of Myst. You play yourself, a character who has placed their hands on to one such linking book. After falling through a swirling constellation of stars, you safely touch down on the island with no instructions, no tutorial and nobody around to tell you where to start. All you can do is start walking to see what clues you can find.

Shortly thereafter, you stumble upon a deserted library with blackened and burned tomes lining the shelves and two other books set apart from the rest: one red, one blue. Inside each is a static-filled video message from a different man, each claiming that the other cannot be trusted and that you must collect the coloured pages of their book in order to set them free from their prison. Until the texts of their worlds are restored by reuniting the lost pages, the books' linking abilities are severed.

The search for the missing pages takes you to the corners of the island and, after some tricky puzzles, beyond. More hidden books take you to other Ages, each home to more clues and coloured pages. You can only carry one page back to the library at a time, so you'll need to think carefully about whom to trust. Pages aside, there are no other objects to fill your pockets: the pieces to each puzzle are kept wholly within a single Age so as not to confuse matters. Every time you travel through a linking book, you do so knowing the puzzles ahead are entirely self-contained.

The primary storytelling is almost completely non-verbal, meaning you have no choice but to wander aimlessly, peering into every nook and cranny and clicking on random objects to see what happens. The loneliness is genuinely unsettling, and you'll often wonder whether you're truly alone. Although there is no threat of death in the traditional gaming sense, you always feel threatened – a mood masterfully conjured up through a combination of the haunting score and visuals that were 1993's equivalent of high definition.

The more you know about *Myst* before playing it, the less impressive it will be. It's a game that has to be experienced first-hand, without advice or much prior knowledge. If there's one warning you should be armed with, it's that obscure logic lies ahead, but under no circumstances should it be tackled with any form of walkthrough. *Myst*'s greatest trick of all is an ending and a subsequent second play-through solution that any developer would be proud to call their own. It's a story reserved for those who've seen it already, and a concept so masterful it needs no further explanation...

N

Release date: 2005 | Platform: PC | Developer: Metanet Software

GOLD-GRABBING, rocket-dodging, gravity-defying ninjas are the order of the day here, and when you've got a combination like that there's no need to justify why you need to play it. Yesterday. We're feeling generous though, so let's kick on.

N is a freeware Flash game where the goal is to guide a stick ninja through 500 increasingly difficult levels. Passing each level involves hitting a switch for an escape door and safely making it through the exit. Levels are bunched into groups of five, which must be completed before the timer expires. Each 'episode' of five starts with ninety seconds on the clock, although recovering gold blocks dotted throughout the mazes adds two extra seconds per piece on to the total time remaining.

Aside from being a frighteningly good lunchtime time-waster thanks to some in-browser variations (although the real game must be downloaded from the official website for the full experience), *N* is a title that can confidently stand shoulder-to-shoulder with 'proper' games. Indeed, remake-cum-sequel *N+* found a premium-priced home on the Xbox Live Arcade service, the Nintendo DS and the PlayStation Portable. Thanks to the inclusion of multiplayer, it instantly became one of the best things on all three formats.

N's ninja is a versatile chappy – he runs faster than Usain Bolt and jumps further than Jonathan Edwards. He also scales walls by bouncing from one surface to another, or by very quickly leaping away and back from and to the same one if there's no wall opposite. They're all handy skills to have, given each map's minimalist approach to platforms, and they're essential abilities given the abundance of deadly mines, lasers, electrified drones and homing missiles that are dropped into these already tricky-to-navigate worlds.

The timer is everything, and *N*'s leaderboards are all focused on speed. The time left at the end of each episode sorts the ninjas from the whingers, and achieving the best times doesn't just involve pegging it through to the level exit as quickly as possible; it requires taking some dangerous side routes to nab as many extra gold pieces on your way to the finish line.

At first glance, *N*'s levels look impossible. If weapons don't kill the ninja, long falls will, and plenty of maps have huge walls and drops to scale and descend as part of the journey to the level exit. But even with inputs limited to left, right and jump buttons, the ninja has plenty of nuances to discover. For instance, dropping on to a diagonal block while moving in the same direction as the downward slant can break falls. Running up a diagonal piece and into a wall, meanwhile, can springboard you up into the stratosphere at ridiculo-speeds. Drops become less frightening when you master the art of leaning into a vertical wall to skid to a very slow descent, although, if you're going for the all-important speed runs, you need to break as late and as little as possible so as not to lose all momentum.

If the 500 levels aren't enough, there's always the level editor. As levels are made from rudimentary monochrome blocks, it's not hard to build maps that look no different from those created by Metanet Software. Fill them with trapdoors, hazards, the trampoline-like springy blocks and some golden pieces and you'll have yourself another *N* level in a matter of minutes, which you can share with other players.

N is the type of game that'll make you have 'one more go' all night long. The difficulty curve is expertly crafted and the momentum-fuelled motions of the ninja are quite simply flawless. But that's all just icing on the cake. *N* had us all playing at 'gold-grabbing, rocket-dodging, gravity-defying ninjas'.

🎮 🎮 🎮

NIGHTS INTO DREAMS...

Release date: 1996 | Platform: SEGA Saturn | Developer: Sonic Team

GIVEN THAT *NIGHTS* was released into a world in which *Super Mario 64* existed, any claims that Sonic Team's cult classic enhanced the gaming landscape are untrue. But, while the famous Italian plumber and his Nintendo 64 outing scuppered any pioneering glories *NiGHTS* might otherwise have enjoyed (the limited-edition *NiGHTS* controller came with an analogue stick that would have been considered groundbreaking had the Nintendo 64 not beaten it to the shelves by two weeks), the game is still an unequalled ode to childhood joy.

The story works like this: when you close your eyes at night and drift off to sleep, you're transported to dream worlds known as Nightopia and Nightmare. In Nightopia everybody's personalities take the form of coloured spheres called Ideya, energy the evil Nightmare ruler Wizeman the Wicked is stealing so that he can rule over Nightopia and break out of the dream worlds altogether. Two jesters called NiGHTS and Reala set out to steal the Ideya for Wizeman, but NiGHTS thinks twice about the evil scheme and finds himself imprisoned by the mean dictator. Later on, upset children Elliot and Claris dream themselves into Nightmare, but discover that they possess the Ideya of courage. The pair rescue NiGHTS and set out on a journey to stop Wizeman.

Wow, you're still here? Sorry about that, but nobody claimed it was Shakespeare. As far as setups go, it's hardly the best: no blue hedgehog grabbing rings just for the fun of it, that's for sure. The story's more quaffle than quality but it's a minor complaint: after all, it serves to put you into seven dreams (read levels) of pure brilliance.

Elliot and Claris run about these levels gathering up their lost hope, intelligence, growth and purity Ideya gems while being chased by an alarm clock. Abstract fun for all guaranteed. But *NiGHTS* takes off when, well, NiGHTS takes off actually. Releasing the jester from prison transfers control to NiGHTS and the magical acrobat is blessed with the power of flight.

NiGHTS's sections are two-dimensional (cunningly disguised as three-dimensional) flights through hoops, magic gates and other obstacles, the goal being to grab as many gems as possible before the flight timer runs out. Snaring twenty blue chips will unlock the children's stolen Ideya, pulling world domination that little bit further from Wizeman's slimy grasp each time.

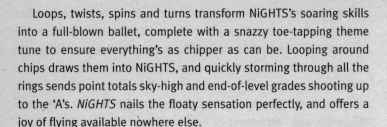

Loops, twists, spins and turns transform NiGHTS's soaring skills into a full-blown ballet, complete with a snazzy toe-tapping theme tune to ensure everything's as chipper as can be. Looping around chips draws them into NiGHTS, and quickly storming through all the rings sends point totals sky-high and end-of-level grades shooting up to the 'A's. *NiGHTS* nails the floaty sensation perfectly, and offers a joy of flying available nowhere else.

Each of the seven dream levels are divided into four 'mare' subsections and an end-of level boss, so *NiGHTS* has plenty to keep you going without even thinking about the score challenges or the Tamagotchi-esque existence of the Nightopian population. And after the main game there's *Christmas NiGHTS* to consider: a winter-themed double-level follow-on with Christmas trees, presents and music, given away free with select games and magazines at the time (which is why it's not really classed as a separate *game*... technically speaking). Play it on New Year's Day or April Fool's and there are extra treats in store.

Though remade for the PlayStation 2 in Japan and reimagined for the Wii in 2007, neither of *NiGHTS*'s follow-ups is a patch on the original. That's not nostalgia talking. At a time when Sonic was saying goodbye to the glory days and ruining his future with tragic 3D shambles, *NiGHTS* was the SEGA Saturn game of choice. A faithful sequel is long overdue.

NO MORE HEROES

Release date: 2008 (2007) | Platform: Nintendo Wii |
Developer: Grasshopper Manufacture

IF *SCOTT PILGRIM vs. the World* and *Kill Bill* were mashed together and turned into a game, the result would be similar to, albeit much saner than, *No More Heroes*. Leading loser Travis Touchdown is a perverted otaku hitman ranked number eleven in the United Assassins Association league of hitmen. When Travis is coerced into a journey to defeat the ten highest-ranked hitmen in Santa Destroy to become de facto numero uno, he grabs his strip-light-alike 'beam katana' (purchased on the web for fun) and begins slicing his way through the higher-ups' bodyguards.

Often referred to as a love letter to gaming, *No More Heroes* is the most fun you could ever hope to have with a Wii Remote in hand. The pop-culture-packed chanbara adventure is so stylish it wouldn't be surprising to find the box dressed in a leather jacket and the disc smeared with Brylcreem. Travis is the video-gaming epitome of cool – a well-dressed man who lives in a fantasy, learns new wrestling moves by watching Pro-Wrestling videos and saves the game by going to the toilet. And, even though the censored European release replaces hoses of blood with disappearing enemies, *No More Heroes* is a dazzling aestheticisation of violence that either wows or offends. There's really no middle ground.

Tracking down the hitmen involves travelling around the open world of Santa Destroy on your Schpeltiger motorcycle, hunting down the top ten and completing odd jobs to earn money for weapon upgrades. The description makes *No More Heroes* sound far more normal than it really is. 'It's gonna be a long, hard road,' shouts Travis in the opening video after he sets the scene. 'But who knows? Could kick ass. Could be dangerous. Could totally suck... you there holding the Wii Remote right now, just press the A button.' Kick ass? Yes. Dangerous? Yes. Totally suck... no. On that count and that count only, Travis is utterly wrong.

The game's control scheme is nothing short of wonderful. Holding the Wii Remote high readies Travis for high attacks, holding it low prepares him for low attacks, and, while swinging the katana is a simple case of tapping the A button, plenty of other actions are born out of your movements with the Remote. Cacophonies of guitar riffs and flashing lights await those who scoop up the beam katana and, once the tutorial has finished, Travis will be able to kick and cut his way through the toughest of crowds with relative ease.

Cleanly striking opponents teetering on the edge of death drags you into a mode called Death Blow – swing the Remote in the direction of the on-screen arrow and you'll carve them up and start a slot machine spinning. If the icons match you'll be warped into an even weirder mode depending on your winnings. Three grasshoppers trigger the one-hit-kill Strawberry On The Shortcake session, three bells bring about a shooting gallery known as Blueberry Cheese Brownie, three bars starts the button-matching Cranberry Chocolate Sundae attack, three 7s opens up access to the Anarchy In The Galaxy bombing mode and three cherries slows the action to a crawl for easier slaying. Grabbing an enemy, meanwhile, brings Travis's wrestling skills into play and forces you to move both hands in set directions to break out some deadly moves.

It's craziness of the highest order but not at the expense of gameplay. *No More Heroes*' quirks make perfect sense in the heat of the moment, and for all its weirdness the core game workings come first. Though not always the case in gaming, here oddness doesn't mean unplayability: *No More Heroes* is as easy and as natural to pick up and play as can be.

Creator SUDA 51 knows gamers like to do stuff and has ensured that every moment is filled with things to play with. When the beam katana's battery runs low, you hold down a button and waggle the Remote to charge it up again. When Travis's phone starts ringing, your Remote starts buzzing – hold it up to your ear and you'll take the call using the speaker on the Remote. When swords clash, you rotate the Remote as fast as you can to overpower the opponent. Even the loading screens are interactive – pressing the B button bounces the loading icon up and down for no reason other than to give you something to tinker with. You're always busy. Always entertained.

That's even the case when it comes to the instruction manual. It's a funny glimpse into the world of Santa Destroy, complete with a neat comic-book prequel to get you in the mood. It's just a taster of the real thing: the world of *No More Heroes* and the ten assassins in particular are too psychedelic to put into words. The odd jobs are too random to understand. *No More Heroes* is to video games what the emergence of punk rock was to music. It's completely insane, and it's the embodiment of everything that's right with gaming.

🐙 🐙 🐙

ODDWORLD: STRANGER'S WRATH

Release date: 2005 | Platform: Xbox | Developer: Oddworld Inhabitants

IT'S AN ODD world indeed. *Oddworld*'s odd world Oddworld is a gaming universe that bleeds charm from every river and sprouts charisma from every branch. To give you an idea of how much personality is packed into *Oddworld*, just be aware of this one fact: even the *ammunition* has attitude.

Stranger's Wrath is an alien take on the Wild West staring bounty hunter Stranger. Think of him as a sort of gruff Creature with No Name type guy (ignoring the part about him actually having a name, that is) out to capture do-wrongers with bounties on their heads and cash them in for moolah to pay for a life-saving operation. Capturing them dead's usually fine, but alive tends to result in better reward sums.

Stranger's Wrath is a half-'n'-half game. Half third-person platform-and-adventure title, with plenty of ledge-clinging, rope-swinging and barrel-smashing antics to soak up; half first-person-shooter, with outlaws to be downed and bountied before they regain consciousness.

Stranger's main weapon is a crossbow that fires little critters instead of arrows. There are nine different creatures in all and each animal has a different power. Spidery 'Bolamites' wrap outlaws in tight, sticky webbing; skunky 'Stunkz' act like stink bombs and make outlaws puke in disgust; chipmunky 'Chippunks' draw enemies away from groups and across levels with foul-mouthed tirades; fireflyey 'Zappflies' shock and stun foes; furbally 'Fuzzles' simply chomp on outlaws; trilobitey 'Thudslugs' are brute-force cannonballs; batty 'Boombats' explode after a few seconds; beey 'Stingbees' attack in rapid-fire modes; and waspy, er, 'Wasps' (how boring!) travel far and fast like sniper-rifle bullets. Seven of these even have upgraded variants with extra power and/or skills (usually involving homing in on the enemy).

When the ammo's not hurling abuse and blowing raspberries at you, it's usually found bouncing around in the Oddworld undergrowth. Apart from the endless supply of Zappflies, you must capture live ammunition before it can be used, giving Oddworld a rather unique two-tiered combat mechanism. Zappflies stun ammo so you can pocket the creatures for later firing, and store-bought attractor potions can be used to draw the rarer species out from their hidey-holes.

Stranger's Wrath is definitely a thinking player's shooter. While you can switch to a third-person viewpoint and bowl groups of enemies over by charging into them, most stand-offs require a little more tact and guile if you're to emerge unscathed. And as Stranger's crossbow isn't exactly a rocket launcher, any straight-shooting competitions are likely to end with Stranger six feet under.

Most ammo types have more than one use and you need to use the creatures in creative ways. Fuzzles can be shot into the ground to act like proximity mines and Zappflies will override electronic panels when given time to charge up. You always earn more money by capturing outlaws alive, but when you spy a pair of chatty bandits palavering underneath a giant boulder-carrying crane and an electronic panel that kick-starts the arm and causes it to crash down on their heads, the temptation to fire a Zappfly its way is almost always irresistible.

While other shooters tend to focus on their shooting mechanics, *Stranger's Wrath* treats combat like a puzzle. An area filled with outlaws should be approached like a brainteaser with one or two prime solutions that result in all the bad guys bagged and tagged with minimum fuss, not as a battleground on which to go Rambo on their butts. This unique approach (plus the snazzy third-person adventuring side of things, of course) sets *Stranger's Wrath* apart from any other shooter you could ever think of. All the *Oddworld* games are about fighting The Man as the little guy, and, as the only shooter of the *Oddworld* bunch, *Stranger* is a cut above the company he keeps. *Stranger's Wrath* isn't just a good action game and a good shooter bolted together: it's a distinctive action game and an exemplary shooter, conjoined by a queer plot and a luscious world untroubled by the competition. No gaming education is complete without a whimsical trip into the peculiar world of the Odd.

👾 👾 👾

PAC-MAN VS.

**Release date: 2004 (2003) | Platform: Nintendo GameCube |
Developer: Nintendo**

IT'S NOT HARD to play *Pac-Man*. Nowadays you need only travel as far as Google for a quick dot-chomping and spectre-dodging fix. The spherical pill-gobbler and his ghostly antagonists rank among gaming's most recognisable brands, and that success has been replicated in a number of remakes and reboots throughout the years for almost every gaming platform under the sun. Pac-Man has appeared in various guises – Ms, Junior, Baby, Professor – but of all the repackaging treatments, there are three versions that can be considered definitive *Pac-Man* titles: the Xbox 360's *Championship Edition* its sequel DX and the Nintendo GameCube's *Vs.*

In its most reduced form, *Pac-Man* is about guiding a compulsive eater around a labyrinth to chow down 240 dots while dodging four ghosts named Pinky, Blinky, Inky and Clyde. Snaffle one of the four bigger pills placed around the map and for a short while the tables are turned: Pac-Man becomes the hunter, the ghosts the hunted. Extra fruit dishes out extra points, and extra points means... a higher score. What, you didn't think it would be prizes, did you? *Pac-Man*'s mechanics aren't that convoluted.

Championship Edition and DX repackaged this basic template into aptly bite-sized chunks. Snazzier visuals are just window dressing. Their real shining glory come from ditching the infinite length and limiting every mode to three- or five-minute bursts. Were it not for *Vs.*, you'd be reading another few paragraphs about these games. As it is, they are worthy runners-up in a close-fought battle.

Vs. – that's 'versus' and not 'vee-ess' – transposes the timeless mechanics on to a multiplayer template utilising a hardware set-up complicated enough to require military planning. Part of *Vs.* intrigue comes from its inexplicably humble existence. In the UK, *Pac-Man Vs.* was mysteriously added as a footnote extra to so-so racer *R: Racing Evolution* on a console where no racing market existed. On top of that, it could only be played with a Game Boy Advance console and the GameCube connector cable. Alas, it was too much to ask for many, which is why *Pac-Man Vs.* is sadly one of the most undeservedly overlooked classics.

The fact that there is no single-player mode gives the game away: *Vs.* is a multiplayer title through and through. One player is Pac-Man. Up to three others are ghosts. It's a straight first-past-the-post race to get the highest score, and the fastest way there is to turn into Pac-Man and start snacking. In principle, it's simple to turn into the yellow blob. All you need to do is touch Pac-Man and swap controllers with the victim, but the beauty of *Vs.* comes down to the asymmetrical nature of the hunt.

If everybody were looking at the same screen, it would be easy to corner Pac-Man, but the television set only displays three zoomed-in segments of the overall maze, each centred on one of the ghosts. The only player aware of the whole playing field is the one playing as Pac-Man, who has a top-down view of everything displayed on his or her private screen via the connected Game Boy Advance console. Back on the television screen, meanwhile, Pac-Man leaves a short trail in his wake to alert any nearby ghosts of his location.

If there are fewer than four players, the spare ghosts mill about harmlessly until another ghost touches them, at which point they're coloured in and 'owned' by that player. It doesn't matter which coloured ghost touches Pac-Man: the moment it happens he is passed over to the catcher. And parallel to this game of tag, you've still got the normal dots, fruit and pills. If Pac-Man grabs a pill and eats a ghost, the score is even subtracted from the devoured player. Ouch.

Nintendo DS title *Namco Museum* has brought *Pac-Man Vs.* back to a new audience, but even now the title is ridiculously underplayed. There is a happy ending, though, if not for *Vs.* then for its legacy. *Pac-Man Battle Royale* is the latest Pac-Man arcade table, and it's a four-player eat-'em-up cross between *Championship Edition* and *Vs.* There are key differences: each player is a different Pac-Man and the ghosts are all computer controlled. It's still possible to swallow other players, though. Digesting pills doubles Pac-Man's size, letting him wolf down any smaller Pac-Men unfortunate enough to stray in his way. It's a fine legacy, but *Battle Royale* is simply dessert to *Vs.* main course.

PAPERBOY

Release date: 1984 | Platform: Arcade | Developer: Atari Games

IT'S A TIME-HONOURED rite of passage – teenagers too young for the minimum wage eager to make a quick buck, and newsagents looking for cheap labour coming together in a beautiful partnership. It's also a comedic plot device in many a family film, with carelessly flung rolled-up newspapers hitting doors, windows and even characters as the paperboy whizzes down a suburban street. But when this menial task collided with the video-game world in 1984, a killer game was born and packaged in a fancy-looking arcade cabinet complete with a set of steerable bicycle handlebars in the place of a joystick.

You are the paperboy, a young bloke laden with papers, cycling through his morning rounds. And just like the stereotypical film paperboy, you don't fancy stopping and getting off your bike to deliver the daily news. You steer left and right as you pedal along the pavement, collecting extra bundles, dodging obstacles and chucking the *Daily Whatever* into the mailboxes of your subscribers as you speed by. Mercifully your route only concerns one side of the street, so you can focus all your efforts to your left.

Simple? Not quite. *Paperboy*'s games span a week and, unlike other games of its time, your actions in the early stages have a huge impact on the states of later levels. The open mailboxes lining the street belong to houses who have paid for their papers in advance. Miss them, smash the corresponding house's windows or otherwise damage the property and you'll lose the customer, turning your target home into a boarded-up house of horrors by the following day, as if one morning without the news has reverted the people inside into uncouth Neanderthals. The more houses you miss, the more customers you lose, and, if too many go in the early stages, you'll have to hit 100 per cent of the mailboxes later on to keep your job. Achieving perfect deliveries will slowly reinstate lost subscribers back into your mailing list, and hurling your issues on to the doorsteps of houses is also an acceptable way of keeping the neighbourhood happy (though you'll receive fewer points than if you hit the mailboxes).

Obviously, striking a mailbox in Easy Street is a much simpler task than doing the same on Middle Road and Hard Way, though come the last day there's no such thing as an easy ride, not least because a paperboy's job isn't as simple as delivering newspapers. It turns out the tabloid-tossers keep pedalling for safety. For some unknown reason, delivering the daily rag morphs you into public enemy number one, and the journey along your choice of street is peppered with obstacles.

It's a head-patting, tummy-rubbing exercise. You need to watch for cars, cats, break-dancers and hydrants up ahead and avoid them when they appear. But forget to sling the scandal sheets at the precise time, or steer into the newspaper bundles to pick up more 'ammo' (and hence avoid running out of papers through careless chucking), and you'll lose subscribers and make the next day's delivery even tougher than it would be anyway.

It sounds like a basic concept and it is, even with the more complex dirt courses complete with ramps and targets that you have to complete at the end of each round for bonus points. But, at the end of the day, committing GBH with a rolled-up broadsheet on the annoying kid who likes to attack passers-by with a remote-controlled car is old-fashioned fun you can't replicate in today's gun-happy games. The paperboy doesn't have the world's most glamorous job, but he has one of the most enjoyable ones.

🐙 🐙 🐙

PEGGLE

Release date: 2007 | Platform: PC | Developer: PopCap Games

PACHINKO MACHINES ARE big in Japan, but to many people the word means only one thing: the basis for the most addictive game in recent years. The idea of the classic gambling device is to launch a metallic ball into a vertical array of pegs, hoping that it will land in a central tray and start a slot machine in an attempt to win some cash. When someone at PopCap Games looked at a pachinko machine and realised the ball-bouncing was more fun than the gambling itself, *Peggle* was born.

Gone is the slot machine and questionable gambling ethics, while the pegs have been fattened up, coloured blue and orange, placed in pretty patterns and promoted from 'annoying obstacles' to 'purpose of the game'. You're put in charge of aiming the ball-launcher at the top of the screen, and your goal is to hit and destroy all the orange-coloured pegs using a certain number of shots. The tray still exists – a small cup that steadily tracks from left to right. Time and angle your shots so that the ball lands on the tray and your shot isn't subtracted from the total allowance, giving you a crucial free ball to play with. Luck, you say? You make your own luck...

That's just the tip of the iceberg. In addition to aiming and launching the balls – watching them ricochet around like on a pinball table filled with bumpers and silently willing them to bounce on to another orange peg – you are given a 'Peggle Master' character who comes with a special skill. The talent varies from master to master, but the power-ups range from explosions to multi-balls to pinball flippers, and the skills can be used twice per level. As more points are awarded for clearing all the blue pegs too, strategic use of these special skills is a must, even when the orange pegs are all well within your grasp.

Because the ball pings off the pegs relative to its initial speed and the angle of the shot, it is possible to set up some outrageously ambitious lines and hope for the best. High scores are awarded to those who go for the crazy bonuses – the flukey shot that tags two pegs either side of the screen, one after the other, or the combo-tastic line of a ball seemingly with a personal vendetta against all of pegkind. In the best lines, the rising chromatic scale of a multi-peg shot even climaxes with a free ball and a barrage of bonus points.

Urging a ball on to a peg or into the moving bucket is a strangely powerful sensation, and something you can get all too easily wrapped up in. At the end of the day, you're just bouncing a ball on to blocks, and yet *Peggle* is a toe-curling, edge-of-the-seat kind of experience that commands just as much, if not more, attention as any other type of game. When the orange pegs are down to just one, time slows to a crawl, drum rolls start drumming and an audience starts gasping every time the ball moves towards the target. If it's a miss, the action returns to normal until the next close shave. If it's a hit, an orchestral rendition of the 'Ode to Joy' bursts to life as the ball falls into one of the newly erected points buckets. It never gets old. Ever.

And good thing too, because the game has more levels than Subway has outlets. When the adventure mode is eventually cleared, 75 Peggle Masters' Challenges await experts eager for more. Their difficulty is such that they'll keep pegglers peggling for weeks before they've cleared them all.

That's *Peggle*: ordered yet chaotic, comprising predictable rules yet random in its outcomes. It's packed with content but easily enjoyed in bite-sized chunks and, though taxing, it's simple, fun and impossible not to love. It's a game of contradictions and a lesson in how incredible presentation can make a good game great. Ultimately it's a riot to play and, unlike the Japanese pachinko machines, you needn't spend a fortune to do so.

👾 👾 👾

PHOENIX WRIGHT: ACE ATTORNEY
Release date: 2006 (2001) | Platform: Nintendo DS | Developer: Capcom

GAMING HEROES COME in all shapes and sizes. There are space marines, there are beautiful archaeologists. There are plumbers and there are blue hedgehogs. Crime lords, cowboys, writers, cats, princes, witches... pretty much anything goes. Yet even in a world with no rules, a *defence attorney* is a bit of a weird one.

Phoenix Wright first appeared in 2001 in the Japanese-only Game Boy Advance game *Gyakuten Saiban Yomigaeru Gyakuten*. Five years later, it gained a side-splitting English localisation and an extra case designed to make the most of the Nintendo DS's unique touch screen and microphone.

Ace Attorney is the opening act of a fledgling defence attorney's rise from training to courtroom legend. Split into different cases, it's your role as the clean-cut and ever-so-clumsy Phoenix Wright to exonerate your client of murder charges and uncover who really committed each crime. Acquittal requires keen investigation of the crime scene and any related locations to gather evidence and clues from witnesses. It then needs careful courtroom cross-examination skills to uncover inconsistencies in people's testimonies. When people are on the stand, Phoenix can press for more information about each sentence of their statements, and he can present evidence that directly contradicts the claims. Sometimes those lies are born out of the killer's guilt, other times they're innocent mistakes of incompetent police investigators (dim-witted detective Gumshoe is a fan favourite) or dopey deponents.

The cases are strictly linear affairs. Phoenix Wright isn't a game with branching paths or a whole lot to do or see off the main investigation's path. Set events in each case's chapters only occur once specific actions have been taken; in the courtroom, evidence must be presented at exactly the right time during a testimony – not a moment too soon or late.

As a result, some issues arise if you anticipate a revelation before it happens. The game doesn't let Feenie jump the gun. The other side of things can be equally problematic: it's possible to find progress halted because you've yet to pick up one vital clue or you're not sure which bit of evidence contradicts a single sentence. The game suffers from a couple of obscure leaps of logic that can turn proceedings into a guessing game. Fitting, perhaps, for a defence lawyer in over his head, but not the best of features for a game to work.

Yet these issues don't come close to keeping the game off these pages. Even though murder and cover-ups (and, later on in the series, suicide too) are deadly serious topics, *Phoenix Wright: Ace Attorney* is a delight to play. It has one of the most chortle-inducing scripts of all time outside of the LucasArts graphic adventure titles, and, though its unwavering linearity means the graphic adventure is more like a book than a game at times, it would be a book of the highest quality.

The English translation is razor sharp – the script, the characters, the frequent pop-culture references and the story itself are what keep you playing, not the hunting and presenting of evidence. It's the characters' reactions to surprise news – the sight of Phoenix sweating on the stand when he says something stupid, or the visual spectacle of a witness crumbling under pressure when their testimony is torn apart. Capcom's localisation team is the best in the entire industry, and the tussles between Phoenix and main prosecutor Miles Edgeworth – a strong contender for one of the greatest antagonists in gaming history – are epic battles of breathless back and forth arguments and counter-arguments.

There's something disarming about the way Phoenix Wright slams his palms on to the table and yells 'HOLD IT!' when mad, or the iconic way he points with his index finger and yells 'OBJECTION!' when singling out a contradiction (and the way you too can yell 'OBJECTION!' into the microphone to trigger Phoenix's outburst). The game is remarkably entertaining and funnier than it has any right to be, but it also shoulders some fairly hefty messages. Beneath all the jokes and buffoonery is a man who fights tooth and nail for truth and justice, and that's rather comforting too. You're not mowing down bad guys with guns and swords, you're putting the guilty behind bars. That you're doing so in a pantomime of a courtroom is irrelevant; there's a strong moral undercurrent to Phoenix Wright and the games deserve to be applauded for more than just the laughs.

While the third game, *Phoenix Wright: Trials and Tribulations*, is home to the greatest case of all, it only makes sense if you've played through the first two games. Creator Shu Takumi has the uncanny and sadly unique talent of knowing exactly what the fans want to see. Though the series has gone downhill after the departure of leading man Phoenix Wright, the original trilogy is an outstanding achievement brimming with returning characters, shock twists and some of the most talented writing the industry has known. Without giving away too much of the surprise, the development of Miles Edgeworth in particular is a masterstroke, and that tale alone is well worth buying all three games for.

That trilogy begins with *Ace Attorney*. It's the finest story never committed to paper and the start of an incredible series that stays with all who play it. And that's a fact that would easily stand up in court. Need the evidence? It's just one DS game cartridge away...

👾 👾 👾

PICROSS 3D

Release date: 2010 (2009) | Platform: Nintendo DS | Developer: HAL Laboratory

PICTURE A CUBE made up from lots of smaller cubes. A Rubik's cube, only much, much bigger. Somewhere inside that cube is a mystery object – it can be an animal, a plant, a household object or some food, even – waiting to be freed. To get it out, you've got to chip away one square at a time like an archaeologist excavating a dinosaur bone from a lump of rock.

Each block is identical to its neighbours, so you don't know which cubes belong to the object and which are parts of the excess rubble until all the gunk has been chipped away and the item remains completely intact. When that happens your object reveals its true colours by, rather fittingly, colouring itself in. And with that you've just conceived *Picross 3D*.

Given that every cube is identical, how do you go about discerning the object from the rubbish? It's a task better explained by *Picross 3D*'s slightly simpler cousin, *Picross 2D*. *Picross 2D* involves a large grid built up from small squares, and at the edge of each row and column is a series of numbers. These numbers tell you how many squares in that row or column make up the object, and whether they are joined together or not. For example, if you're playing on a 10x10 grid and one row has a 9 by the side of it, you know that the middle eight squares of that row have to be part of the object along with one of the two end squares.

If a column on the same grid were to have 5 4 written above it, you know that there are two blocks of 'object' squares with a gap of at least one rubbish square in between them, and that the first block is made up of 5 squares and the second of 4. On our 10x10 grid there's only one solution, and it involves a single discardable block on the sixth square down.

Sometimes it's not immediately clear from looking at a single collection of numbers what goes where. A 2 2 tells you there are two blocks of two separated by at least one bad square, but on a row 10 blocks long they could fall anywhere. And that's where *Picross*'s appeal lies. It's about singling out the lines that you can figure out straight away, and using those set blocks to deduce which other columns and rows you can start piecing together.

Picross 3D obviously extends this idea into the third axis, giving you more clues (but also more headaches) on the way to the solution. Like Sudoku it's a remarkably simple concept, and like Sudoku it's a fantastic way to pass the time when at home or on a long (or short if you're super clever/don't mind using the DS's sleep mode to pause the puzzle) journey. If you do ever make a mistake, you're not penalised for it. Blocks can be scratched out and reinstated at will. Going wrong will make it harder for you to see the solution and backtrack to a correct position. It won't ruin the puzzle, though. There's no such thing as a fail state in *Picross*.

Just because a product comes on a gaming console doesn't mean its status as a game is a given. Look at *Wii Fit* or *100 Classic Book Collection*: one a home fitness planner, the other a selection of famous literature. Some people would question *Picross 3D*'s status as a game. Those people would be completely wrong to do so. For unlike Sudoku and to a lesser extent *Picross 2D*, *Picross 3D* couldn't exist on anything other than a gaming machine. It's not possible to print the game in a newspaper or to play it with a pad and pencil as there's no way to visualise the cube you're chipping away at. *Picross 3D* clearly isn't as glamorous a title as a *Super Mario Galaxy* or even a *Pac-Man*, but it's an important part of a healthy and balanced gaming diet. You don't always want to be advancing an army or taking part in a sporting tournament during a quick play on the bus or the train. You often want to sink your brain into a one-off puzzle. Plenty of titles aren't design to be played in short bursts. *Picross 3D* is, and it absolutely thrives on it.

🐙 🐙 🐙

PLANTS VS. ZOMBIES

Release date: 2009 | Platform: PC | Developer: PopCap Games

TOWER-DEFENCE GAMES work like this: you have a base you need to protect from waves of enemy onslaughts and your only defensive options involve erecting stationary 'towers' at key locations to push them back. Different-flavoured towers and different enemy types interact in unique ways and it often takes a well-measured approach, not to mention several crossed appendages to juggle all the keystrokes, to survive later assaults. There are thousands of games like this in existence, but when PopCap's *Plants vs. Zombies* grabbed the concept with two rotting hands and shambled straight into a flowerbed of killer geraniums, it rendered all others obsolete. This is partly because this fight for the ages involves cutesy plants and comedy zombies. If there's a funnier, more appealing spin on the tower-defence concept, we'll eat our brains.

Laughs isn't all *Plants vs. Zombies* has going for it, though. The strategy game shies away from the concept of feeding enemy forces through mazes and keeps things basic by restricting zombie movement to five or six parallel lines, bowling alley-style. While the zombie masses are shuffling along the lawn towards your house, it's your job to plant chlorophyll-powered protectors into spare grid spaces to defend your home and your brains from the slow, shambling legions of undead.

There's no downtime in *PvZ* to bubble wrap the spare china and hammer a few extra boards over the windows: while plenty of tower-defence games let you get your house in order before releasing the enemy hordes, *PvZ* starts both sides off simultaneously. A quick, green-fingered approach is vital, although if you do mess up on one of the lanes a one-time-only lawnmower can be called into action to slice and dice everything in its path.

No breathing space and no downtime, that's *PvZ*'s secret. Continuous garden management is the key to survival; replacing the plants munched into mulch or planting a second projectile-pitcher on rows with long queues of zombies. Quieter seconds are best spent organising sunflower ranks to earn more sunlight (the game's currency) to buy more offensive seed packets, or planting emergency potato mines in case any zombies break through the first lines of defence and need to be turned into a mountain of mash before wreaking more havoc.

The main adventure mode spans five long chapters and is spent meeting new zombie breeds and buying new seed species from Crazy Dave the neighbour. There are forty-nine plant varieties and twenty-seven zombie types in total, with unique problems to work around depending on whether you're battling on the front lawn, the backyard or the rooftop. (In the backyard, for instance, only aquatic plants can be placed in the swimming pool unless there's a lily pad for a regular seed to rest on.)

The plant and zombie combinations and permutations seem endless. Magnet-shrooms weaken strengthened zombies by removing pickaxes, screen door shields and bucket heads. Similarly, big wall-nuts called tall-nuts stop pogo-sticking and pole-vaulting zombies from leaping over defences. Bungie zombies nick random plants but can be countered with umbrella leaves or cob cannons, but cob cannons only appear when two kernel-pults are placed in adjacent squares... For a so-called 'casual' game, *Plants vs. Zombies* is deceptively hardcore.

The flowers are healthy and the zombies are still upbeat in their own special, mouldy sort of way, long after the adventure mode is but a distant memory. Entertaining diversions such as 'walnut bowling' and 'whack-a-zombie' (both as fun as they sound) and a *PvZ*-themed *Bejeweled* spin-off named *Beghouled* keep the rotting humour undead, while the raw challenge of the survival mode – complete with infectious looping soundtrack – captures the kernel of the tower-defence genre's appeal.

While other games can claim to match (though not overtake) *PvZ* in the mechanics department, PopCap has the race for presentation all wrapped up in Hazmat gear. When there's little to set substance apart, style does matter, and *PvZ* registers as a must-have on both fronts. The actions of its tower-defence mechanics will be what keeps you playing – the mark of any good game. But the irrepressible smile while you're doing so is a direct result of the lurching bobsleigh zombies and the hypno-shroom. The timeless battle between cute, multicoloured shrubbery and obliterating swarms of varied, cunning and often hilarious undead is just something every self-respecting gamer owes it themselves to experience. Go get your fingers green.

🐙 🐙 🐙

POKÉMON RED/BLUE

Release date: 1999 (1996) | Platform: Nintendo Game Boy | Developer: Game Freak

RED, BLUE, YELLOW, Silver, Gold, Crystal, Ruby, Sapphire, FireRed, LeafGreen, Emerald, Diamond, Pearl, Platinum, HeartGold, SoulSilver, Black and *White*. Add *Green* to the list for the original Japanese launch in 1996 – three years prior to the European release. It's ironic that the famous Pokémon tag line 'Gotta Catch Them All' could just as easily be applied to the number of game iterations. And then there's the dozens of spin-off titles: *Snap, Trading Card Game, Pinball, Stadium, Colosseum, Ranger, Mystery Dungeon, Trozei!, Channel*... you get the picture.

Pokémon is short for Pocket Monsters. Well over 500 of them, to be precise, though just 151 animals existed in the glory days of *Pokémon Red* and *Blue*, back when Pokémon qualification checks were stringent. Nowadays it seems any old work-experience boy's scribble is being morphed into a Pokémon: slap two googly eyes on to a hairbrush, call it Brushy and it'll probably pass the filters. The original assortment remains the best. What's more, it was well within anybody's grasp to follow through on the series' motto and actually catch them all.

Pokémon are cutesy animals who mostly live in harmony with humans. They come in different types – grass, fire, ground, flying, etc. – they hatch from eggs, they don't age but evolve into new Pokémon types, and they all possess unique superpowers. Obviously this is all pretty weird, which is why professors worldwide devote their lives to studying them, and why Pokémon trainers like you are determined to catch and befriend them all.

Pokémon Red and *Blue* are two sides of the same role-playing coin. The games that started it all differ only when it comes to 24 of the 150 creatures hiding in the game's grassy areas (151st Pokémon Mew cannot obtained without cheating or exploiting glitches – it was handed out at specific Nintendo events). Twelve are exclusive to each game cartridge colour, forcing gamers to connect Game Boys to friends' consoles with a link cable to trade Pokémon and complete their sets.

You play a Pokémon trainer, which means you can pretty much mirror the brilliant cartoon's plot. You choose your first Pokémon from a selection of three, meet your future rival and leave home on a quest to become the greatest Pokémon trainer of all time. You travel around the world, hopping from town to town and collecting Pokémon in the grasslands in between settlements. Along the way you'll trade creatures and battle with other trainers, and the only way to push forward is by defeating each town's gym leader to earn your Pokémon training badges.

Pokémon trainers sound awful: they search for wild Pokémon, trap them in small spheres called Pokéballs and train them to attack other Pokémon. But in practice it isn't as barbaric as it sounds. It's a game about three core elements: exploring, collecting and nurturing. When Pokémon fight, the battles are good-natured and free from pain. If a Pokémon loses its health, it faints instead of dying. There's no blood. No hint of stress. Battles are simply playtime for the creatures.

To become the best trainer you need to capture weak Pokémon and train them up until they can take on better Pokémon. Then you capture those and train them up and so on. The cycle continues until you find a team of six Pokémon you wish to stick with eventually to take on both the world's greatest Pokémon trainers and your friends.

Getting to know your Pokémon teams is unspeakably rewarding: there's something comforting about knowing at which level Diglett evolves into Dugtrio, and which Pokémon can learn Surf to take you across the sea on its back.

Different breeds of Pokémon appear in specific patches of grass along the way, usually in unlimited numbers, apart from the Legendary Pokémon: rare sightings that you encounter only once. Blow your chance of capturing them by letting them flee or faint and you'll never have another chance.

More and more combat layers are introduced throughout the thirty-something-hour lifespan. The fighting system takes the main workings of your average Japanese role-playing game's attack/ defend/item combat (Pokémon adds the 'swap' command to that list to change the active monster) and keeps it simple. On a basic level, there's a rock, paper, scissors system at play. Certain Pokémon types are weaker against others – fire loses out to water, for instance – so picking the right Pokémon during battles is crucial. Every Pokémon can then learn up to four moves, and these moves are also filed into the same category types as the creatures themselves.

Keeping a balanced party is the key to success. In later games, it's possible to breed Pokémon capable of learning non-native move sets, but this just muddies the waters too much when it comes to fighting friends. The pure mechanics of *Red* and *Blue* are unspoiled by the sequels' complications with their needless beauty contests and Pokémon mutations. You know where you are with *Red* and *Blue*: coordinating with friends to ensure you all evolve Eevee into its different adult forms, and swapping monsters to max out your Pokédex encyclopaedia, is as good as it gets.

There are a number of reasons why *Pokémon* became an overnight success. A solid concept, a snazzy cartoon series, a theme tune you'll sing in the shower each morning... The beginnings of the entire multi-billion-dollar franchise, however, are the very first *Pokémon* Game Boy games, and they're titles that still rank high among the greatest creations in the gaming universe. You don't have to play them all to understand the Pokémon craze, but once you've started *Red* or *Blue*, you'll probably want to.

PORTAL

Release date: 2007 | Platform: PC | Developer: Valve Corporation

IT'S NO COINCIDENCE that *Portal* is the fourth Valve Corporation title in this book and the second of the quartet to hinge on the brilliance of a single weapon. While *Half-Life 2* has its gravity gun, *Portal* has its Aperture Science Handheld Portal Device. It doesn't take a genius to work out precisely what the portal gun can do, but as there's no minimum IQ requirement to buy this book we'll play it safe. The portal gun is a weapon that fires blue portals and orange portals and links them with magic and space dust. Or, erm, science or something. Step through one portal and you step out of the other. Pedal back through the gateway and – as if by magic – out the first portal you come.

Only one portal of each colour can exist at any one time – firing a second will wipe the previous portal from existence – and portals only open on solid surfaces (and select ones at that). Walls, floors and ceilings can all be portalified. If you want to create an endless tunnel by positioning portals on the floor and then on the ceiling directly opposite, you can.

You begin the game knowing as much about your situation as clueless, silent protagonist Chell. She's a test subject dressed in an orange jumpsuit with metallic jumping stilts fixed to her legs to protect her from long falls (although Portal is played entirely through Chell's eyes, we know this by placing portals on either wall of a corner and peeking through like a self-voyeuristic peeping Tom). Trapped in a sterile cell, you discover you're in an 'Enrichment Centre' as part of a science programme for a company called Aperture Science. Unfortunately, before you learn the whole truth, the computerised voice explaining it all becomes garbled and the cell door slides ominously open. There's no option other than to begin the tests.

Your journey through *Portal*'s test chambers is lonely save for the automated voice of the Genetic Lifeform and Disk Operating System (GlaDOS), an artificial intelligence monitoring your progress. Every chamber is a self-contained puzzle designed to use the portal gun in different ways, and the goal is simply to make it to the end of the room and into the lift that takes you to the next chamber.

'Simply' isn't the right word, actually, because, although your only skills involve firing two coloured portals, jumping and picking up the occasional crate, Valve Corporation's puzzles are fiendishly tricky. It's amazing what you can do by linking two unique points in space-time together with the portal gun, and it's only by 'thinking with portals' that you'll be able to pass through each room – some of them terribly dangerous – unscathed.

A typical puzzle involves trying to cross a deep ravine where every surface on the opposite side is padded and therefore cannot be manipulated by the portal gun. The solution is beautifully quaint: place one portal high on the wall facing the exit and jump down to the bottom of the pit, being sure to fire a portal into your landing spot before you touch down. The momentum of the plummet then fires you horizontally across the gap back at the top of the room and towards the level end.

Without giving too much away, Aperture Science isn't quite what it seems. Occasional glimpses behind the scenes suggest something is amiss. The automated sentry guns shoot on sight but come with a suspiciously polite demeanour, and the omnipotent GlaDOS seems to know more than she's letting on.

You just can't submerge quality design. Away from the action-packed City 17 of *Half-Life 2* and the zombie-stricken streets of *Left 4 Dead*, Valve

Corporation manages to let its quality shine through other means. *Portal* is a tiny game (three hours absolute tops) set in a stark world, yet more is made of every inch of those bare white walls than in most other titles. Even with meagre ingredients, *Portal* ends up as a sometimes touching, often hilarious adventure that ranks among some of the smartest games ever devised. Only *Portal* could turn a humble crate into a major character you genuinely care for. And only *Portal* could end with a quirky song that has been adopted as a gaming anthem.

Even when *Portal* was but a distant memory, the fun didn't stop. When Valve Corporation announced *Portal 2*, it didn't just bung a press release on the internet: it pushed extra content into the first game. New radio transmissions playing Morse code messages and secret images hidden in the updated game files all pointed towards a follow-up, something that was confirmed when Valve Corporation modified the ending sequence of the game.

If that wasn't enough – and it really is – *Portal* comes with extra challenge rooms and modes. Full developer commentary, meanwhile, lets you play through the game while its creators explain the thought processes of the design and implementation of the puzzles. The extra features are the icing on the cake of a three-hour masterpiece that would shame most other full-length titles. Just remember to tear up the rule book and think outside the box when you give it a go. Scratch that, think with *portals*.

🕹 🕹 🕹

PRINCE OF PERSIA: SANDS OF TIME

**Release date: 2003 | Platform: PlayStation 2 |
Developer: Ubisoft Montreal**

SPEAK TO A clued-up gamer about *Prince of Persia: Sands of Time* and they'll probably say one of three things: that it was one of the greatest games of its generation, that it was unfairly lumbered with terrible, sell-out sequels or that it didn't receive enough acclaim on its release. On all three counts, they'll be wrong. But these aren't false claims intended to sway opinion, they're honest thoughts of people cleverly duped by a game so hypnotising it would leave Derren Brown lost for words.

Memories lie. For starters, *Sands of Time* is a tiny, tiny morsel of a game expanded by ruddy naff fighting. The hair-tearing combat is so shonky it nearly ruins everything. The eponymous Prince is an acrobatic fellow armed with a scimitar and a big fan of flipping, flopping, twirling and generally making a nuisance of himself, but, when placed in a room full of burly enemies who keep respawning, he's trapped in an ugly and infuriating dance of death. Combat is just a test of patience and the ability to abuse the same cheap tactics over and over again. There's little gratification in *Sands of Time*'s fighting. The only plus point is the knowledge that, after much suffering, each battle, eventually, ends.

Onwards with the great selling job: its sequels were better. They were bigger, they featured more creative puzzles and level design, and their combat mechanics were generations beyond that of *Sands of Time*. Anyone who plays the classic *Sands of Time* trilogy (now a tetralogy thanks to a belated addition to the series after one horrible reimagination tried and failed to take it in a new direction) in one long go would begrudgingly have to agree.

But there's a reason everybody looks back on *Sands of Time* so fondly and there's a reason why it's listed in this book. It's this: the game possesses more charm than a leprechaun's bracelet. It's as charismatic as they come, and anybody subjected to the game's magnetism is utterly helpless to resist believing the hype. The charm negates all faults bar none, and said charm is sadly missing from the sequels, hence the widespread belief that *Sands of Time* is the superior game.

Charm stands for a lot. In *Sands of Time*, it all stems from the story, the lead character and an Arabian soundtrack that manages to hit both mellow and energetic strides at precisely the right times. The game is one giant flashback, a retelling of the Prince's journey through the city of Azad, narrated by the Prince himself.

There are (terrible) battles and (decent) puzzles along the way, but the main meat of the game is the gymnastics. Azad's engineers were clearly off their heads on opium when building the city, and the only way to traverse the towers and palaces involves wall-running and jumping over and under spinning spike traps and guillotines. There are plenty of chances for the Prince to induce his flippy fantasies here, but be warned: between the circular saw blades and the crumbling ledges that make up the platforming side of *Prince of Persia*, there's not a lot of room for relaxation.

In any other game these brutal acrobatic challenges would be one frustration too far, but the well-spoken Prince in his progressively tattier clothes holds the Dagger of Time, a mystical weapon capable of rewinding time a few seconds to erase death-yielding mistakes. Rewinds are limited by the volume of sand stored in the dagger. As the whole game's a retelling, death is paradoxical. Expiring when there's no rewind power left leaves the narrator shaking his head and sighing, 'No, no, that's not how it happened.'

One of the original trilogy's biggest sticking points is the transformation of the Prince from a polite, sometimes cheeky nobleman into an angsty emo for the sequels. The relationship between the Prince and female adventure-mate Farah in *Sands of Time* is delightful to watch unfold. It taps into that c-word again: charm. All failings on *Sands of Time*'s part are wholly forgivable, simply because the game is too alluring not to fall in love with. Anybody who disagrees is dead inside.

PUZZLE QUEST: CHALLENGE OF THE WARLORDS

**Release date: 2007 | Platform: Nintendo DS |
Developer: Infinite Interactive**

A STUNNING FUSION of two wildly different concepts, *Puzzle Quest: Challenge of the Warlords* mixes the maddening addictiveness of Connect 4-alike *Bejeweled* (which is sort of 'Connect 3') with a traditional role-playing game's scale and scope. *Challenge of the Warlords* imbues a simple puzzle game with a motivation other than high scores, and proves that, while games don't need stories to be successful, almost any title can be hugely improved upon by joining it with a smartly conceptualised and masterfully implemented tale.

The core game involves swapping the positions of two gems on a filled grid to create rows and columns of three or more identical jewels. Lines of gems vanish, shunting higher gems down to fill the free space and pushing more jewels into the grid from the top. Clever matching results in a chain reaction as falling blocks trigger and destroy more rows.

Normally, this would all feed points into a score system, but *Puzzle Quest*'s role-playing leanings are fused into every single move you make. The game is the story of the quest of one man (or woman, if you choose) through a ye olde kingdom beset with evil warlords and mystical monsters. Each puzzle is a fight between your adventurer and some beastly foe – skeleton, vampire or other. The two parties take it in turns to trade blows using the same gem board, and the victor is the fighter who wipes out the other's health bar first.

The gems on the board come in a variety of flavours. Skulls deal direct damage to health bars relative to the number in the row and the number of multiplier bonuses in the group. Four colours, meanwhile, feed into a player's 'bank' once matched. Every character has a variety of spells at their disposal, which need a minimum expenditure of specific coloured gems to cast. The banked jewels act like magic points, letting characters forgo the gem board and cast a spell instead. Depending on which skill is cast, the effect could be anything from damaging the enemy to removing all gems of a specific colour from the board. Careless swapping that doesn't lead to a row is punished – the silly fighter will lose a chunk of health for their misdeeds.

Match more than the minimum three gems at once and you'll earn another go before the turn ends. It therefore pays to try to set up potential lines of four and five gems, but it's even more beneficial to sabotage your foe's similar plans.

In addition to the skulls and colours, there are money blocks and purple balls. Money gives you money, obviously, which can be spent on better equipment for future attack and defence bonuses among other statistic boosts. Purple gems are experience balls, which are used to level up your character's skills and stats.

It means matches aren't just about killing your enemies. That goal's still the main focus of *Puzzle Quest*, but wherever possible you need to emerge victorious with enough bonus money and experience to put towards new gear and perks. Failure to do so will make later puzzling much, much harder than it should be.

The overwhelming popularity of identical puzzlers *Bejeweled 2* and *Zoo Keeper* proves beyond any doubt the power of *Puzzle Quest*'s match-three principle on its own. That it's combined with a role-playing mechanic in which you travel the world, chat to people, buy equipment and animals, take on missions, build castles, save those in need and fiddle about with more inventory details than you'll find in your typical role-playing game, is in equal parts daunting and exciting. The game is nothing short of an inspired work of genius and combines two ultra-addictive themes into one mega time sink, which drags you in like quicksand and holds on like a starving python. Puzzle games are brilliant. Puzzle games masquerading as role-playing games are dangerous threats to spare time.

RESIDENT EVIL 2

Release date: 1998 | Platform: PlayStation | Developer: Capcom

THE THEME OF any zombie fiction is escalation. Vampires tend to be a rather stable species – turning a few people here and there but rarely reaching the sort of numbers that would be considered an infestation. Werewolves, too, aren't ones for spreading their gift. Too many of the victims wind up dead rather than simply bitten, so population rise is minimal. Zombies, on the other hand, get everywhere fast. The infected turn quickly, and because a measly bite spreads the disease but the zombies themselves are often too slow to overpower and kill all on whom they munch, there are plenty of short-term survivors whose bodies are a ticking z-bomb.

So it is with *Resident Evil*. The first game – a stunning horror rightly high on many people's personal favourites list – is the story of a zombie outbreak in a country manor and the efforts of two Special Tactics and Rescue teams to investigate and neutralise the threat. Things went boo (or to be wholly accurate: gwaaahhhrrghhhh), other things went squelch and everybody was in agreement that, between the zombies in the cupboards, the killer sharks in the basement and the Edam-cheesy acting, *Resident Evil* was the cream of the horror crop.

Escalation is the name of the game for the second reanimation: the infection has spread from one little house in the woods to an entire city. Fictional Midwestern American metropolis Raccoon City is the doomed municipality in question – a place where the hills are alive with the sound of groaning and the streets are hostile enough to make Hull city centre look like paradise.

The saga begins with new characters Leon Kennedy (a fresh-faced police recruit arriving for his first day on the force) and Claire Redfield (younger sister to the first game's leading man, Chris) travelling to Raccoon City, meeting up and finding themselves separated by a burning wreck. You choose who you play as first, and that choice has a profound impact on how the game plays out. *Resi 2* ships on two discs. One is Leon's story, the other is Claire's and each one is longer than either of the two adventures found in the first game.

Play Leon's tale first and Claire's story will be markedly different from the experience you get if you play Claire's first and then Leon's. As will Leon's. Still following? The A and B stories for each have twists and turns depending on the order of play, and just to be clear: Leon and Claire have entirely different experiences set in (some) unique locations with bespoke horrors, weapons and characters for each. The game is designed to be played with one scenario following the other, and the true ending only reveals itself once both stories are complete. This isn't like the first *Resident Evil*, where the choice between protagonists means playing through pretty much the same game from two different viewpoints – *Resident Evil 2* can be considered to be two games. Or four if you want to be generous and count each person's 'other' order version as a separate game.

Crossovers between the two characters' journeys are few and far between. The B character will find the odd puzzle completed by the A character and may or may not be able to collect certain equipment depending on whether character A nabbed it earlier. Otherwise, the stories are distinct and always surprising as a result.

The lurching undead and the fixed camera angles are the main trademarks of the early *Resident Evil* years, but episode 2 has some extra special moments of its own. The whole city has turned gnashy and that's bad news for you, especially because zombies are the least of your worries. Seeing Raccoon's monsters flood the streets and tear the remaining survivors apart is a haunting memory, but clamping your eyes on monsters like the Licker and Mr X for the first time is a thousand times worse. There are great stories behind both entrances but to tell them would simply ruin the surprise for anybody yet to give it a go.

Inventory and puzzle mechanics seem a little antiquated by today's standards, but the minor – almost imperceptibly so – imperfections are just a product of the game's time. *Resident Evil 2* managed to squeeze four different versions of a gigantic story into one title and each one on its own effortlessly embarrassed the competition. *Resident Evil 2* ups the ante, ups the visuals and ups the stakes in a game that has absolutely everything – even an unlockable mini-game starring a running, squeaking slab of tofu who needs to make it to an escape chopper. From drawn-out, tension-building, door-loading sequences to giant tarantulas and head-popping zombie/shotgun combos, *Resident Evil 2* is the number-one zombie game in this book, and the number-one zombie game of all time.

👾 👾 👾

RESIDENT EVIL 4

Release date: 2005 | Platform: Nintendo GameCube | Developer: Capcom

IF BUNGIE STUDIOS or Microsoft had played any part in *Resident Evil 4*'s development, there's a good chance it would be known today as *Resident Evil 4: Action Evolved*. Before the *Resident Evil* horror series had a chance to stagnate, Capcom stepped in and ordered a total reboot of their undead standard-bearer. The resulting rebirth of the *Resident Evil* brand is as influential to action games as *Halo* is to shooters. That it's often considered to be the game of the Xbox, PlayStation 2 and GameCube generation – trumping *Halo* and *Shadow of the Colossus* to that coveted title – goes to show how successful the premature reimagination of the popular franchise really was. Trace back the roots of any modern-day action title and they'll all lead here.

Resident Evil is a series revolving around flesh-eating zombies, but *Resi 4* bravely ditched the series' fascination with reanimated corpses and started afresh with a new tale and a new threat to mankind. It made no attempt to wrap up all past plot strands and didn't worry about filling in any of the blanks left hanging after *Resident Evil Code: Veronica*. 'This is five years later,' it would defiantly proclaim if it had a voice. 'The world has moved on. Get over it.'

It could easily be argued that *Resident Evil 4* stepped away from the series' horror background and morphed into an all-out action title. Such arguments should be reserved for another place and time. What really needs to be discussed is the way in which *Resi 4* delivered a new breed of game and an alien setting (that would be rural Spain – how many other games do you know set in Spanish forests?) and created a monster of a game that's had countless imitators but has still yet to be bettered.

Resi 4 has it all. The Spanish woodlands and gothic castles take the relative comfort zones that were western cities and research facilities from previous *Resi* titles, scrunches them up into a ball and tosses them blithely over its shoulder. It puts a bullet in the brains of the slow, shambling, groaning zombies and places the Ganado in their places: sentient locals armed with throwing knives, pitchforks and dynamite, capable of organising coordinated, *intelligent* attacks and breaking through any blockade you can throw in their path. Then it adds to their ranks a super-powerful chainsaw-wielding freak who will terrify you every time you hear a petrol engine rev as he is capable of lopping off heads in nanoseconds.

Resident Evil 4 still piles more and more monsters on top of those. Too many to mention, really. *Lord of the Rings*-style cave trolls, lake monsters and unkillable spike monsters join the assailant line-up. And traps too: trip wires, bear traps and lava pits, all waiting for a careless human to call their friend.

These are all ingredients that could have theoretically been worked into the old *Resident Evil* template. Locations and enemies makes for different artwork, not for different games. *Resident Evil 4* is a different game to its predecessors. The camera is unhinged from its previous fixed locations and firmly attached just behind and above protagonist Leon's right shoulder for a more involved view of the world. This is a camera position adopted by most action games since, and its intimacy opens up a whole new combat system. Old *Resident Evil* titles worked on a spin-on-the-spot-and-fire-up/straight/down policy. *Resident Evil 4* asks you to target every attacker precisely, right down to shooting their torso to knock them back, their shins to make them stumble or their weapons to prevent their attacks (or, in the case of the dynamite-chuckers, to make them and their mates go boom!).

Resident Evil 4 introduced a monetary system to the series, and a mid-level shop. It ushered the idea of weapon upgrades – not a new concept to other games by any means – into the franchise. It relied heavily on action buttons and so-called quick-time events (flashing controller buttons on-screen that need to be pressed to stay alive) further to enhance action set-pieces and to transition between chapters, but did so in a way that fitted the fiction. Chapters and acts – more new elements right there. All these features were alien to horror titles and rarely featured in standard action shooters. They are now common in games belonging to both genres.

And then there was the wise-cracking merchant character who'd pop up from time to time to offload new weapons and items – the most fondly loved meme to originate from games. Nobody knew where he came from or why he appeared in *Resi 4*. Years on, nobody's any the wiser.

Escort missions – a groan-inducing set of words if ever there were any – play a huge role in *Resident Evil 4*. Chaperoning a helpless character through dangerous territories was a true gaming frustration until *Resident Evil 4* arrived with its boxes. *Resi 4* lets you order your 'package' – in this case, the President's kidnapped daughter – to hide inside a giant box until the coast is clear. If the unthinkable happens and she is grabbed, all you need to do is blast at her abductor until they release her. Simple, smart, ground-breaking.

As if that wasn't enough, Capcom kindly tagged an extra mode (and then even more in the subsequent PlayStation 2 and Wii releases) on top. Mercenaries is *Resident Evil 4*'s key juices squeezed into an hourglass and tipped upside down. It's a score-attack mode that would be worth buying were it a stand-alone game, and it was thrown in as a small bonus to try and bolster a package that had already wiped the floor with every other game on the GameCube. Why? Because, in *Resident Evil 4*, Capcom enjoyed its finest hour.

REZ

Release date: 2002 (2001) | Platform: Dreamcast
Developer: United Game Artists

SLIP ON A pair of headphones or crank up the surround sound and *Rez* will take you to an isolation tank fitted with the greatest light and sound show ever devised. It's a game insomuch as there are levels and scores, but some would argue that *Rez* is much more than that; a whole other state of mind, even.

In a gaming library where every title must have a concise label summing up its parts, *Rez* would be tagged as a musical shooter. It's an on-rails trip through virtual reality with an electro-synth trance soundtrack. Your speeding journey through this world is pre-programmed, but you have the ability to slide a square targeting reticule around the screen and shoot down any attackers intent on blocking your path.

In the future all data are handled by a supercomputer known as the K-project, a network monitored and controlled by artificial intelligence called Eden. Predictably Eden goes all Skynet, forcing a rogue hacker – that would be you – to dive inside K-project and abort her suicidal shutdown sequence. Turns out K-project is like Tron crossed with

Kandinsky's 'On White II', an alternate reality where firewalls and viruses are given vibrant computerised bodies and physically attack intruders. Cities and tunnels are built with wireframe vectors, all splashed with neon paints.

Tumbling down the network's rabbit hole blitzes your ears as much as your eyes. *Rez*'s pulsating bass notes encourage head-nodding, finger-drumming and foot-tapping to get you in the mood. Then the harmonious intertwining of the shooting and the music aims to make synesthetes of us all. Run the targeting cursor over an enemy and you'll add bleeps to the music track. Fire a shot and notes will play. You can track and fire on up to eight targets in one go, and the resulting eight notes play a little tune if you do. You'll need to combo your shooting as much as possible for the points, but you'll *try* to combo your shooting just for the music. It's a key difference.

The emergent risk/reward system is finely tuned. Do you unleash a volley of seven shots to clear a screen of bugs or wait for an eighth to hear that final note play, knowing full well that you could be attacked while you procrastinate? Rhythmic shooting is rewarded with character and level evolution, piling more and more music and visual effects out of the speakers and screen. Taking hits results in devolution and a disappointingly sparse audio treat. Again, you play for the sensations, not the score counter in the corner of the screen.

You can see *Rez* isn't quite the game Tetsuya Mizuguchi intended to make: his vision was hampered by hardware limitations. *Rez*'s PlayStation 2 release came with an optional Trance Vibrator, a pocketable device that throbs in time with the music. *Rez*'s HD re-release on the Xbox 360 lets you use four controllers to simulate the music's thrum through even more palpitations. Yet you can see Mizuguchi's vision for *Rez* lies beyond the simplicity of vibrating controllers. The vision *is* that isolation tank *Rez* takes you to. If he could have got away with it, there's little doubting Mizuguchi would have created a full-body vibration suit to use in conjunction with *Rez*.

Rez's Microsoft Kinect-enabled sequel is *Child of Eden*, a game boasting futuristic *Minority Report*-style hand-waving controls. It's another step towards Mizuguchi's goal of a full-body experience, but *Rez* will always be the first to tread in that direction. You shouldn't play *Rez* before you die; you should look beyond the controller and *experience* it.

ROCK BAND 3

Release date: 2010 | Platform: PlayStation 3 |
Developer: Harmonix Music Systems

WITH EIGHTY-THREE anthems on one disc, fingertip access to over 2000 more songs, lead guitar, bass, keyboard (for the first time ever in the series), drum and vocal tracks to master, plus a difficulty mode that teaches you how to apply all your gaming skills to playing real instruments, *Rock Band 3* is more than just a music game. The *Rock Band* brand may come on a disc in a box like every other title, but don't be deceived: it's an entertainment platform, and it's a gaming institution.

Rock Band is the game for everybody who wishes they were a rock star. More than that, even, it's for everybody who enjoys music that isn't limited to just classical or techno. It's a game to practise over and over, until practice makes perfect, and it's also the game to stick on for a spot of fun during a friendly gathering. It's a real chameleon of a title and can be all things to all people. Hardcore score-'em-up or casual background entertainment for a sing-song? It's both.

This duality is echoed in the game's modes. On one level it's a beat-matching rhythm-action title that simplifies music-playing by reducing every song into half a dozen basic inputs. You pick your instrument of choice and play along to the selected songs. Plastic guitars have five brightly coloured buttons and a strum bar; drum kits have four coloured drum pads and a pedal; keyboards come with twenty-five keys (banded into five groups coloured to match the guitar buttons); and microphones, well, they're just standard microphones. There's not much else it could do to make things less complex.

The game displays scrolling coloured bars that must be struck at the right time to play the notes and earn points. On easier difficulties you won't be expected fully to simulate a shredding guitar solo or a ten-minute drumpocalypse, but on expert toughness things can get hairy, even with just the five coloured notes to worry about. Singers are judged on timing and pitch, with higher difficulties clamping down on the acceptable range to 'pass' a bar.

Whether on your own or in a band of seven – drums, lead guitar, bass guitar, keyboard and three singers – belting out classics such as 'Break On Through', 'The Power of Love' and 'Bohemian Rhapsody' is top-notch entertainment. *Rock Band* parties are commonplace, and it's not tough to understand why.

On the downside, all these instruments cost money and some people would rightly point out that they're not a million miles away from Fisher Price toys. Thankfully, as the game is backwards compatible with all the old instruments from previous *Rock Band* and *Guitar Hero* games, it's not too tough to cobble together a garage band of odd guitars and drums from titles past for a snip of the price. They all work so it makes financial sense.

As for the plastic-toy issue, *Rock Band 3* has an answer: a mode that elevates it above cheesy simulation and into full-blown music tutoring. It's worth pointing out right now that the standard game mode is still ridonkulously great fun and is more than enough to secure its place in any Must Play collection. But Pro mode attempts to go one better and bridge the gap between fantasy and reality.

The five-buttoned guitars can be traded out for either 102-button beasts with six short strings on the base, or a genuine electric guitar with extra gubbins squeezed inside to make it compatible with the game. Three extra cymbals can also be added to the drum set-up to take that track up a notch also. Pro mode teaches you how to play with these real instruments so the game can one day be left behind for dreams of a real stage with a real band for a real crowd. Like the standard game, it comes with different difficulties, meaning you needn't be a pro to play Pro mode – it's there to help everybody, regardless of their starting ability.

The synthesis of fantasy and reality is a landmark step in the genre, and one taken by a developer who had already established itself as so far ahead of the competition they're out of sight. And just remember: even if you don't have aspirations of learning how to handle a genuine instrument, the game still has the classic mode to enjoy, with Career, Party and Challenge modes so deep *Rock Band 8* will be on the shelves before it's all been exhausted.

🕹 🕹 🕹

THE SECRET OF MONKEY ISLAND
Release date: 1990 | Platform: PC | Developer: Lucasfilm Games

PIRATES OF THE CARIBBEAN proved to be a surprise box-office smash when it wowed cinema-goers in 2004, but its success is nothing compared to the lasting legacy of similarly themed point-and-click pièce de résistance *The Secret of Monkey Island*. Created by the triumvirate of talent Ron Gilbert, Tim Schafer and Dave Grossman, the first *Monkey Island* game has forever secured its place in the hearts of point-and-click aficionados.

It's the story of wannabe swashbuckler Guybrush Threepwood, a floppy-haired halfwit whose quest to become a feared pirate forces him to undertake three dangerous trials on a pirate outpost called Mêlée Island. Only by mastering the three goals of sword fighting, thievery and 'treasure huntery' will he earn the rank of pirate, be allowed to hire a crew and set sail for the forbidden shores of Monkey Island.

The Secret of Monkey Island came smack bang in the middle of Lucasfilm's point-and-click (or, as the pirates of Mêlée Island would say, pointery-and-clickery) drive. Powered by the company's iconic SCUMM engine and featuring the standard array of Pick Up, Talk To, Open and so on input commands, there's not much on the surface that suggests *Secret of Monkey Island* is any different to the other Lucasfilm games. There's the standard array of taxing puzzles (nothing too obscure just for obscurity's sake, mind) and red herrings, and the adventure is neither longer than nor especially different in format from its competition.

An unshakable soundtrack plays a big hand in its success, but the real stars of the show are the laugh-out-loud funny script and an ensemble of characters nothing short of perfect. Eminently quotable dialogue has ensured *The Secret of Monkey Island* is a real front runner in the contest for the funniest ever game. For every joke that falls flat, there are half a dozen that strike gold.

Where else, for instance, could you ever hope to clash swords in duels that depend more on traded witticisms than fencing prowess? The sharpest weapon in *Monkey Island*'s sword-fighting mini-game is the tongue, and the only way to defeat Mêlée Island's sword master is by collecting witty responses and insults from other pirates and using them at the appropriate times. 'Nobody's ever drawn blood from me and nobody ever will,' says one pirate. The winning response? 'You run THAT fast?'

Other puzzles test your chortling skills as much as your brain. You collect a useless totem early on in the story, and, when sheriff Fester Shinetop tries to stop hilarious hero Guybrush from reaching Monkey Island, he tethers him to the idol and hurls them both to the sea bed. Daggers and cutlasses and broken bottles lie just out of reach, meaning there's no way to cut yourself free from the idol anchoring you down. But the solution is one big joke: for hours Guybrush has been carrying the idol in his pocket. All you need do, therefore, is just pick it up again.

The bumbling pirate in training is at his best when talking to others. People like Stan the used-boat salesman, who would flog his own grandmother for a gold coin or two, are well-rounded characters who make for some memorable conversations. Despite having two different endings, *The Secret of Monkey Island* wouldn't exactly be worth replaying were it not for a non-stop succession of ace conversation after ace conversation, with characters as colourful as rainbows. Humour is worked into every line, every piece of narration and every item's multiple uses along the journey, transforming *The Secret of Monkey Island* from a smartly put together point-and-click into the most memorable one of them all. The real secret of Monkey Island is as unmissable as a three-headed monkey: its script is written by the best writers in the business at the peak of their development careers.

🐙 🐙 🐙

SENSIBLE WORLD OF SOCCER

Release date: 1994 | Platform: Amiga | Developer: Sensible Software

THE BEAUTIFUL GAME of the beautiful game. The wide world of football, management and all, condensed into one gloriously simple simulation. Modern footy games (*FIFA* in particular) have reached a stage where they can replicate every minutiae of the world's favourite sporting event, but behind every feint, every back-heel and every shoulder barge is a game that was first perfected with a little project fans have come to call *Sensi*.

Sensi encapsulates everything you need to recreate a solid football game in one easy-to-grasp system. A zoomed-out camera covers a large portion of the field at once, letting both players spot formation weaknesses, and a one-button-does-all control scheme subtracts any confusion from the game. Everybody knows how to play football, *Sensi* says, so the same should apply to a football game as well. *SWOS* is the pinnacle of pick-up-and-play sporting games, a lesson that's now being brought back into modern football titles with the inclusion of two-button control schemes.

Hundreds of clubs and thousands of players make *Sensi*'s 20-year-long season mode one of the ultimate gaming tests and one of the most rewarding campaigns ever to grace the sporting genre. Nobody really cares that Liverpool's star players are McMenemen, Radknepp and Fiwlar, or that their bitter rivals are called Manchester Red. *Sensi*'s lack of licences gives the game a personality of its own and the thrill of weeding super-obscure foreign stars out from the clubs and leagues you've never even heard of and putting them to work in a championship-winning squad is as powerful today as it was back in 1994.

SWOS habits die hard. The game teaches the value of passing by hacking down players enjoying extended dribbles, often injuring them and forcing you to make a substitution. In *SWOS*, ball and player movement are two independent quantities (something modern games still struggle with), so every run and jink needs to be timed just right to keep possession of the ball. Player movement is restricted to eight directions: compass points and the four mid-points in between. Ball movement is restricted to your ability to pick a pass or to apply spin to a shot.

Each misplaced pass is a jab to the gut. Every shot curled just wide caused by slightly too much aftertouch control is a slap on the cheek. A conceded goal is an insult to your skills, or lack of them. The line between winning and losing is finer than piano wire. The optimal shooting angles are there for those who work to find them. The long-range net-busters exist for the daredevils and the replay mode for the show-offs. The perfect goal is within reach of anybody who can string twenty passes together without getting caught in possession. Through balls and lobs have to be weighted expertly if they're to reach their targets: skills only perfected through hours and hours of practice.

Sensi is much more than a football game. It's a title about testing theories and pushing the limits of what's possible to showboat at every available opportunity. Perfection isn't a goal reached easily in *Sensi*. It's rarely reached at all. *SWOS* is an onion: the more layers you peel back, the more it has underneath. Tactics need to be mixed and matched. Every kick of the ball needs to be carefully considered. Not bad for a game with just one button.

SWOS is lacking the licences, the photo-realistic graphics and the skill moves of the modern titles. It's lacking the stadia and the different modes. It's lacking the players of this generation, quite obviously. It doesn't need any of it. *Sensi* still has the soul of a football game, and that's all it needs to stand the test of time.

👾 👾 👾

SHADOW OF THE COLOSSUS

Release date: 2006 (2005) | Platform: PlayStation 2 | Developer: Team Ico

THERE ARE THREE types of people in this world: those who think video games are an art form, those who think video games aren't an art form, and those who don't really know why some people are so adamant it must be one way or the other. It's the debate that just refuses to die and invariably it's undertaken by people who want a so-called educated discussion on games and yet always end up squabbling and yelling over petty points in order to gain the upper hand. This book isn't concerned with that row other than to say this: if you do believe the games equal art argument and you ever want an example to whip out mid-debate to back up your opinion, *Shadow of the Colossus* is the only game you'll want to reach for.

Shadow of the Colossus is a coming-of-age tale unlike anything else. It's a game never seen before or attempted since. A real one-off in an ocean of remakes and copycats. It begins with a young adventurer visiting a forbidden kingdom and begging the gods to bring a dead girl (sister? lover? you never do find out) back to life. It can be done, but life must be sacrificed for life and the scales need to be weighted heavily towards Satan's side for an exchange this major. The task is set: journey into the surrounding lands and slay sixteen wild beasts to revive the girl.

These beasts are the colossi: walking, swimming and flying behemoths that tower above all other beings. Their fearsome qualities are purely physical: behind their enormous statures are innocent lives. Yet you've got to pluck up the courage and the strength to track them down across expansive landscapes and slay them in cold blood. The rolling world is largely barren and your horseback journeys are generally free from distractions, giving you plenty of time to focus on the task ahead and reflect (as well as marvel) on past events. The trips are free from cluttered displays too – the only way to navigate the world is to stop and hold your sword in the air. Light bounces off the blade in the general direction of the next target.

Each colossus is a giant conundrum to solve. Slaying them is a matter of watching their movement and learning their behaviour, of targeting their weak points and devising schemes to reach them. The colossi aren't your average video-game bosses. They're organic platforming challenges: to take them down, you need to clamber up legs, across shoulders and tails and around midriffs until you're in a position to deal some damage.

To scale each animal successfully you need to cling on to fur and growths that can double as handholds. Your presence won't go unnoticed, though. The creatures will try to scratch and shake you off like a dog ridding itself of ticks, and the only way to hold on is through careful rationing of your grip meter's strength.

Everybody who plays it will encounter at least one moment where they have to release their hold to recharge the grip meter and are thrown from the colossus thanks to an unexpected lurch, but through some minor miracle will be tossed on to another part of the leviathan where there's a stray hair to clutch to avoid certain doom. If it happens to occur on one of the few flying colossi, you'll instantly file the sequence among your finest gaming moments of all time. Guaranteed.

The adventure brings out emotions no other game has come close to tapping into. Every felled colossus adds a slice of life to the girl at the cost of more and more of your own soul. The beasts you're murdering aren't evil. Their only crime is to exist. You're the interloper invading their homelands and cutting them down in the prime of their life, and the game makes sure you know it. Each time you plunge your sword deep into soft flesh, your quarry howls in pain and confusion. You'll need to battle through the guilt and slam the sword home again and again. Is one girl's life really worth that of sixteen beautiful titans? That's the question *Shadow of the Colossus* poses, and only by playing it first-hand will you be in a position to give an honest answer.

👾 👾 👾

SHENMUE

Release date: 2000 (1999) | **Platform: Dreamcast** | **Developer: SEGA**

SHENMUE HAD PROBLEMS, none greater than its unrestrained ambition. The first entry in a trilogy that never had a chance to finish, *Shenmue* wanted to *be* everything and *do* everything in an age where the hardware could barely cope. In the course of its development, it became the most expensive game ever made (a record that has since been surpassed numerous times), and transformed from a role-playing game spin-off of SEGA fighting classic *Virtua Fighter* into a phenomenally epic stand-alone saga, as well as one of the most tragic gaming stories of all.

Spread across three discs, the first of the two *Shenmue* games is the story of Ryo Hazuki's first steps on a quest to avenge his father's murder. Ryo's investigation takes him all over the Japanese city of Yokosuka, which is where creator Yu Suzuki's lust for 'everything' really shows. The city is huge, every character is fully voiced (with some deficient acting sure to elicit real belly laughs) and every object is interactive.

Such features were groundbreaking. Ryo's quest mainly involves conversations and complex martial arts fistfights by the dozen – sometimes both at the same time – but the interactive objects opened up whole new avenues of gameplay. Vehicles, dartboards arcade cabinets – all leading to races, mini-games and even complete SEGA arcade classics. Shenmue pushed the Dreamcast to the limit but somehow managed to make it all work.

A constantly ticking clock dictates what happens. At night the shops close and the bars open, during the day there are errands to run and jobs to be done. Transport systems run like clockwork and different days bring about different weather systems. Ryo needs to sleep at appropriate hours and seek out clues at the right times. You're made to feel like a very small fish in a very big pond. You live by the game's rules and the city will carry on with its daily life whether you're there to quiz people at the right hour or not. Whenever a games company is trying to build up the realism of its environment it always tends to wheel out the same old tired phrases about a 'living, breathing world'. *Shenmue* was a game that could use the term unashamedly and without a hint of irony.

Shenmue also invented the term 'quick-time event' for all those moments in cutscenes where an image of a button flashes on-screen and you must quickly press the corresponding button to carry on. In *Shenmue*'s case, this means punching somebody before they punch you. It's a great system when used in moderation and not as a mechanic to centre an entire game on (looking at you here, *Dragon's Lair*), so *Shenmue* deserves love letters and hate mail in equal parts for showing the world how it should be used properly. Love letters because after *Shenmue*'s example some truly brilliant games went on to use quick-time events in some jaw-droppingly awesome ways. Hate mail because so did every other game in existence and their sisters too – and not so sparingly, either. The quick-time event epidemic was the industry's equivalent of the bubonic plague. It's only just recovering...

SEGA has replaced the *Shenmue* games with the rather splendid and somewhat similar *Yakuza* series. The trouble is that *Yakuza* is *Yakuza* and it's just not *Shenmue*, and gamers can be fickle folk opposed to unnecessary changes. The *Shenmue* series is like *Star Wars* if George Lucas hadn't been allowed to make *Return of the Jedi*. *Shenmue* burned brightly and then it was gone. The original must be appreciated, if not just to understand the aspirations of its developers, then to fully appreciate the game that won a place in fans' hearts through forklift-truck racing and suggestive phrases about sailors.

🐙 🐙 🐙

SILENT HILL 2

Release date: 2001 | Platform: PlayStation 2 | Developer: Team Silent

FREAKIER THAN WATCHING a midnight marathon of *Blair Witch Project*, *Ringu* and *[REC]* in an abandoned asylum, *Silent Hill 2* is the game to turn to when you want your shivers transformed into borderline convulsions. An arguably spookier game does exist – haunted freakfest *Project Zero* is all about taking snapshots of spectral boogiemen in a rotting mansion – but *Silent Hill 2* has the added bonus of smuggling a brilliant core game with smart puzzles and a thought-provoking storyline beneath its startling, taboo-shattering exterior. While *Resident Evil* was pussyfooting around with zombies and tyrants, *Silent Hill 2* aimed for much more disturbing territory.

The first return trip to Silent Hill is an unsettling tour de force of scares. The ostensibly deserted mid-American town first debuted on the ageing PlayStation two years previously in a game almost too ambitious for the console to run. In *Silent Hill 2*, the overly foggy town – murky for atmospheric reasons, this time, rather than to conceal creaking visuals – is a horrific hotbed of paranormal activity, with nightmarish denizens cutting lines through the soupy air at every turn. It goes without saying that clerk-turned-hero James Sunderland is a little out of his depth in this one.

Silent Hill 2 masters the craft of turning your imagination against you. The gangly, deformed monsters exist – you fight them with lead pipes and kitchen knives and, if you're really lucky, a couple of guns as well – but the game wheels them out sparingly, opting to tread a more cerebral path on many occasions. To pass safely through Silent Hill and its hellish parallel dimension version (which does the seemingly impossible and transforms the town into an even scarier place), you'll need to scamper silently through bloodied hospitals and apartments, fetching keys and puzzle pieces to open doors and meet 'friendly' characters.

Like in the first game, *Silent Hill 2*'s item of choice is a portable short-wave radio – a little gizmo that blurts out static whenever you stray close to a creature cloaked in the gloom. Hear static and it won't be long before a bubble-headed succubus in a skin-tight nurse outfit might shuffle jerkily into view. The best way to deal with them often involves turning off the flashlight and shuffling past in the pitch black. Whether you'll be brave enough to do this is another matter entirely, and in some instances it's impossible to perform tasks when the flashlight's switched off, so you can't hide forever.

The gratuitously sexual nurses aren't even the most iconic enemies in *Silent Hill 2*. Pyramid Head is the man who carved the horror masterpiece into the memories of thousands of terrified gamers: a humanoid terror with a giant, metallic, pyramid-shaped head and an even bigger knife. The monster is all that is unholy about *Silent Hill 2*, a murderous evil who assaults and slaughters anything in his path. As violent as anything in *Saw* or *Hostel*, and as unworldly as any horror produced by Asian cinema, Pyramid Head's popularity has outgrown the game.

Silent Hill 2 isn't above toying with its prey. Close encounters with monsters wheel out a trick called noise effect, something invented specifically for the second episode in the series. It's a visual filter that warps and corrupts the screen to torture the mind even more. But just when you think there are plenty of warning signs, the game likes to shatter your nerves even further. Glistening headless mannequins fail to trigger radio static, so there's zero warning of their approach and absolutely no chance of finding a comfort zone.

Just before it all becomes too much to bear, *Silent Hill 2* shows a lighter side to its personality. Easter eggs and secret endings (including one where James is abducted by aliens and bundled into a UFO, and a second which reveals the horrors are all the master plan of a dog sitting at a control panel) await keen searchers. To see it all involves withstanding some of the nastiest content ever burned on to a disc. Only the bravest need apply.

SIMCITY 2000

Release date: 1993 | Platform: Apple Mac | Developer: Maxis

FOR THE FULL *SimCity 2000* story, you need to travel back some ways to 1984 and a helicopter shoot-'em-up called *Raid on Bungeling Bay*. During its development, creator Will Wright allegedly enjoyed playing with the game's terrain and urban editor more than the actual game itself, prompting Wright to make *SimCity* in 1989 – a notable year that also saw the release of fellow 'God sim', *Populous*.

SimCity casts you as the mayor of a patch of unspoiled land and asks you to design and build the perfect metropolis. You lay down power stations and squares of residential and industrial zones (usually in batches of eight to design economic ring-donut shapes) and link them all with power cables and roads. Soon fields become villages, villages become towns, towns become cities and you'll have a bustling megalopolis with taxes to juggle, traffic jams to erase and natural disasters to recover from. All the fun things a mayor and his aides have to deal with, plus a few more besides.

If *SimCity* has one real limitation, it's the small pool of city features to pick from, something successor *SimCity 2000* – the undisputed pinnacle of the series – more than makes up for. Libraries, museums, zoos, hospitals, schools, prisons and a whole host of other buildings are all part of *SimCity 2000*'s creation tools, with power-station options including exotic solutions such as hydroelectric dams for cities built in close proximity to waterfalls.

The same underlying infrastructure principles still apply, but in *SimCity 2000* everything is taken to the nth power. Power stations still need to be linked to everything with cabling, but they have lifespans and need to be monitored and replaced over time. Pipes must be installed for clean water and sewerage, and decayed buildings must be flattened and replaced sharpish so as not to anger the locals.

Unless you plan with foresight, the chances are your city's growth will highlight problems with early development layouts. New subways can help ease congestion issues, as can buses and trains. Richer and poorer areas can be allotted different taxation bands and boroughs can be smartened up or made even more exclusive with fancy constructions like marinas and arcologies.

What goes up must come down, usually by the hand of God.

Hurricanes and fires can decimate cities and put grandiose construction plans on hold. Because every tiny detail is rendered in astonishing clarity, it's possible to see your city literally crumbling under the stress of a natural disaster. More than just spanners in the works, the catastrophes are the focal points of individual recovery scenarios. These scenarios are *SimCity 2000* at its best. They place you in charge of a prefabricated city in its prime, then unleash floods, recessions and giant killer robots (no, really), some based on actual historic events, some not. The goal is to clean up the mess and make the city prosperous once more, usually by weeding out the old infrastructure from around the building husks and starting anew. (When the tragedies strike, they strike big.)

Recognising the appeal of affliction and recovery scenarios, Maxis released the *Great Disasters* expansion pack to push even more into the game. Everything from UFO attacks and terrorist nukes to chemical spills and out-of-control satellite beams and... drunken lawyers? Yes, they all ravage re-creations of some of the world's most famous cities so that you can stroll in and save the day through careful rebuilding schemes and more than a few gutsy calls when up against it.

SimCity 2000 takes the relatively dull task of running a city and makes it exciting. The original appeared at a time when games with no clear end goals or win/loss criteria were unheard of, and soon proved you didn't need Game Over and Complete screens to make a successful game. Somewhat fittingly, *SimCity 2000* uses its predecessor's template and builds the perfect simulation on top. There are hundreds of good simulation games in existence (*Theme Park* and *RollerCoaster Tycoon* are two hugely popular and fun series) but in a land of giants, *SimCity 2000* is the tallest skyscraper of all.

THE SIMS

Release date: 2000 | Platform: PC | Developer: Maxis

DUBBED A 'people simulator', *The Sims* is a Tamagotchi for grown-ups, starring grown-ups. Like real life there is no overall goal, only personal targets and dreams: theirs and yours. Content with holding down a job, feeding the kids and having an extra-marital affair with the next-door neighbour? Fancy rising up the social rankings and becoming the most popular person in town by throwing parties in a freshly renovated pad every week? Want to cash in the old place and upgrade to a giant mansion with a television set in every room? So be it. Whether your Sims reach these goals is entirely up to you. Whether your Sims survive, even, depends on your actions.

The Simlish-speaking Sims aren't the smartest bunch of computerised people in the world. They're little human-shaped husks with zero brain cells. The people-simulator dubbing mentioned earlier... yeah, that simulation aspect applies to *everything*. Your little guy, gal or mixture of the two (as in a family of Sims, not one single transgender) obeys your every command. They eat when told to, sleep when told to and even visit the bathroom on cue. Forget to send a Sim to the toilet and they'll have a nasty accident that'll need to be cleaned up sharpish.

You control everything from job types to relationships (same-sex permitted) to looking after pets and paying the bills. Keep your Sims inside during non-office hours and they'll become socially awkward and depressed. Your Sims have feelings, so, if you want to stick with the same family for the long run, it pays to treat them well by providing everything they need or by helping them help themselves. If relationships turn sour through neglect, couples will split up and Sims will leave forever. If children are ignoring their homework, they'll be packaged off to military school for more discipline. The game doesn't need to tell you explicitly that you've failed as a parent for you to know when things have gone awry. Keeping life rosy for your family is motivation enough to keep playing.

But nobody says you *have* to be kind to your little guys. It's a game with no goals, remember. Send a Sim into a swimming pool and remove the ladder and they'll drown. Put them in a room and brick up all the doors and they'll starve. Leave a nasty virus untreated and they'll kick the bucket too, their ghosts remaining in the house to haunt the next owner. Sims don't grow old (a feature later corrected in the sequel) but they can snuff it if you're not careful or have a wicked streak. Between torture and monkeying around with ideas such as getting steamy in the shower every hour and removing all the toilets, there's plenty of fun to be had by just messing about.

Sims start life with a pocket of money and little else. You can buy property or land, build or redo a house and fill it with furniture that your Sims will like. Even the biggest sceptic will have to admit it's a fairly therapeutic game to toy with. Property deals alone can keep people going for weeks.

The Sims went on to become the bestselling PC game of all time and made EA a truckload of money through seven add-on packs that bolted extra content (such as characters, careers, clothes and furniture) on to the basic game framework. *The Sims 2* corrects shortcomings such as the lack of weekends and even turns Simville into a fully three-dimensional world, but the essence of the people simulator is at its purest in the first *Sims* game and its expansions.

👾 👾 👾

SONIC THE HEDGEHOG CD

Release date: 1993 | Platform: SEGA Mega-CD | Developer: Sonic Team

WHILE SEGA'S BLUE hedgehog is a gaming mascot who needs no introduction, his finest game certainly does. Despite the overwhelming popularity of *Sonic the Hedgehog 2*, it's the criminally under-played Mega-CD instalment that stands head and shoulders above the rest of the series – even though it's responsible for adopting the Sonic graphic novels' forgettable love interest Amy Rose into the game series.

Sonic's place in the annals of gaming history has long been cemented by the blisteringly fast, left-to-right gameplay seen in its early two-dimensional days. Levels are multiple routes threaded together into convoluted labyrinths teeming with secret spots, all masterfully tweaked until they can be raced through by doing little more than holding the right button. Depth is there for those who long to explore and are partial to the left direction too; ramps and loops exist for those who simply want to enjoy the speed. It may sound crazy now but nearly two decades ago gamers earnestly squabbled over who was better: Sonic or Mario. Somewhere on certain SEGA forums, those discussions still continue.

Developed in tandem with *Sonic 2*, *Sonic CD* is an off-shoot to the main series. There are moments where you wonder if Sonic Team's designers needed to exercise greater self-restraint when copying and pasting traps and springboard pads in the level editor, but the cruellest Sonic game is also the most thought-provoking. *Sonic CD*'s stand-out feature is its time-travelling mechanic. Activate one of the many time posts scattered about the colourful levels, hit top speed and maintain your pace for a few seconds to go all Marty McFly and warp to a new era.

There are four realities in all – past, present, good future and bad future – and actions in the past alter future states. The result is a Sonic game unlike any other. Fans of the regular series will recognise all the key ingredients (speed, rings, power-ups, more speed...), but the methodical approach needed to save each zone from Robotnik's slash and burn industrialisation encourages different tactics. Getting to the end of each level is no longer the goal; it's about how you get there, and whether you managed to travel back in time and destroy Robotnik's robot generators along the way.

It's a fine balancing act. The past's main perils are the robots you're trying to destroy. Shiny and new, they're all fully functioning. Flash forward to the present and future and those machines are either less effective thanks to corrosion, or they're gone altogether. However, neglect your job of sabotaging Robotnik's key apparatus in the past and you'll be up against hordes of robo-puppets and decimated environments teeming with hazards in the 'bad' future instead.

In recent years, good boss battles have become something of a lost art, but here too *Sonic CD* pioneered the way forward. For once Dr Robotnik – and these are the good years when rotund Dr Robotnik was still Dr Robotnik and not Dr Eggman – doesn't just appear in elaborate armour suits with easily memorised attack patterns. Fights involve various different skill sets such as navigating pinball tables or racing against new nemesis Metal Sonic.

Sonic CD was fundamentally still *Sonic* (albeit with a couple of new moves), but it proved to be a whole new gaming experience for fans, with a soundtrack as good as anything else SEGA has produced. The only reason for its relatively poor following was its release on SEGA's doomed Mega-CD – a failed console about as profitable as an Antarctic ice-cream parlour. Sadly, *Sonic CD*'s wealth of ideas has remained unique since its time-travelling template was abandoned by Sonic Team in a sorry acceptance of the game's commercial mediocrity. Yet where 3D Sonics have failed to recapture Sonic's essence, *Sonic CD* was and continues to be an experiment that successfully takes the icon in new directions. Whether it's as an introduction to the Sonic catalogue or a reminder of the speedy urchin's halcyon days, *Sonic CD* is SEGA at its best.

SOULCALIBUR

Release date: 1999 | Platform: Dreamcast | Developer: Namco

WHILE THE *Street Fighter* franchise has the 2D fighting genre all wrapped up in its battle-worn mitts, the 3D fighting crown belongs to Namco's banquet for the eyes, *Soulcalibur*. Though arguably bettered by its first sequel (a game that saw console-exclusive characters appearing on the PlayStation 2, Xbox and GameCube versions – the most notable of which being *Legend of Zelda*'s Link on the Nintendo platform), the first *Soulcalibur* is the purists' game of choice, not only because it introduced some revolutionary concepts but also because it provided alternative avenues of winning for non-fighting experts. Technical showpiece *Virtua Fighter 2*, all-round class act *Tekken 3* and multi-tiered-stage stunner *Dead or Alive* are worthy of a mention, but it's the flashy weapon-based brawler *Soulcalibur* that edges it.

The 8-Way Run system is *Soulcalibur*'s lasting legacy. Attempts at 3D prior to *Soulcalibur* primarily focused on sidestepping incoming attacks to shuffle the 2D fighting plane slowly about pivot points. *Soulcalibur* defied conventions by opening up true three-dimensional movement in the battleground. Characters can run in any of the eight major directions, making the most of all the fighting arenas.

In 2D fighters, arenas are primarily pretty backgrounds with little to no influence on the actual fighting. (Granted, there are a few exceptions, such as in *Mortal Kombat*.) Stages are bordered by walls at set distances along the x-axis and, when one fighter is backed into a corner, they'll be pressed up against the edge of the screen and the fight will continue. Certain 3D fighters, however, often have arenas with edges, and knocking your opponent over these boundaries brings about the same result as depleting all their health: a victory.

Soulcalibur doesn't just let you run ragged in sprawling zones – it gives you freedom of movement in areas that, while all differently themed and styled, are predominantly small. This feature gives rise to the holy grail of fighting games: accessibility. There's a worrying tendency for fighting-game developers to focus all their efforts on pleasing only the hardcore fan base. The net result is that most fighters are far too complex for newcomers to penetrate. With each tougher iteration, fewer people can claim to understand and get a firm grip on the mechanics and the fighters' combo moves.

By setting *Soulcalibur* in small zones, Namco opened the floodgates for all players across all skill levels to come and play. A relative newbie really can go toe-to-toe with a combo-master by employing wildly different tactics – as one player tries to unleash the big moves, the other can try to lure them towards an edge and bash them off the sides with a single strike. There isn't a funnier sight in fighters than stepping to one side like a matador as your opponent comes charging in with a baseball slide only to plop off the playing field for a suicidal Ring Out.

Even though the arenas play a large part in shaping *Soulcalibur*'s legacy, every fighting game is ultimately defined by the roster of its characters. And on this front *Soulcalibur* is just as strong as the competition. True, some of its fighters are partial clones of others, but the extensive choice of battlers covering a wide range of shapes, sizes and skills covers all bases. From big, lumbering brutes equipped with giant axes and swords to small, nimble, bouncy men and women with faster attacks, *Soulcalibur* ticks all the right boxes. Every character is memorable for some reason or other. Ivy's sword-whip, for instance, is a prodigious weapon to wield, and Voldo (returning from Namco's previous Soul game *Soul Blade*) is a harrowing freak whose snaking movements are somewhat disturbing and whose gauche dress sense makes Lady GaGa's outfits look like Marks and Sparks' new summer range.

Above all else, and this is something all the above feeds directly into, *Soulcalibur* isn't above putting fun over tight fighting systems. Other fighters may be concerned with frame-perfect input strings to unleash monster combos, but *Soulcalibur* is more forgiving with its moves and more approachable as a result. The game wants to entertain, nothing more and nothing less. There are plenty of mission, survival and time-trial modes for the single players, but *Soulcalibur* really comes alive with a group of friends, two controllers and some established house pass-the-pad rules (winner stays on is usually the best). *Soulcalibur* sticks two fingers up at the games that only come alive after memorising hundreds of pages of complex move lists. It's a fighter for everybody and its invitation is just too tempting to decline.

SPACE INVADERS

Release date: 1978 | Platform: Arcade | Developer: Taito Corporation

MANKIND IS OBSESSED with extra terrestrials. Hollywood horrors, television terrors, literary nightmares, autopsy tapes, abduction accounts, UFO spotters... we've even beamed messages into space so intelligent life can learn about Earth and track us down. It was always inevitable that interactive entertainment would look to the heavens for inspiration. When it did, gaming hit the big time.

Make that the huge time. *Space Invaders* took gaming up twenty notches at once, convincing suits and developers-in-waiting alike that the hobby known as gaming had the potential to power a worldwide industry. *Space Invaders* cabinets wormed their way out of dingy arcades and into department stores, and it became a key factor in sparking the eighties' golden age of arcades. The ramifications of *Space Invaders* cannot be ignored. Shoot-'em-ups – vertical-scrolling shmups in particular – owe a lot to *Space Invaders* (although *Spacewar!* can rightfully claim to be a more original influence for 'regular' shooters). Popular culture frequently looks to *Space Invaders* as a source of inspiration, and it appears on everything from television shows to t-shirts.

Even the art world likes to fall back on *Space Invaders'* pixelated extraterrestrial intruders. If you've ever spotted a mini-mosaic of an alien stuck to a wall, it might be the product of French artist Invader, who travels the globe sticking the aliens on walls of major cities. London, Manchester and Newcastle have all succumbed to the attack. Even Los Angeles' famous Hollywood sign is under alien control.

Inspired by bat and ball game *Breakout* (think *Pong* but with a brick wall where each struck brick disappears), *Space Invaders* features five rows of eleven oceanic-looking aliens gradually slithering and snaking their way down to Earth. Unfortunately, the global economic meltdown evidently punctured a few too many holes in the defence budget, as Earth's only hope rests on the fate of one solitary cannon (and a couple of spares should it take a hit) and a few spongy shields for it to duck behind.

These were the days before *Independence Day*, so we'll let them off...

The metronomic plod of the sinking alien ranks, the pew pew pew of the cannon and the withering shields with holes punched from top to bottom are sights and sounds forever burned into the memories of those who play. There's a visceral edge to *Space Invaders* that isn't touched upon in other arcade games.

The menacing inevitability of the invaders' plummet paints a harsh geometric picture. Left, down, right, down, left, down and so on. *Pac-Man* has square 'loops' to enjoy. *Breakout* has diagonal balls. *Space Invaders* is all down, apart from a feeble cannon and its pathetic horizontal track and its even more pathetic little bullets.

But that's what makes *Space Invaders* so compelling to play. You're Earth's final defence and you're saving the world. By the skin of your teeth at times – it can get pretty desperate – but you're saving it nonetheless. Look, you're even ratcheting up high scores to prove you must be doing something right. Knowing there are three more aliens to go and only two drops left to snare them is riveting stuff. Getting that number down to two a few seconds later is heart-in-the-mouth gaming. Intensity doubles when it's just one left. You versus it. You know where it's moving. You overshoot, you undershoot and at the last minute you wipe him out and save humanity. You're on top of the world.

And then the next wave attacks, and it starts all over again.

👾 👾 👾

(TOM CLANCY'S) SPLINTER CELL: CHAOS THEORY

Release date: 2005 | Platform: Xbox | Developer: Ubisoft Montreal

WHEN MICROSOFT SHUT down the original Xbox servers in April 2009, it almost wiped out one half of *Splinter Cell: Chaos Theory*. The Xbox version of the third *Splinter Cell* game boasts a campaign that out-Solid-Snakes *Metal Gear Solid*'s finest hour, but that wonderful campaign plays second fiddle to the experience of the almost-dead asymmetrical multiplayer mode Spies vs. Mercs.

Spies vs. Mercs is the ultimate game of cat and mouse. Two against two: spies must stay silent and hidden, cover their tracks with smoke grenades while creeping around in third-person view. Mercs have the power of a small army at their fingertips: guns, 'nades and remote mines, not to mention spy-hunting kits, but are restricted to a first-person view and don't have access to the cat-like vaulting and crawling skills of the spies. Spies want to hack nodes, mercs need to defend them. *Aliens versus Predator* gave the world a legendary and unforgettable aberrant multiplayer mode; *Splinter Cell: Chaos Theory* gave the world a perfect one.

Spies vs. Mercs – a jointly competitive/cooperative adventure that runs on a different game engine to the main campaign to ensure a smooth, lag-free experience – is the main reason to play *Chaos Theory*. Its labyrinthine maps take no prisoners and nor should they. The mode is the ultimate test of stealth, instinct and skill. The hunters and the hunted, locked tightly in a battle of wits and nerves. And Microsoft killed it by pulling the plug on the original Xbox Live service.

Almost. While the PlayStation 2 and PC modes are still limping along online, the superior Xbox mode still exists offline thanks to the wonders of the long-lost art of system linking. Hook four machines up with a tangle of ethernet cabling to a local area network and Spies vs. Mercs is as gripping as back during those first days of release.

Timeless, unbeatable, irreplaceable: Spies vs. Mercs à la *Chaos Theory* is the top of the pile. Xbox 360 sequel *Double Agent* tried to make the mode more accessible, inadvertently diluting the mixture beyond repair and wiping Spies vs. Mercs off the plans altogether for the much-delayed 2010 follow-up *Splinter Cell: Conviction*.

Though *Chaos Theory*'s technologically troubled cooperative story doesn't fulfil its potential, the game's supposed main draw – the single-player campaign – almost equals Spies vs. Mercs' dominating qualities. Round Three of the Sam Fisher years packs our greying hero off to East Asia in 2007 to intervene in an escalating war between North and South Korea, which is heating up exponentially due to Chinese and Japanese involvement.

Chaos Theory's single player trades up its Unreal Engine technology for the extra horsepower of Unreal Engine 2, and puts the more capable coding to great use. *Splinter Cell* is a series all about silently sneaking around in the shadows, keeping tabs on multiple light sources and spending time in dingy, murky locations or hanging from ledges and drainpipes. When Ubisoft developed *Chaos Theory*, it went all out to create the most impressive environments it could. New texture-wrapping techniques and high dynamic-range rendering helped paint staggeringly detailed locations with marvellous sights like swirling mists and torrential downpours.

Chaos Theory's level designs are classic Ubisoft Montreal working flat out to prove the series belongs in Canada (the same studio developed the first *Splinter Cell* game, but Ubisoft Shanghai was handed development duties of sequel *Pandora Tomorrow*). The team added a noise meter underneath the light display to force you to stay whisper quiet as well as cloaked in darkness, and hands the Korean-calmer the gift of takedowns by snapping necks while hanging above an enemy, or by yanking them off the side of a walkway down on to the floor/rocks/sea way below.

It's Sam's unique theory of chaos that makes the campaign an irresistible slice of modern gaming: the toying with genuinely smart enemies before picking them off one by one, Batman style. Sam can whistle to grab a guard's attention then run and hide in the shadows or, better yet, jump up the wall of a high corridor and stand split-legged, balanced between the walls of a narrow hallway before dropping down on to a curious guard and knocking him out cold. His gadgets give him the upper hand at all times: he can temporarily knock out electric lights from afar with an electronics-busting Optically Channelled Potentiator device; snake cameras poked under doorways reveal who's waiting on the other side; and sticky cameras fired at walls will monitor locations for incoming patrols and knock them unconscious with gas if need be.

Splinter Cell: Chaos Theory is the ultimate in realistic stealth titles – he's Bond, Bourne and Bauer all rolled into one, with a touch of the Caped Crusader's ability to melt into any shadow unseen to stay out of the spotlight even more. The single-player campaign alone would be enough to secure *Chaos Theory*'s place in history. So would the multiplayer Spies vs. Mercs. Combined together, the package is almost unfairly brilliant.

STARCRAFT

Release date: 1998 | Platform: PC | Developer: Blizzard Entertainment

BRITAIN HAS DAVID Haye, a punching machine capable of beating a giant in the ring to become heavyweight champion. Switzerland has Roger Federer, tennis-player extraordinaire and winner of, at the time of writing, sixteen Grand Slam singles titles. America has Michael Phelps, a man so efficient at emulating a fish he holds seven world records and fourteen Olympic gold medals for propelling himself through water. And South Korea has Jaedong, a man capable of hitting his keyboard more than 300 times a minute in order to command an army of dribbling aliens to win national, televised *Starcraft* tournaments seven times. Jaedong has been dubbed 'Legend Killer' by followers of his career as a professional 'eSport athlete'.

Not many games can or ever will attain the type of popularity that Blizzard's real-time strategy (RTS) classic has in South Korea. Played by just about everyone, the only reason many South Koreans stop playing *Starcraft* is military conscription. Even that doesn't stop them picking the title back up as soon as they return to civilian life.

Thankfully for the country's perceived sanity, it's a wise choice of game to elevate to the status of a minor deity. Blizzard Entertainment spent years perfecting their RTS design of build workers/use workers to collect two types of supplies/use supplies to fuel your expanding war machine formula with previous gems *Warcraft* and *Warcraft 2*.

Before *Starcraft*, the done thing for RTS games was to have opposing, technically similar armies. This is how *Dune 2* set up its stall when it pioneered the genre in 1993 and, well, it was easy for developers to fall in line and balance their games in this way. *Starcraft* rocked the boat by featuring three armies with *very* individual skills, yet somehow managed to fine-tune the mixture exquisitely so that no army has a clear advantage over the others out of the blocks.

First up, the salivating, insectoid aliens known as the Zerg. A very nimble race, the Zerg favour numbers over abilities and are able to produce a scary amount of units cheaply in order to plug holes and keep pressure on the enemy. The Zerg's structures also lay 'creep' on the battlefield – a devastating fertiliser needed to construct buildings. Expanding Zerg forces are terrifying sights to behold as they visibly devour the battlefield.

On the other hand, the squid-faced, god-fearing Protoss are very technologically advanced. Their units are few in number but more versatile than the rest thanks to varied abilities. All units sport a regenerative shield to withstand heavy enemy barrages, and the Protoss use 'pylons' to power their incredibly futuristic, glowing buildings. These pylons also double up as teleportation networks, making the Protoss an unpredictable force in the right hands.

The human Terrans complete the trio of races. All about country guitars and speaking with Texan accents, they sit comfortably in the middle of the other two. *Very* comfortably, in fact, behind their long-distance ordnance and waves of marines. The Terrans are the most approachable race for newcomers but that doesn't mean they're lacking in party tricks – when the fertiliser hits the turbines, they can lift their bases off the ground and hightail it out of Dodge like any well-minded tactician.

The key to *Starcraft* is how different all three races are from one another, not just in terms of building structures and organising armies, but in terms of countering and repelling. The three different races are unique to control and unique to battle against. A Terran versus Zerg match requires completely different tactics to a Terran versus Protoss scrap. Matches against equally skilled opponents are tense games of action and counter-action, with both players vying for map control and desperate to scope each other out.

No matter how you try to analyse Blizzard Entertainment's wizardry, Bob Dorough has already beaten you to the punch. Three really is the magic number. Blizzard Entertainment's following RTS, *Warcraft 3*, proved that too many armies ruin the fine balance of a trio of armies, and other RTS series have been playing catch-up ever since. (Even *Command & Conquer* has muscled in on the *Starcraft* act by introducing a third race in *Command & Conquer 3*.)

It took Blizzard Entertainment twelve years and a constant revenue stream from 11.5 million *World of Warcraft* addicts to pluck up the courage for a sequel. South Korea, with its televised eSport coverage and nationwide fanatical devotion, would accept nothing less than the second coming, and Blizzard Entertainment's appreciation for the Eastern following is telling in just how few risks they took with *Starcraft II* so as not to butcher the formula. *Starcraft* managed to capture the imagination of an entire country, and any game with that kind of power must be played by all. Just hope you don't meet Jaedong online...

STAR WARS: KNIGHTS OF THE OLD REPUBLIC

Release date: 2003 | Platform: Xbox | Developer: BioWare

STAR WARS HAS had a pretty torrid time when it comes to video-game treatment. There have been a couple of exceptional games in the past (*Star Wars: TIE Fighter* in particular) and a few decent recent showings (*LEGO Star Wars* and, to a lesser degree, *Star Wars: The Force Unleashed*), but by and large if a game has Star Wars in the title, you can usually be sure it isn't the greatest.

Unless, that is, the game in question happens to be set 4,000 years before the *Star Wars* saga we all know and love and is developed by *Baldur's Gate* guys and gals BioWare, in which case you've got a stunner of a role-playing game on your hands. *Knights of the Old Republic* is everything you'd want from a *Star Wars* game and plenty more besides. It's an epic adventure that, along with its rousing original score, sits among the best additions to the extended *Star Wars* universe of any media type.

Life starts as a character of your choosing aboard a Republic ship under attack from Sith forces. The round-based combat is accessible without being overly simplistic, and the opening action is suitably frantic until you can get away and regroup. The ensuing journey through *KOTOR* takes you on a galaxy-wide trip across richly detailed planets and meeting posts in a quest to become and train as a Jedi.

Your party expands as you meet and impress new people, and your character is as customisable as a create-your-own pizza: you can adjust everything from fighting abilities and attributes and proficiency with certain weapons to individual skills such as droid-repair capabilities and computer hacking. Then there's the little matter about something called the Force...

While other Star Wars games plonk you on one side and tell you to fight for their cause, *KOTOR* lets you make up your mind. Whether you want to be a benevolent Jedi and channel the light side of the Force, or you want to be a prize a-hole and rollick in the dark side, *KOTOR* lets you get on with it.

A large deciding factor in your moral-o-meter is dialogue. There are hundreds of characters to chat to and you can steer conversations in the direction you fancy. Stroll around cussing people out and betraying potential friends and you're a dark lord in waiting. *KOTOR* will recognise this fact and bestow you with appropriate Jedi powers and, eventually, a fitting ending.

Though many *Star Wars* games are slaves to the fiction, BioWare manages impressive creative licence without incurring the wrath of LucasArts. The 4,000-year cushion gives the game plenty of breathing space to tell a story free from compromises. There are even games within the game. Swoop Racing and Gunner Stations are two fun diversions from the normal lightsaber-swinging and lip-flapping content, and card game Pazaak is an addictive variation of Blackjack played to twenty (and with negative and wild cards to make things a little more interesting).

As is the case with *Batman: Arkham Asylum*, take away the licence and the foundations are so solid it would hardly spoil the game. *KOTOR*'s success is a direct result of the base role-playing game, not the iconic overlay that gets the fanboys all flustered up. Yet *Star Wars* it is, and it's a *Star Wars* product sitting just below the original trilogy of films in terms of greatness. BioWare has since taken its sci-fi RPG knowledge to pastures new with the eminent *Mass Effect* series, but even that cannot compare to the wonder and amazement of becoming the Jedi of your dreams – or nightmares.

🐙 🐙 🐙

SUPER BOMBERMAN

Release date: 1993 | Platform: SNES | Developer: Hudson Soft

IT'S NOT WHAT you're thinking. No, wait, that's not right. It's *precisely* what you're thinking. *Super Bomberman* is indeed a game about trapping and blowing people up with bombs. Oh boy, this is going to be fun...

On paper, it seems like a controversial premise for a game, but *Super Bomberman* appeared in a different world to the one we live in today. *Bomberman* first appeared on the ZX Spectrum in 1983 and, after a few sequels and spin-offs, it found a home on the SNES under the guise of *Super Bomberman*, a game so successful it spawned a sub-series of *Super Bomberman* games. The cute visuals betray the game's dark secret: it isn't about killing, it's about saving yourself, and indeed the world, with comic weaponry. *Super Bomberman* is no more a glorification of violence than Wile E. Coyote and his ACME arsenal.

Nobody plays *Super Bomberman* for the story mode and you

shouldn't either. Not that it has a bad story mode – quite the opposite, actually – but it's like visiting the Natural History Museum and spending all day in the gift shop. It's not what you came for. *Super Bomberman*'s battle mode is the true main event and the only real reason to play the game: a four-player party mode of the highest quality that can also be enjoyed on your own during the lonelier days.

Battles all take place on simple grids filled with obstacles. Bombermen move vertically and horizontally around the map's indestructible blocks and lay one bomb at a time, which blasts through weaker obstacles. Sometimes a wrecked obstacle will leave behind a power-up – one-round-only skills that increase a bomb's blast radius or let you plant more than one explosive device at once. The four players each start in a corner of the screen and as the obstacles are slowly destroyed they begin to meet. The victor is the last Bomberman standing.

Anybody caught in the fallout of an explosion is instantly frazzled like a calculator in a microwave. The longer a round goes on, the trickier it gets to avoid said explosions. When everybody has picked up the speed-boost, multi-bomb and blast-radius power-ups, the screen will be filled with bombs, each ticking down and unleashing a stream of fire almost as wide as the map itself. While it's true that the bombs all have a short fuse, any ticker caught in the fire of another device will immediately kaboom, potentially sparking a chain reaction of detonations.

Once laid, bombs can't be picked up. The thrill of the battle modes is in cornering and trapping another Bomberman while trying not to succumb to the same fate. Foolhardy bombing will get you killed, and careless play can easily lead to suicide. Should fights extend beyond the ninety-second mark, the screen will rapidly fill with indestructible blocks in a sudden-death mode designed to force all survivors into the middle.

To really enjoy the game at its fullest you need four players.

Computer-controlled opponents are all well and good, but *Super Bomberman* thrives on the banter and chitchat of people getting together and tripping each other up. And as any SNES connoisseur will know, the console only has two controller ports. Step forward the Super Multitap, a device that turns the console's second controller port into four individual sockets.

Super Bomberman was the first SNES game to dabble with four players (the series would go on to support a fifth gamer) and it still holds up as the best use of the SNES Multitap. The simple concept and even simpler controls mean absolutely anybody can play it competitively with zero practice. There is no better nineties multiplayer game.

SUPER MARIO GALAXY

Release date: 2007 | Platform: Nintendo Wii | Developer: Nintendo

FOR OVER A decade, nobody believed platforming sensation *Super Mario 64* could ever be matched, let alone beaten; that the magic of exploring the Mushroom Kingdom for the first time in three dimensions, or the thrill of playing with an alien control scheme, could ever be topped. For many, 1996's *Super Mario 64* marked the first steps into a bold new world of gaming. In 2007 the world discovered that, compared to those small steps, *Super Mario Galaxy* is one giant leap.

Super Mario Galaxy was destined for greatness the moment the first chords of the symphony orchestra warmed up with what can only be described as the sensation of waking up on Christmas morning condensed into sound form. The plumber has grown up, the aura boasted, only he really hadn't at all. In the same way that Pixar's *Toy Story* films bring out the inner child in every adult, *Super Mario*

Galaxy takes you back to your fondest gaming memories and rewrites them all. Warm nostalgia sweeps over everybody who plays it, and the hairs on the back of your neck stand up and start jumping so violently they nearly pull free. *Super Mario Galaxy* is the unthinkable: it's Super Mario made *Superer*.

When one planet became too small to contain Mario's fame, Nintendo did the only thing they could and shipped the moustachioed plumber off into space to conquer worlds new. Think Captain Kirk but with a wrench instead of a phaser. Mario's staple diet of collecting pocket money and bouncing on enemy heads is all present and correct, of course, only this time it takes place across an array of celestial bodies instead of just the one. Some are big, others are small. All are the dreamiest playgrounds ever invented.

The game is chopped up into forty-two galaxies, each home to one or more of the 120 Power Star collectibles that need to be hunted down through cunning jumps, races, boss fights and old-fashioned treasure hunting. These galaxies are then home to smaller planets and various inhabitants. Every planet in *Super Mario Galaxy* has its own gravitational pull. Whether it be donut worlds or snaking worlds or simply the traditional sphere, Mario runs up and down and all around (and even *inside* in some cases thanks to the odd Dyson shell) without trouble. A quick brain rewire is needed fully to grasp the circumnavigation and the resulting puzzles: you'll need to be thinking in new dimensions to avoid one-way trips down killer black holes.

The familiar Bowser-kidnaps-Peach plot is dutifully wheeled out once more, but it's just a vehicle to justify the game's existence. As soon as Mario jettisons off across the cosmos on a rescue mission, he meets star-gazer Rosalina and becomes entangled in a brand-new and altogether more captivating story than is normal for the series. Plot isn't the reason you ever play Mario, though. Level design is, and Mario's creators really outdid themselves with their inspired level choices (a feat they'd later repeat with the equally blinding *Super*

Mario Galaxy 2). The uniqueness of the Wii Remote controller and its varied inputs allows for a controller parity with Mario never seen before, even letting a second player join in on the fun.

Time after time after time, *Super Mario 64* has been described as perfect. Yet *Super Mario Galaxy* has strong-armed it out of its assured place in this list. It's not just because *Super Mario Galaxy* is newer and therefore more technologically impressive, but because it's the game that best captures the plumber in his element. It's a playroom spread across a succession of varied worlds each more incredible than the last, and it's a game that embraces Mario gaming from the modern day right back to its two-dimensional roots.

Super Mario Galaxy is a celebration of everything Nintendo stands for. A celebration that's literally out of this world.

🦑 🦑 🦑

SUPER MARIO KART

Release date: 1993 (1992) I Platform: SNES I Developer: Nintendo

LIKE A WIDE-LOAD trailer defiantly hugging the middle of a dual carriageway, the daddy of all karting games hasn't been overtaken in all its time on the road. *Super Mario Kart* founded and defined a genre of kart racers and did such a marvellous job that, despite some close-ish run-ins, no sequel or spin-off has managed to recapture the *Super Mario Kart* magic. The reason: because every follow-up has tweaked minor or major features to justify a release, and every change is a short step away from the original's greatness.

The racer pits eight differently skilled Nintendo favourites against each other on twenty perfect little courses in frantic battles for the Mario Kart tournaments: Mario, Princess Peach, Bowser, Koopa, Luigi, Yoshi, Donkey Kong Jr and Toad. Four tournaments, five races per tournament, five laps per race, top-four finish guarantees progress to the next round and anything lower loses a life. That this isn't still the modern *Mario Kart* formula is to the detriment of the series.

Super Mario Kart doesn't have the sprawling courses filled with shortcuts, but it doesn't need them either. The micro-circuit coin-collecting races of old haven't lost a microcosm of playability and are made even more intense with some brilliant weapons. Crucially, they're completely unspoiled by the overly powerful power-ups of later iterations. Collecting coins ups top speeds slightly, getting tagged by weapons loses coins and slows you down. There's not a hint of game-breaking, first-place-destroying unfairness to be found to unbalance the blend.

While recent *Mario Kart* games are dogged (for the record they're still great fun) with exploitative tricks, cheap homing weapons (first-place-seeking blue shells are a travesty) and rubber-banding computer characters who can catch up no matter how much you outclass them, *Super Mario Kart* relied on no cheap tricks to pack its races with thrills. Hopping and power-sliding are brilliantly simple moves to master, and there's no cheap 'snaking' manoeuvres to give anybody unfair advantages. It's one of two *Mario Kart* titles, along with *Mario Kart: Super Circuit*, where racing lines really matter. Races and tournaments are won on timely hopping and expert corner-taking, not spamming artificial boost bonuses that are by-products of later games' drifting techniques.

The three difficulty levels are based on engine powers, so the better you are, the faster the karts you'll be handling. The final cups are frantic tussles in the single-player mode and complete madness in two – a superb multiplayer addition that bucks all conventions and lets you unlock content that would normally only be unlockable in single-player mode.

The exclusive multiplayer Battle mode is the final feather in *Super Mario Kart*'s cap. (This fictional cap has so many hypothetical feathers it could easily be mistaken for a dead bird.) Both players are released into one of four gladiatorial arenas with a trio of balloons tied to their chassis and a selection of power-ups to collect. Every successful projectile strike pops a balloon and the first person to lose all three is crowned the grand chump loser of the round.

Given the multiple additions of the sequels, it would be wrong to label *Super Mario Kart* as the kart racer with it all. Instead, it's the kart racer with just enough. Just enough features in the right doses to make it a riot whether it's 1991 or 2011, and not enough features to dilute the elements that make simple karters so much fun in the first place. *Super Mario Kart* is proof positive that Mario's rightful place at the top of the gaming pile doesn't apply exclusively to the platforming genre.

🕹 🕹 🕹

SUPER MARIO WORLD

Release date: 1992 (1990) | Platform: SNES | Developer: Nintendo

ANY GAME RELEASED alongside a brand-new console needs to showcase what the new hardware is capable of, and *Super Mario World* fitted the bill perfectly. It took all the popular features from the earlier *Super Mario* titles, stripped away the excess material and added a couple of new elements to keep the fans happy. Moreover, it looked stunning. The game was rendered in colours never seen previously on a home console. One of the oddities of video games is how certain titles age, while others are timeless. The 3D titles of the late nineties look positively ancient now, but, more than twenty years since its release, *Super Mario World* is still a pleasure to ogle.

After rescuing Princess Peach from arch nemesis Bowser for what felt like the millionth time even back then, Mario and company waved goodbye to the Mushroom Kingdom and took a well-earned break in the infinitely more prismatic Dinosaur Land. Of course, nary five minutes had passed before Peach was snaffled by Bowser one more, raising all sorts of questions about her royal guard, Bowser's motivations and, more than anything else, whether Peach actually *enjoyed* being kidnapped. *Super Mario World* was another quest to free the princess, only this time it involved enlisting the help of everybody's favourite friendly dinosaur Yoshi, who fast became a series regular – even if he did lay questionable bum eggs after nomming on too much fruit.

The excursion across Dinosaur Land is the plumbing duo's finest joint adventure. Whether played in single player or co-op, it's a game not of highs and lows but highs and higher highs. Whether it's collecting one of the new winged capes and flying for the first time (really flying, not fluttering about awkwardly as in *Super Mario Bros. 3*) or tip-toeing around haunted castles with ghostly music wailing out of the speakers, the game doesn't put a single foot wrong. New features such as the spin jump became crucial elements in Mario's later titles, and tracking down all the secret exits and navigating Dinosaur Land's hidden passages is a game in itself. Playing *Super Mario World* is like reacquainting yourself with an old friend, regardless of whether you've played it before or not.

It's rare that a title can tick every box. Looks, longevity, level design, music and mechanics: there isn't a misplaced feature among them. To be fair to other franchises, the *Super Mario* series did have a few entries' practice before it perfected them all (some of the earlier titles came mighty close, though). But that shouldn't take away from *SMW*'s accomplishments.

It's important not to confuse a game's legacy with its individual quality. Mario was already an icon come *SMW*'s launch, but, if he wasn't, *Super Mario World* would have catapulted him to instant stardom. If tragedy had struck and for some reason *SMW* was the end of Mario, its stand-alone quality would still outshine all pretenders to the throne. To this day *Super Mario World* remains the best 2D platform game ever seen or played. In many circles, the '2D' in that statement is redundant: *Super Mario World* is commonly considered to be the single greatest Mario title of them all. For a series so loved and praised, that's an accolade that can't be topped. The best of the best.

🐙 🐙 🐙

SUPER METROID

Release date: 1994 | Platform: SNES |
Developer: Nintendo/Intelligent Systems

IN THE PREMIER League of Nintendo's most powerful franchises, *Mario*, *Zelda*, *Donkey Kong* and *Pokémon* are the clear Champions League spot holders. Few would disagree. The four brands are Nintendo icons known to gamers and non-gamers alike, and therein lies one of the biggest tragedies of all: *Metroid* isn't up there with them.

With barely a minor dip in quality registered during its twelve-game tenure, *Metroid* is Nintendo's most consistently brilliant franchise. Among many other honours, the first *Metroid* combined game styles in ways never seen before, creating a unique open-world template that birthed titles such as *Castlevania* and even inspired fellow 100 bed-mate *Batman: Arkham Asylum*. It also shattered conceptions of the roles women should play in games. *Metroid* ignored the damsel-in-distress role of games past and cast a female character in the leading role. Brilliantly, alien-blasting bounty hunter Samus Aran was only revealed to be a woman right at the end of the game, a shocker up there with finding out who Keyser Söze is, what Soylent Green is made from and the truth about the planet run by intelligent apes.

If *Metroid* set the stage and Game Boy follow-up *Metroid II: Return of Samus* warmed up the crowd, third entry *Super Metroid* stole the show, performed the encore and collected every award. *Super Metroid* was an adventure title created so far ahead of its time audiences were sadly swayed by more traditional gaming offerings and left Samus's finest hours largely untouched. A ravaged space station filled with eerie music, a giant boss fight, an escape from a self-destruct sequence while the level is listing from side to side... *Super Metroid* pushes all the right buttons, and that's just the opening three minutes.

Music: above and beyond. Looks: (for the time) above and beyond. World design: so above and beyond it's untrue. Samus's scrap against the evil space pirates and Mother Brain (which is, exactly as you'd expect, a giant brain in a tank) takes her to the planet Zebes and its miles of underground hallways. The world feels real, its lost history is there to uncover. And its gritty themes are incredibly mature, especially for a company famed for colourful plumbers and warp pipes and fruit-eating dinosaurs. But what really sets *Super Metroid* apart from the rest (barring its two predecessors, that is) is the open nature of the world.

Zebes is one giant tangle of corridors. *Super Metroid* has a clear A-to-B route, but that path forces you to backtrack, loop and skip about the underground research base like a rat in a maze. Rooms usually have multiple exits, some of them blocked off until Samus recovers a vital piece of new equipment (letting her blast through reinforced doors with missiles or roll through tiny crevices with the power to morph into a tiny ball, for instance), others secretly hidden behind nondescript bits of scenery, hiding incredibly helpful but ultimately non-vital goodies away from prying eyes. The pattern of regular enemies, giant boss, new equipment, new area and repeat is a tried and tested formula that flourishes in *Super Metroid*'s open-world format. But the element that has secured *Metroid* as a cult favourite is a little trick called sequence breaking.

Games aren't perfect. It takes a lot of time to code a game, and an awful lot of testing and bug-fixing to get it right. Even then issues slip through, especially when you're dealing with an open world like *Super Metroid*'s, whose template locks areas away from the player until they have the ability to jump high enough or travel fast enough to reach them. The art of sequence breaking is a phenomenon synonymous with *Super Metroid* and all following *Metroid* titles, and it involves playing through the game in an order other than that intended by the developer.

Through secret wall jumps, dashing and other hidden talents, Samus can obtain skills out of sequence and bypass some bosses altogether. Samus's gathered powers can be stacked in custom formations for different effects to access more areas, and you can learn tricks from the wildlife of Zebes to break through the game's barriers even further. A community of sequence breakers circled around *Super Metroid* to try to collect weapons and suits in ways Nintendo never dreamed of. Their findings are beyond belief.

Sequence breaking isn't a prerequisite to enjoying *Super Metroid*, and neither is it a suggestion that the game is broken, buggy or somehow incomplete. The stability of *Super Metroid* during sequence breaking suggests the coders had some idea that the exploitations were possible and ensured gamers wouldn't get stuck or wreck their game by using them. Whatever order it's played in, *Super Metroid* is Nintendo at its most mature – a sight sadly seen all too rarely. It's also Nintendo on top form. *Metroid* is the only major Nintendo brand without a bad game under its belt. *Super Metroid* really lived up to its name.

SUPER MONKEY BALL

**Release date: 2002 (2001) | Platform: Nintendo GameCube |
Developer: Amusement Vision**

TWITCH GAMING REFINED. *Super Monkey Ball* does exactly what it promises – trapping super monkeys in hermetically sealed transparent balls and unleashing them in a series of devious mazes and contraptions. The game began life in 2000 as an arcade cabinet game with a joystick styled like a banana, but it wasn't until the home console release in 2001 that most gamers realised it was superior to its 1984 spiritual precursor *Marble Madness*.

Unlike most other rolling games – let's call them roll-'em-ups – you control the floor, not the ball. The analogue stick tilts each maze and your monkey rolls along accordingly. He or she will jog at first, but if the acceleration's too great you'll soon unbalance your primate and leave them flailing about like they're locked into a gyroscope.

Apart from the occasional secret gate that teleports you past select stages, each maze has just one safe exit. There are, however, countless ways to fail. Levels float in the ether and rarely have sides to keep you from falling. Imagine resting a marble on top of an elevated glass chopping board and cutting giant holes out of the glass. Playing *Super Monkey Ball* is a bit like rolling the marble from one side of the board to the other and into an eggcup glued to one edge.

Fall off and you lose a life. Dawdle long enough for the bomb-shaped timer to hit zero and you lose a life. Collect 100 bananas carelessly left lying about and you gain a life. And that's as complex as it gets for the main game. There's nothing as fancy as a jump button or power-ups; *Super Monkey Ball* is a purist's dream game perfected thanks to 1:1 parity between stick movements and level tilting.

Three difficulties sort the marmosets from the tamarins. Multi-tiered levels creep into the frame early on, and by the time you've reached the latter stages of Expert you'll be balancing on fibrous wires, dodging speeding obstacles and catapulting yourself across chasms and on to atom-sized platforms. Actually, make that *if* you reach those stages: Expert *Super Monkey Ball* is one of the toughest gaming challenges ever constructed. The intensity of the frustration drawn out by yet another failure is second only to the overwhelming elation of finally cracking a rock-solid mission.

Like many games, it's better in multiplayer. Both alternating and simultaneous competitive play complete the experience, though it's the pass-the-pad mode that really brings gatherings to life. On your own, your face will be a picture of concentration, your hands will be tensed up and you'll be feeling the sweat drip on to the controller as you frantically try to rescue a balancing act that starts to head south.

With others watching, the pressure will double. Triple, even. You're not just trying to beat the game clock; you're trying to beat everybody else's time as well. And then you've got to factor dirty tactics into the equation too. The jokes and the distractions. Willing somebody else to fail or succeed in *Super Monkey Ball* is no different to urging on a horse at the races: the difference between success and failure is marginal and until you know which side you'll land on, there's no time to relax.

Away from the core arcade mode, you'll find six mini-games, some of them frighteningly similar to *Wii Sports*. Monkey Fight and Monkey Race are weak sauce, but Monkey Billiards, Monkey Golf, Monkey Bowling and Monkey Target (roll down a huge ramp, open the ball up to glide towards a series of dartboards floating in the sea and close the ball to drop and land in high-scoring zones) each boast the longevity of a full-priced game.

The *Halos* and the *Rock Bands* and *Wii Sports* of this world are all obvious candidates for any gaming get-together, but the best party game of them all is *Super Monkey Ball*. Its appeal is as powerful now as it was a decade ago and shows no sign of diminishing with time over the next decade or two.

SUPER STREET FIGHTER IV

Release date: 2010 | Platform: Xbox 360 | Developer: Capcom/Dimps

IN THE CROWDED landscape that is the fighting genre, all roads lead back to *Street Fighter II*. The one-on-one duelling game is the common ancestor of every successful fighting game and most unsuccessful ones too. Two characters squaring off in a small 2D arena in a bid to knock the other unconscious first in a best-of-three fight. No weapons allowed, just punches, kicks and a few special moves involving fireballs and electric shocks.

Knowing it was on to a good thing, Capcom pumped out iterations, revisions and sequels like there was no tomorrow. Naturally, there have been more than a few shockers, but it's a real testament to the Capcom teams that plenty of the follow-ons were brilliant, and against the odds the best and most accessible of all appeared almost two decades after the might of *Street Fighter II*.

Super Street Fighter IV is the ultimate battleground for two people to fight head-to-head in a test of pure skill. Completely faithful to its great-grandfather *Street Fighter II*, it leaves the core fighting systems untouched and innovates only in the areas that needed changing. From six building blocks – light, medium and heavy kicks, light, medium and heavy punches – *Super Street Fighter IV* builds a moves list longer than Santa's naughty or nice records.

While it's true that complex combos await lightning-fingered fighters, *Super Street Fighter IV* isn't just for the hardcore gamer. With a roster of thirty-five unique characters, there's somebody for everybody. Some are more powerful than others, nobody's grossly better than everybody else. Each fighter has a weakness, and it's up to the opponent to exploit it to its potential. That the roster is pieced together with characters from all off-shoots and spin-offs of *Street Fighter*'s past speaks volumes for the accommodating nature of the game engine. Nobody's out of place – something that highlights the outstanding fighting engine's breadth and depth.

The widely different fighting styles appeal to all crowds, and even the worst gamer in the world could pull off a Hadoken or a Shoryuken. The inputs for *Street Fighter*'s famous techniques are forever ingrained into the mind of everybody who plays it, and knowing how to throw a fireball and a dragon punch is enough to hold your own in any fight.

Playing *Street Fighter* is like riding a bike. Once you've learned the rather basic ropes, there's no forgetting them. Of course, a newcomer isn't in with much of a chance against somebody with a twenty-year head start, but *Super Street Fighter IV* has a few tricks to even the score.

Obviously, as with any self-respecting fighter, there's a handicap slider to adjust life bars. There's also an Ultra Combo meter that fills up when characters take a bashing. Unleash this at the right time and the screen turns into an explosion of neon as the daffiest volley of over-the-top moves is unleashed on to the unsuspecting opponent. At heart, *Super Street Fighter IV* is all about skill: about blocking and dodging at the right times and picking your attacks wisely. There's nothing quite as tense as two hardened fighters with a sliver of health remaining each battling out in the dying throes of the final round. Occasionally, however, it's about the luck of the fight and every now and then a novice is capable of pulling an unexpected win out of the bag.

Budget release *Super Street Fighter IV* is a fine-tuning of *Street Fighter IV* (look, there are a *lot* of games in the series...) with more characters, more arenas and more everything. For a year after *Street Fighter IV*'s release, Capcom monitored the best players and deduced which characters were too powerful and which were too weak. *Super* takes that range and shrinks it right down, cobbling the strongest fighters and upping the strength of the weakest for a fairer fight for all. There's just one word of warning: fighters are arcade games at heart and suffer when played with a controller. The accompanying arcade-quality Tournament Fight Stick is as expensive as another games console, but it's the only way to play. Take the stick out of the equation and you might as well take the game out of this book too.

There are too many features to list them all. Story, Practice, Time Attack and Survival modes are the main offerings, and online spaces include Tournaments and Team Battles. Between the replays and the collectibles, *Super Street Fighter IV* is bursting with extras, and it's all done in a gorgeous visual style that knocks bells out of the competition. Capcom defined the fighting genre with *Street Fighter II*. Twenty years of practice lead to perfection with *Super Street Fighter IV*. It won't be the last in the series, but it'll always be one of the best.

👾 👾 👾

SYSTEM SHOCK 2

Release date: 1999 | Platform: PC |
Developer: Irrational Games/Looking Glass Studios

'IN 2072 A rogue artificial intelligence lost her mind. In her limitless imagination, SHODAN saw herself as a goddess destined to inherit the Earth. That image was snuffed out by the hacker who created her.'

Before the days of *Bioshock*, there was 1994's *System Shock*: an intelligent first-person shooter-cum-RPG that sealed you in a space station with SHODAN. It was a quiet revolution for first-person games. The ability to free-aim and the emphasis on story were huge advancements in the genre unfairly overlooked because of (Bungie Studio's) *Marathon*'s similar features. In 2114, forty-two fictional years after the events of *System Shock*, an alien infestation takes control of a military ship and its prototype consort. Those first three sentences are your introduction to *System Shock 2* – seeds that hint at a return of SHODAN. Boy, do those seeds sprout.

System Shock 2 is more of the same with the added benefit of five years' worth of improved technology and two incredible development teams working in tandem. Newer team Irrational Games focused on horror elements and forged spaceships teeming with infected, monstrous crew members and not enough ammunition to deal with them all – not to mention the added shocks of degrading weapons that break if neglected and not promptly repaired.

The first game's hacker is dropped for new playable characters. Depending on your career choice, you can play as a gun-happy marine, a tech-savvy marine or a psionic agent. The career paths and the subsequent skill choices make for some very different games. Regardless of your choice, you always feel like the underdog. *System Shock 2* is the first shooter that successfully made you fear what's lying in wait around the corner. When you're not around, the ship's crew go about their business and lurch around their shadowy lairs out of sight. There's nothing predictable about what the game throws at you: a truly terrifying feature then as now.

This time around, you've got company via radio. Fellow survivor Dr Janice Polito is your partner, to a point, and she guides you through the game pointing you in the directions you need to go and feeding you hints you need to press forward. The help provides a solid narrative streak that runs in tandem to the entire game. The most advanced shooters at the time were still dealing with mid-level cutscenes and the odd line or two of dialogue with a handful of non-playable characters. *System Shock 2* took a match to the acceptable story blueprints and started over with a narrative that which never fails to tease and surprise.

In 2007, *System Shock 2* made a comeback in all but name. Underwater masterpiece *Bioshock*, widely considered to be the best game of its year, is really just *System Shock 2* recycled with prettier graphics, set in an underwater dystopia instead of a desolate spaceship. Its audio logs, ghostly apparition clues, hackable vending machines and its persistent voiceover partnership – right down to the eventual twists that particular road leads to – are all ripped straight from *System Shock 2*. The plasmid superpowers are *System Shock 2*'s psionic skills and the enemy research mechanic also hailed from SHODAN's second lair. Admittedly, *Bioshock* uses a research camera instead of *System Shock 2*'s chemistry kits, but nobody's fooled: a wolf in sheep's clothing is still a wolf.

Happily, wholesale thievery is entirely justified and fair given both projects were Irrational Games' babies and not enough people bought and appreciated *System Shock 2*'s greatness. The overwhelming plaudits *Bioshock* received should really all be directed at its under-loved, under-bought, space-based precursor. Everybody knows and adores *Bioshock* – it's time the secret behind its success enjoyed the same attention.

☗ ☗ ☗

TEMPEST

Release date: 1980 | Platform: Arcade | Developer: Atari

DEFINITION TIME: A tube shooter is what you get if you take a vertical shooter like *Space Invaders*, map the game on to a sheet of paper, roll that paper around a cylindrical object, tape the sheet's longest ends together, turn it back into game form and then look down the tube like you would down a telescope. Take a moment to digest the concept and prepare yourself for a pop quiz: guess what genre *Tempest* belongs to?

Correctamundo. *Tempest* is a tube shooter and being from the eighties it's quite fitting to tag it as a real 'tubular' title. Geometrically speaking, its levels aren't all that cylindrical. They've got steps and angles and trapezoids and halfpipes and all sorts going on, but, as any name other than tube shooter just isn't as catchy or as widely recognised, *Tempest* is to all intents and purposes a tube shooter.

While its sequels went on successfully to mix the shooting action with psychedelic hypno-music (all down to visionary designer Jeff Minter who made such games as *Llamatron* and spiritual *Tempest*-a-like *Space Giraffe*, 'nuff said), Dave Theurer's *Tempest* is a rather straight take on the tube-shooter theme. It features a ship trapped on the near edge of the 'tube' and enemies emerging from the tube's vanishing point and rushing towards the screen.

Every level takes place on a different tube shape, each one comprising a number of long strips. Your ship hops between these strips with a twist of the arcade cabinet's 360-degree rotating dial and fires straight down the current strip at the press of a button. Your ship also warps forward to the next level as soon as every enemy has either been wiped out or has reached your edge of the tube. If a baddie on your edge touches you, however, it's bye-bye to one life. To help avoid those nasty situations, you have a superzapper bomb in addition to your regular gun, which annihilates every attacker on the screen.

Different enemies cycle through distinct behaviour patterns and it really pays to know your foes. Some zig-zag down the tube and fire bullets, others electrify entire strips or leave spiked mines that are deadly during the end-of-level warp. Later in the game the frenetic jumble of levels and enemies provide a twitch-gaming masterpiece: dodging and downing them all takes incredible skill, and survival is something to feel genuinely proud of. *Tempest* tests the memory as much as it tests your reflexes. Death is always one silly mistake away, making *Tempest* a genuine one-more-go title every time you're halted by the Game Over screen.

Tempest's contribution to the industry doesn't just stop at one amazing game, some zany sequels and being the first game to utilise a colour vector screen – not a bad list to have on one's CV. In previous arcade games, dying meant restarting from the beginning, but Atari's Skill-Step concept allows players to buy another credit after death and resume the game at a level of their choosing. It's the first ever example of the 'continue' in action, and some choose to define the choice of starting level as the first instance of difficulty selects too.

Tempest lets people dig deeper and deeper into its ninety-nine levels than most people would ordinarily have reached. Naturally, those later levels are ferociously tough, to ensure people still pay up for the privilege. The concept of the continue system would later be adopted by pretty much every arcade game ever produced. It's a huge landmark in the history of gaming, but *Tempest* is worth playing for no other fact than this: it's just worth playing.

👾 👾 👾

TETRIS

Release date: 1990 (1989) | **Platform: Game Boy** | **Developer: Nintendo**

WHO COULD POSSIBLY have imagined the impact four little squares would have on the gaming industry before *Tetris*'s release? Four little building blocks that grew up to star in the most famous puzzle game of all time. A game, according to Guinness World Records, with more known variations (both official and unofficial) than any other.

Stack the four blocks in a line and you have an 'I' shape. Chop an end square off and stick it to a free side of the (now) middle square and you have a 'T'. Slide that square up or down a place and you can make both 'L's and 'J's. The 'O' is a simple object to construct: it's a 2x2 square. From there you can then slide a row of two one way or the other for an 'S' and a 'Z'.

These are the seven governing shapes of *Tetris*, formed from every conceivable orthogonal joining of the game's four little atoms. Collectively, they're known as the tetrominoes and they're the root of all of *Tetris*'s glory. This wasn't always the case: an early concept involved five-block shapes based on the board game Pentomino rather than just the four blocks.

The aim of *Tetris* is simple. The seven types of tetromino slowly fall down the screen one at a time into a deep well ten squares wide. Every tetromino can be rotated through 90 degree angles, shunted horizontally and made to drop faster. The goal is to fill horizontal rows, which then disappear, causing pieces higher up to fall one place lower. The higher the level and the more rows you clear, the higher the score. Let the tetrominoes stack up to and above the top of the well and it all ends in tears.

Tetris's rocky history began five years before the 1989 Game Boy release, involving legal battles, confused copyrights and a Russian law that prevented creator Alexey Pajitnov from receiving any profit for creating the most famous puzzle game of all time for twelve years. But it's the Game Boy version that has been bestowed with the honour of a place in this book: a game that shifted millions of Game Boys on its own and kick-started the handheld gaming revolution.

Der, der-der der, der-der der, der-der der, der-der der, der-der der, der der, der der. Don't pretend you don't know how it goes. There was nothing better than sitting in the sun with a chunky grey Game Boy and dropping blocks for hours at a time. The constant sound of 'Korobeiniki' – *Tetris*'s adopted anthem – soon became synonymous with the handheld wonder.

Explaining *Tetris*'s rules takes seconds. Over twenty-five years on, there hasn't been a better pick-up-and-play game and there's unlikely ever to be one. While throwaway games like *Snake* (which rode the mobile-phone wave of the late nineties like nothing else) have been and gone, *Tetris* has outlasted every fad since its release to remain the people's puzzle game of choice.

Tetris wasn't just a lonely game either; the Game Boy version opened the door for multiplayer handheld games, letting two people connect consoles with a Game Link Cable for competitive fun. Clearing rows adds rows on to the other player's screen, edging them closer and closer to certain doom. In the late eighties, gaming didn't get better, and there's a very convincing case that argues things haven't changed today.

Tetris didn't just put Game Boys into people's hands; it *kept* the consoles in those hands. Years after release, it was still selling consoles and still keeping gamers amused for hours. The game's irresistible pull has yet to fade. Tetris lives on in the form of the stonkingly great remixed puzzle game *Tetris DS*, but the DS only exists because of the Game Boy, and we all know what started the Game Boy movement. Handheld gaming owes it all to the little puzzler they dubbed 'From Russia with fun'.

👾 👾 👾

TIME CRISIS II

Release date: 1998 | Platform: Arcade | Developer: Namco

THE LIGHT-GUN shooter is the game for every kid who ever played Cops and Robbers in their backyard. It's the ultimate test in skill. The ultimate test in reflexes. The ultimate test in precision. And perhaps most importantly of all, the ultimate test in badassery. Who can claim they've ever played a light-gun game and *not* felt like they've been teleported into the middle of a Chuck Norris classic? No one, that's who.

Time Crisis II isn't technically the greatest light-gun game ever made, but it features the two best innovations the genre has ever seen: branching multiplayer and the foot pedal. Forget about the home console port, because the only way to play it is in an arcade or a cinema foyer – the louder the better – with a partner helping you out on the second screen. *Time Crisis II* is a constant sensory bombardment. The narrator is forever yelling at you to press forward when the coast is clear. The ticking timer is a constant reminder of the need to hurry up. The flashes and the explosions are warnings of danger and rewards for smart shooting. And the relentless pounding of the light gun's recoil mechanism thunders against your wrist with every shot fired. Each clack of the blowback accompanies a jolt down your arm, one that needs correcting to ensure the next target isn't spared. You're a cop: you can't afford to let the bad guys walk free.

The hokey plot may have enough cheese to feed an army of rats but it doesn't matter. If anything, the corniness of *Time Crisis II*'s exaggerated story and its bicep-bulging bosses adds to the charm. Importantly, it rattles along at a breathless pace, dragging you through three acts (comprising three scenes apiece) of town squares, boat chases, speeding trains, forests and factories. While the first *Time Crisis* was an unfair money pincher, robbing people of their credits with its near-impossible, instant-game-over time limits and harsh kills, *Time Crisis II* is a fairer shooter but one that feels just as frantic. Your arms are given much-needed rest time in between the action, but the frenetic cutscenes ensure the pace never lets up.

The foot pedal is your trump card. Release the pedal and you duck behind cover, where you can hide from danger and reload your weapon. Press it down and you spring from safety to take down the terrorists, either directly with a shot to the body or by blasting a nearby propane tank. The first *Time Crisis* instantly made pedal-free shooters antiquated, and *II* builds on its lead with an extra warning system to force you into protection.

What *Time Crisis II* gives you over the first game, apart from a fair chance of surviving past the first act, that is, is a second character with their own screen. Two cops means twice as much fun, especially when each law enforcer has a unique path through the shrapnel storm. Sometimes both players are attacking the same areas from different angles; sometimes the pair are split up and forced to go it alone. Either way, each gunner has plenty of opportunities to save the other from taking a hit. Blasting a terrorist just as he's about to shoot your teammate between the eyes is a rewarding moment for both players, and the game actively encourages communication to take down the most dangerous foes. Not that it's too difficult to spot who to target first: inspired design choice means the deadliest enemies are instantly recognisable by their outfit colours. Always shoot the red soldiers before the blues...

When the story's over, the co-op system comes into play once again. Two radically different paths means *Time Crisis II* is actually two bespoke games for each player. Mastering one route is only half the challenge; there are two branches each with their own enemies to battle and secret pick-ups to find. Of course, the second path doesn't come for free, but who'd begrudge paying again for an alternative trip through the most smokin' gun game to ever hit the arcades?

👾 👾 👾

TOMB RAIDER ANNIVERSARY

Release date: 2007 | Platform: PlayStation 2 |
Developer: Crystal Dynamics/Buzz Monkey Software

TEN YEARS IS a long time in gaming-technology terms. Three different console generations can emerge within a decade – Nintendo's N64, its humble GameCube and their industry-changing Wii all appeared in that window – and the resulting advances in technology open gateways to games believed impossible ten years previously. So to celebrate the tenth anniversary of gaming's first lady Lara Croft, Crystal Dynamics (the studio who inherited development duties from creators Core Design four years previously) looked at Lara's original creaky waltz into gaming and decided to nip, tuck and fully modernise the first game with a complete remake.

Lara's had plenty of causes for celebration in her time. She's received multiple Guinness World Records, she's featured in two major Hollywood films and she's even had a Derby ring road named after her.

Unfortunately, the anniversary party was rather embarrassingly delayed when a planning miscalculation meant the game didn't emerge until nearer Lara's eleventh birthday. By then, of course, the name had been revealed, and, as one insider didn't admit, 'Tomb Raider Anniversary... And A Bit' was just too long to fit on the box, so they stuck with the original title.

Thanks to an aggressive advertising campaign targeting young men (show us another archaeologist who wears hot pants on their expeditions), Lara Croft stands alongside Mario, Sonic and Pac-Man as one of gaming's few icons to step into popular culture. But the roots of Miss Indiana Jones's success weren't bedded in Lucozade adverts or lads'-mag appearances; they emerged from the very first *Tomb Raider* game.

While later *Tomb Raiders* pitted Lara against increasing number of enemies and took her to some rather uninspired environs, the début game focused on one key element: *tomb raiding*. Combat played second fiddle to the exploration of sealed burial chambers and forgotten kingdoms for hidden treasures. Death-traps and perilous leaps of faith were the main antagonists, not gun-toting goons, and when the occasional enemy did attack it was a bat or a wolf or a tyrannosaurus rex – hardly common gaming fodder. *Tomb Raider* was *different* to other titles, and the excitement of treading through cobwebbed corridors wasn't lost during the remake process. In fact, after years of progressively worse sequels, the magic of the original was further enhanced.

Tomb Raider Anniversary isn't just the finest *Tomb Raider* title dragged into modern times, it's a corking update of the defining adventure game of the last twenty years. Retro favourites often disappoint when replayed because they date so rapidly, but *Anniversary* is more inventive, more elaborate and far more impressive than the game first released in 1996. *Anniversary* breaks *Tomb Raider*'s ideas free from the restrictions of the original hardware and transforms Lara Croft into an athletic heroine with more moves than a trained gymnast. The grand designs dreamed up for the original could finally be realised. Thirty-foot-high cliff faces suddenly grew to two hundred feet, and bottomless pits lived up to their names rather than ending abruptly after a short fall.

Crucially, already great puzzles and platforming sections could be expanded upon. For all its great level design, the first game was built from bulky cube and pyramid building blocks. *Anniversary* wowed everybody with its corners and rope – fancy geometries alien to gamers back in 1996. The return journey through Peru, Greece, Egypt and Atlantis was as familiar as old shoes but edgy too, a balance tough to perfect.

The merchandise machine may well have turned Lara Croft into a household name, but it's only by exploring her first game – the precursor to all current adventure titles – that you can fully appreciate the impact she had on the gaming world. The best way to do that is through *Tomb Raider Anniversary*, a remake completely faithful to the source material but assiduous in its modernisation.

🕹 🕹 🕹

TONY HAWK'S PRO SKATER 3
Release date: 2001 | Platform: PlayStation 2 | Developer: Neversoft

IT WAS THE first PlayStation 2 game with online capabilities, but that's not what made it great. It was the final American game ever released for the wonderful Nintendo 64, but that's not what made it great. It let you play as Darth Maul *and* Wolverine but, no, that's not what made it great. What made it great was an aligning of the stars. It was just the right product at the right time in a series with enough previous games in the bag to iron out any issues and not enough games in the bag to flog the proverbial dead horse.

Pro Skater 3 is a coming together of everything that's great about the now-abysmal Tony Hawk franchise. It has the most refined trick system of any skater (the only decent ability it's lacking is the spine transfer), and it's the last Tony Hawk game with a timed career mode framework. It's also the last Tony Hawk game that didn't force you to chat to 'witty' locals who are as funny as a punch to the groin. To lapse into skater speak for a second, it's the 'sickest' skater of them all, and the only extreme-sports title to better snowboarding sensation *SSX*.

Tony Hawk's Pro Skater 3 takes you back to a time when NOFX, Sum 41, Alien Ant Farm and Papa Roach were hip (believe it or not, they were in 2001). And if they're not your bag it doesn't matter, you've Motörhead's 'Ace of Spades' and the Ramones' 'Blitzkrieg Bop' to rock out to instead. Reverend Horton Heat's 'I Can't Surf' isn't as famous but deserves a special mention.

One button to jump, one button to flip trick, one button to grab trick, one button to grind on rails and shoulder buttons to spin. *Tony Hawk's* controls are faultless. The previous game added manuals (the skateboarding equivalent of a wheelie) to link different trick spots together. *Tony Hawk's Pro Skater 3* crams two more extras on to the pad: flatland tricks to seriously bump points during manuals, and a little move called the revert.

The revert is simply a twist you perform when landing in a quarter pipe, and this little spin alone makes *Tony Hawk's Pro Skater 3* the best game of the series. It allows skaters to link huge lines together (without abusing the stupidly powerful tricks or nonsense off-the-board antics introduced in future title), and it makes it possible to travel from one side of a level to the other without breaking a combo. The revert is the key to stringing vert moves and flatland moves together. Before the revert, the halfpipe tricks and manuals were two separate skills. The revert lets one lead into the other.

The last Tony Hawk game to focus on two-minute-long levels is the ultimate test in skating skill. Working out how to climb up high to grab the secret tapes when there's no way to step off the board is a head-scratcher. Figuring out the best line to collect the floating S-K-A-T-E and C-O-M-B-O letters is another tricky challenge. Beating the high-score targets is a true test of vision – levels are put together so expertly that when you're in motion you positively flow around the world.

High grinds drop down smack bang on to low grinds. Ramps boost you up on to lips and ledges above. Settle into the groove and *Pro Skater 3* almost turns into a rhythm-action title: hit jump at the gap, press grind when the pipe whizzes into view... Comboing around the levels is a zen-like experience no Tony Hawk game has replicated since.

After every area has been rinsed (no easy task, especially not when there's hidden levels to unlock too), there's even a skatepark editor to prat about with. Admittedly, it isn't as streamlined as other editors, but it's functional enough to design death traps too dangerous to make it into the next *Jackass* movie.

Anything you construct is just a bonus, though. Neversoft did an exemplary job of crafting worlds fine-tuned to maximise every potential combo line. EA's wonderful *Skate* games are all about replicating real-life skating as closely as possible, but *Pro Skater 3* added just enough zaniness to make every second on the deck a second Tony Hawk himself would be proud of. Games rarely comes as instantly gratifying as this.

👾 👾 👾

UPLINK

Release date: 2001 I Platform: PC I Developer: Introversion Software

REGARDLESS OF WHAT the movies suggest, real hacking never involves guessing three- or four-letter passwords while Angelina Jolie drapes herself over the monitor. It's not that glamorous a trade, sadly, and if it were a good ninety per cent of gamers would have swapped hobbies years ago. Slurping on flat cola and munching pizza while desperately squinting at multiple screens and trying to reroute FBI tracer programs as quickly as possible, however? Yeah... truth be told that's a little Hollywood lie too, but, as it's nearer to reality and infinitely more believable than the alternative fiction, it's precisely the image *Uplink* strives for.

Uplink is a fictional black-cap hacking game desperate to cloak the gamey part of it all. New games aren't started: fresh agents are registered and hired instead. It begins by auto-logging you on to a remote system, telling you what hardware you're running, handing you a loan and then pointing towards a jobs list and ordering you to make a living as a freelance hacker. There is no CG avatar and you're not some character in a computer; you are you, and your equipment is your own keyboard and mouse. Fiction and reality blend into one.

You can take or leave jobs at your discretion. An online notice-board tells you what each job involves, how dangerous it is and, most importantly of all, your fee. There is a central plot line but it can be entirely ignored should you choose to stick with the regular requests. Further details are delivered via the in-game email system, and missions end only when you bounce back a reply with any relevant files attached. Complete a few requests successfully and you'll rise through Uplink Corporation's ranks, earning access to more profitable ventures. Make mistakes and the opposite occurs: Uplink will strip away privileges and you'll be forced to transfer funds from your in-game bank account to your captors as compensation.

Early work involves accessing low-level systems to copy or delete a few files, but soon you'll be falsifying user logs, committing major industrial espionage, funnelling money streams into personal accounts and preventing or unleashing major viruses depending on which story path you choose to follow. To reach this point, you'll need to stop fooling around with *Minesweeper* and *Solitaire* and spend some of those hard-earned credit chips as each ranking boost brings with it increasingly complex hacking systems. New equipment, job postings and advice live on your employer's servers, meaning every job begins with you logging on to the corporation's extranet using the name and password you registered when creating your account. The login box is a small touch but a brilliantly understated way to reinforce the game's alternate reality.

Tougher security measures come with every level upgrade. Everything from upgraded software programs to new hardware and internet gateways are up for sale to crack passwords and bypass firewalls as quickly as possible. Integral to your infiltration is the Trace Tracker, a nifty bit of software that lets you know how close the authorities are to zeroing in on your location. Even if you've bounced your work off various nodes around the world, you're never safe from detection. Sever the connection before the time's up and you're safe, provided you've covered your tracks well. Tricky jobs demand multiple actions at once, so CPU priorities need to be juggled on the fly while emails are checked and rechecked to ensure the right files from the correct archives are being targeted.

It's all false, of course. You're as much on the internet as you would be out in the park with a pen and paper, but the deception is so good it's difficult not to be taken in by it. More than that, you actually want to believe it all. The choices are yours – *Uplink*'s story goes in whatever direction you want it to, just like it would in real life. Make of it what you will.

🐙 🐙 🐙

VIB-RIBBON

**Release date: 2000 (1999) | Platform: PlayStation |
Developer: NanaOn-Sha**

AFTER CUTTING ITS teeth on rhythm-action rapping game *PaRappa the Rapper* and its guitar-based sequel *UmJammer Lammy*, Japanese developer NanaOn-Sha turned its gaze towards a music game without boundaries. While other rhythm games are restricted to the tracks on the disc, *Vib-Ribbon* loads itself into the PlayStation's free memory and lets you eject the disc and replace it with a CD of your choosing.

It isn't much to look at, but *Vib-Ribbon*'s crudely scratched lines marked a breakthrough music game that should have sparked a revolution in the industry. Six preloaded songs can be complemented by a potentially infinite number of extras, the exact number limited only by your personal music collection. The music isn't just background noise either. *Vib-Ribbon* is a platform game of sorts, and each level is morphed to fit around the music that plays.

Wire-frame rabbit Vibri is the game's star, and it's your job to guide her from one side of an obstacle-filled ribbon to the other. In her way are blocks, spikes, pits and loops, each of which needs to be dodged by pressing the correct button. R1 sends Vibri round a loop, L1 makes her hurdle a block, Down lets her step over a pit and X ensures she snakes past the spikes. The layout spreads the controls to all four corners of the control pad, keeping everything nice and simple to remember.

Twenty dodges in a row turn Vibri into Super Vibri: a high-scoring, winged, angelic being. On the flip side, nine mistimed dodges devolve her into Frog Vibri and, if failure persists, Insect Vibri.

Slow music is easier, fast music is tougher: a pretty simple idea reinforced by the six incredible J-pop tracks on the disc. However, speed isn't the only factor that plays a part in each level's ribbon formation. Each of the four obstacles can merge with one other depending on the note, bringing the total trap count up to ten. And the only way to clear these mutations is, of course, to press the two corresponding buttons at the same time.

So not only has Vibri got blocks, spikes, pits and loops to contend with, she has loops on top of blocks, pits within blocks, pits within loops, spiky blocks, spiky loops and spiky pits too. High-tempo tracks can be a nightmare to clear, let alone run through on score challenges.

Two Japan-only sequels let you play with calligraphy and even your own pictures (holiday snaps were morphed into trampolines of all things!) but neither can claim to be as groundbreaking as *Vib-Ribbon*. Stick figure though she may be, ever-happy Vibri has more personality in one of her rabbit ears than most other characters can muster up over a fifteen-hour game. Every wrong move jolts the controller and punishes Vibri with a small electric shock. Even though you're actually just pressing buttons in time to music, you feel invested in Vibri's welfare.

It's stunning to think *Vib-Ribbon* was more forward-thinking than any music game that's been released since with the exception of PC 'racer' *Audiosurf*. Maybe nobody else wants to follow suit and release a title with personal music capabilities because it'll make any future sequels entirely redundant. The beauty of *Vib-Ribbon* means we're seeing unique levels created every single week when a new CD is released, and in twenty years, when all the current music games have been relegated to the history books, *Vib-Ribbon* will still be inventing more and more new content. That's longevity you just can't buy any more.

WARIOWARE, INC.: MINIGAME MANIA

Release date: 2003 | Platform: Game Boy Advance | Developer: Nintendo

ON PAPER, THE WarioWare concept seems as promising as a glass trampoline: a succession of five-second micro-games, one after the other, involving such taxing tasks as shaking a dog's paw or picking your nose. The plot – Wario twigs that video-game sales are on the rise and so wants to capitalise on the popularity by designing and releasing any old rubbish to make a quick buck – sounds too much like real life just to put down to creative thinking.

If it's really a cash-in, though, it's one of the most unintentionally brilliant and bonkers ideas stamped on to a game cartridge. The game spawned not one but two successful series: the *WarioWare* games and the more musically focused *Rhythm Paradise* franchise (*Rhythm Tengoku* for the Japanese-only original). It also became the inspiration for such micro-game-focused titles as *Half Minute Hero*.

Wario's game idea is a selection of over 200 mini-games ranging from the eccentric to the so-bizarre-the-designer-should-be-committed. Some ask you to leap over barrels in *Donkey Kong* or jump on Goomba heads in *Super Mario Bros.*; others are all about killing flies as they land under a swatter or deploying airbags in crashing cars at the right time in order to protect the crash-test dummies inside. The rule is that there are no rules. Mundane tasks such as hammering a nail are ripe fodder for games. And if one isn't so enjoyable, who's going to complain when it only lasts five seconds?

Only a handful of the mini-games are Wario's creations. Turns out making mini-games, even five-second ones, is harder than it looks, so Wario tasks his radically diverse set of friends with helping out. Nintendo fan 9-Volt recreates his favourite Nintendo games, disco fan Jimmy T devises sports games, child ninjas Kat and Ana base their titles on nature and so the list continues. Come the end you'll be playing remixed categories that pull games from every single group. How does Wario come to be friends with all these people? That much is left unexplained.

The mini-games are played in batches that speed up over time. One-word hints are the only instructions you get. 'STEER!' it demands. Steer what exactly? A paper plane around some walls as it happens, though you don't know that until the game starts. 'SNIFF!' begins another. This one involves snorting up a runny bogey (nobody said it was pleasant) before it drops to the floor.

Sometimes these games are created with crude drawings, sometimes it's photographs of real things. The overall collection is a wacky pick-'n'-mix of insanity.

Boss rounds conclude each friend's batch, and these typically last a lot longer than the throwaway microgames, though aren't exactly complicated either. *WarioWare*'s all about fast reactions, not thinking. Pressing a button or a direction's as complex as it gets. Once you've completed a round without failing, it'll turn into an infinitely long high-score-a-thon. Mini-game orders are randomised each time, so don't expect to learn any patterns.

WarioWare's final distinction is a pleasant one. The series is now seven games strong and, in what must be a first for a franchise as busy as this, each game adds a major new feature to the series. *Minigame Mania* is the first, *Mega Party Game$!* adds multiplayer modes, *Twisted!* utilises a tilt-sensor cartridge and is controlled by rotating the Game Boy Advance, *Touched!* makes the most of the Nintendo DS's touch screen, *Smooth Moves* uses the Wii Remote, *Snapped!* involves the DSi camera and *D.I.Y.* allows you to design and create the mini-games yourself. All cash-in statements are now officially retracted.

👾 👾 👾

WAY OF THE SAMURAI

Release date: 2002 | Platform: PlayStation 2 | Developer: Acquire

DEATH RARELY MEANS much in modern games. Since game saves were first introduced a few console cycles ago, death is simply a hitch that forces you to reload your last save. Sometimes dying doesn't even boot you out of the game and back to your last save – checkpoints and continue screens now makes croaking a minor inconvenience at worst.

Way of the Samurai doesn't play by the rules. Every time you load the game, your single save file is wiped. The only way to replace it with another is to put your head down and press on to the next save screen. Cop it before you get there and it's time to start all over again. In *Way of the Samurai*, reckless actions come with seriously major consequences.

Shoehorn this mechanic into a gigantic game and you've got a terrible idea designed to punish and anger people who slip up dozens of hours into their stories. The chances of them returning to the game afterwards would be zero. But *Way of the Samurai* is designed from the ground up to fit around the save system. Going back to the beginning is all part of the fun.

Weighing in at just two fictional days long it's a relatively short game, but its longevity is boosted by tremendous depth. Every decision you make leads you down a different story path and feeds into one of six possible endings (later games in the series have fourteen and twenty-two endings), providing you survive that long. You don't play *Way of the Samurai* to see the end; you play it to see everything – all the decision permutations, all the finales and all the item rewards.

Your choices predominantly fall into the good/evil categories, with the crucial ones focused on fighting or aiding the perceived bad guys. The game is set in 1878 during the last days of the samurai, and warring clans are at each other's throats. Everything starts with you witnessing a kidnapping on a bridge. Whether you choose to help the girl in trouble, her attackers or just walk on by sets in motion a sequence of wildly different events.

No matter which story paths you choose, you'll be forced to fight other samurai. Your starting samurai sword is weak, but over forty new weapons are up for grabs by slaying other people and completing certain tasks. Better blades come with better attributes and better moves and soon the basic weak attack, strong attack, kick and block inputs will be joined with strings of more powerful combos.

You can carry up to two swords at once, which is a very handy skill; but, if you ignore your swords' hardness meters during combat, they could shatter forever.

Decisions all stem from conversations. Decline to join somebody's ranks and you'll fight to the death. If the battle's not going your way, you can beg forgiveness and ask to reconsider. When you health is whittled right down, your foes will often give you the chance to renounce your earlier decision and turn to the dark side. You don't have to – you can gamble it all and fight for honour if you think you can still win or if you're prepared to sacrifice your life. The further you press into the second day, of course, the less inclined you may be to stay defiant to the end.

If and when you do restart the game, you aren't simply hurled back to minute one. Swords collected throughout the adventure and handed to the game's Swordsmith are placed in your personal warehouse to be carried over to the next play through. They unlock new skills and new options early on, and hence a better chance of winning those early confrontations. Swords collected and not placed in your warehouse are lost when you die, piling even more weight on to your decision to fight or yield when the going's tough.

Completions also add points to a score total. When milestones are passed you unlock a multiplayer fighting mode as well as new characters and character-customisation parts. Again, *Way of the Samurai* is built for multiple play throughs. It shatters the concept of finishing a game by simply seeing the ending, and it makes for an inspired break from the norm. If there's one game in this book that demands to be played more than just the once, this is it.

WII SPORTS

Release date: 2006 | Platform: Nintendo Wii | Developer: Nintendo

WII SPORTS IS officially the bestselling game in history, although the fact that it comes bundled with every Wii console sold has something (i.e. everything) to do with the record. It's also the game that ushered in a new generation of movement-centric titles and consoles. If it weren't for the Wii and *Wii Sports*, there would be no PlayStation Move, no Microsoft Kinect and half the games on the horizon wouldn't be controlled by waving our arms about in the air like a semaphorist tanked up on energy drinks.

Everybody with decent upper-body movement knows how to play *Wii Sports*, but the game's real success was how it got many of them up and experimenting with video games in the first place, in some cases for the first time in their lives. The game nullified anybody's fear of complicated gaming controllers and their millions of buttons. TV remotes aren't scary, so what could be daunting about picking up a dinky remote-a-like object and waggling it about?

Of course, that psychological trickery is the main appeal of the Wii in general, but *Wii Sports* showcased it better than any other game on the platform for two key reasons. One, it's a simple collection of five basic sports that can be mastered in minutes. And two, as mentioned before, it comes free with the console, meaning it's most people's first taste of the Wii controller. It's also worth highlighting the overlooked fitness mode too, a feature that paved the way for exercise-simulator sensation *Wii Fit*.

Tennis, golf, tenpin bowling, baseball and boxing are the five games on offer, and, though they all use the controller in markedly different ways, they're a mixed bunch. Boxing's a messy waste of time, included only because it demonstrates how the Nunchuck controller add-on can work in conjunction with the Wii Remote. Golf and baseball are OK in short spells, but after a while they tire and hurt respectively. Tennis and tenpin bowling are the real highlights, capable of getting everyone up on their feet and participating.

The most impressive feature of all, however, is how *Wii Sports* levelled the playing field like no other game. Here's a title with a funky new controller and a bit of a weird name, and because of the marketing strategy it's going to be pitting Johnny fast-fingers who's been playing games every night for all his teenage life against his mum who doesn't know the difference between *Final Fantasy* and *Final Fight*. In any other game, our friend Johnny would have trounced his mum in seconds as she got to grips with the controls, but past gaming skills count for next to nothing in *Wii Sports*.

Sit most non-gamers down with a copy of *Halo Reach* or *Street Fighter* and their one experiment with the game will end in a pummelling and no insight as to the title's appeal. But even if Mum, Dad or Gran loses in *Wii Sports*, it doesn't really matter because there's a natural connection between swinging your arm in real life and seeing your character – a 'Mii' representation of you – swing their arm on the television.

As it happens, *Wii Sports* doesn't demonstrate everything the Wii is capable of. That responsibility fell to the sequel *Wii Sports Resort* three years later, which comes bundled with the Wii MotionPlus – an accessory bolted on to the Wii Remote base that detects the device's rotation. And because motion-sensing floor mat and glove games had existed for twenty years previously, claims of motion-based originality on *Wii Sports*' behalf are questionable. It did, however, become the first real motion-powered home-console game successfully to sidestep the gimmick label, and was therefore the sole pioneer for the future movement-centric games. Nothing much, then...

THE WORLD ENDS WITH YOU

Release date: 2008 (2007) | Platform: Nintendo DS |.
Developer: Jupiter/Square Enix

IF YOU HEAR the words 'role-playing game', it's only natural to expect one of two things: an antiquated fantasy world that may or may not have crazy monsters and/or steampunk references, or a 'futuristic' science-fiction universe (that *could* be set in the distant past for extra quirkiness) spanning multiple planets and space stations. There's usually very little middle ground.

Then there's *The World Ends With You*, a contemporary story set in modern-day Shibuya, starring grumpy and introvert teenager Neku. The tale kicks off with Neku seemingly tripping over and discovering a fashion pin badge in the middle of the Tokyo shopping district, though clues later point towards a more sinister origin tale. Irrespective of the truth behind the mysterious start, touching the badge transports Neku from the 'Realground' into a parallel universe known as the 'Underground' – a world where Neku is invisible to the Realworld Shibuya civilians but can read everybody's mind.

The situation quickly escalates from there. Slimy creatures called Noise also live in the Underground and congregate in areas where the Realground citizens' negative energies are the strongest. They're deadly beasts and Neku must slay them all to win the week-long games he's enrolled in. Fail to pass the games' tasks and Neku is erased from existence forever.

Games, you say? Er, yes – that part's thrown out there rather quickly. To cut a tangled story short, much to his confusion (and our amusement) Neku ends up taking part in seven-day games to fight for his survival. Orders are sent via text to his mobile phone (very modern!) and older teenagers called Reapers are on hand to oversee everything. The Reapers' standout feature? They're all menacing hoodies. Ooh-er!

Neku eventually grows stronger and with great power comes no responsibility. At the start of the game, he's a lonely, confused fifteen-year-old who only cares about the music track currently pumping out of his headphones. By the end of *TWEWY*, he'll be plucking thoughts out of one person's mind and implanting them in another, and psychically moving Ouija boards to influence the characters in the Realworld. He'll also be playing dress-up. (Paying attention to each Shibuya sub-district's fashion trends and dressing appropriately results in stat boosts.)

So far so confusing, and unfortunately there's a little more strangeness to plough through yet. Before you can say 'ASBO', *TWEWY* reveals that Noise exists on two planes of existence at any one time, and the only way to defeat them is to team up with another character and fight the Noise at one location each.

Here *TWEWY* really makes the most of the Nintendo DS's features – beginning with the two screens – and starts claiming its place in Must Play territory. One battle takes place on the top screen and the other on the bottom, and it asks you to manage both simultaneously. It's called the Stride Cross Battle System: the bottom screen is managed by rubbing the stylus around, the top screen is handled by tapping the DS D-Pad rhythmically in specific directions. Stylus strokes move Neku and attack the Noise, D-Pad presses trigger combos for your partner.

To add more complications into the mix, the two fighters toss a magical frisbee to one another. Timing each attack with the frisbee's movement builds up combo power and deals more damage. It's a lot to juggle at once and *TWEWY* definitely neglects to usher beginners in gently.

The hardware maximisation doesn't end there. Neku gains extra experience relative to time passed on the DS's internal clock, so any tough areas are made progressively easier with breaks in gaming. The wireless mode, meanwhile, not only lets you trade items with other *TWEWY* players, but factors in how many DS consoles are in close proximity and hands out bonuses irrespective of the games the nearby users are playing.

Development collaborations can sometimes be risky business: one project split across two different studios can end up being pushed and pulled in opposite directions, resulting in a confused and diluted game. Part of *TWEWY*'s craziness stems from spreading production over two separate teams, each with a hand in shaping the game. Fortunately, its resulting zaniness is almost entirely positive. Both conceptually and mechanically, *TWEWY* is a game that flies in the face of everything that's gone before, and is a rare RPG in that there's genuinely not another title in history that's similar. In years to come, it'll be a certified collector's item.

☻ ☻ ☻

WORLD OF WARCRAFT

Release date: 2005 (2004) | Platform: PC |
Developer: Blizzard Entertainment

11.5 MILLION GAMERS can't be wrong. At least, that's what *Warcraft* creator Blizzard Entertainment likes to preach. 11.5 million real people logging in to the virtual world known as Azaroth on a daily basis to improve their own character through fighting monsters, interacting with other humans, gathering resources and battling more monsters. On paper, many of the standard massively multiplayer online role-playing game (MMORPG) features read like a cure for insomnia. In practice, well, 11.5 million gamers *can't* be that wrong, surely.

It all starts innocently enough at level one. You create a hero fighting for either the Alliance or Horde faction, and choose their type. From the fire-hurling Mage and shape-shifting Druid, to the demon-summoning Warlock and hard-hitting Warrior, every class brings with it a unique set of abilities that will help you in your future endeavours as a *World of Warcraft* citizen.

And then you take your first steps into Azaroth. It's not long before you realise just how World of Warcraft has enthralled so many. It's a labour of love. The visuals have been so finely tuned that, regardless of its now-dated polygon counts, the locations still emanate a real sense of beauty (helped out massively by a gorgeous lighting engine). It's a credit to Blizzard Entertainment's craft that temples *feel* old, Night Elf woodland sparkles with magic, and Scourge-pillaged towns (Scourge are undead) are visibly drained of life.

And that's *WoW*'s not-so-hard-to-spot secret. Everything about the game screams quality, and it's Blizzard Entertainment's attention to detail that propels it into many gamers' hearts. Every corner of the world is home to something new to investigate. Sometimes it's a link back to *Warcraft*'s early days as a real-time strategy, sometimes it's a particularly good quest line, and other times it's simply a funny pop-culture reference.

It would be for nothing without a game to base these details on, and luckily *World of Warcraft*'s skeleton is a sturdy one. There's repetition and legwork galore, and your path up the ranks isn't the fastest experience in gaming, but ultimately the *World of Warcraft* journey is what keeps those 11.5 million people logging on to the servers every night. The story steadily introduces new abilities and game mechanics across its seemingly never-ending timeline. Certain new skills are useful, some are less so, while character professions add depth to your avatar and encourage that all-important social aspect.

It's the multiplayer interaction that takes the core *World of Warcraft* adventuring and elevates it to greatness. The unpredictable human encounters add a layer of spontaneity you just don't see outside of MMORPGs. Jigsaw-snug combinations between different character classes mean working with other players is always a satisfying experience – an important feature considering *World of Warcraft* thrives on cooperative play.

The game comes alive when you join a 'guild' of players. You'll forge friendships and rivalries, help and be helped by others, march in armies to take on towering foes and find yourself written into the *WoW* history books by playing a part in world-shifting expeditions and raids.

And then there are all the other ingredients that make up the whole; the compulsive, Pokémon-like 'vanity pet' collection, the player vs. player battlegrounds and arenas, the seasonal holidays, the fishing, the cooking, the rare-gear drops... The world is crammed with hundreds of hours of entertainment and it even comes with an achievement list designed purely to make any completionist cry.

World of Warcraft's reach extends far outside the gaming world. Spin-off novels, mangas, board games, an upcoming film from Sam '*Evil Dead* and *Spider-Man*' Raimi and an entire *South Park* episode proves the MMO has hit the big time. The game almost single-handedly spawned gaming rehab clinics: a sign it's been doing something right... *ish*.

But explaining all the ins and outs of *WoW*'s features would double and possibly treble the length of this book. You don't need to know everything, though. Just know this: 11.5 million gamers can't be wrong.

👾 👾 👾

WORMS

Release date: 1995 | Platform: Commodore Amiga | Developer: Team17

IF YOU HAD to pick an animal – any animal – to arm with Uzis and cluster bombs and star in a brutal war game, what would you pick? A shark, maybe? It's certainly vicious enough, although the water situation might be a bit of an issue. A gorilla, then? An obvious choice, perhaps, given its intelligence. Whatever it may be, though, we're betting an earthworm wouldn't be your first choice.

But it was Team17's first choice when it looked to follow in the footsteps of artillery-based strategy games like *Artillery*, *Artillery Duel* and *Scorched Earth*. (And oddly enough it was Shiny Entertainment's pick a year previously with *Earthworm Jim*.) Vertebrates be damned – *Worms*' angry but oh-so-funny stars have proven to be better than any other creature on the planet.

The game pits up to sixteen worms against each other in a team-based last-worm-standing duel to the death. Battles take place in randomly generated two-dimensional levels, with teams evenly spread across the undulating terrain. Everybody takes it in turns to control one worm at a time and has a strict time limit to move and perform a single action, be it building or tunnelling or taking a shot at an opponent or three. Hearing your friends beg and plead for mercy is an irreplaceable feeling. *Worms* thrives on the short-lived truces and the double-crossings of friends playing together, trying to convince one another to attack certain players. Judas acts aren't soon forgiven...

While later *Worms* games introduce hall-of-fame-worthy weapons like the Holy Hand Grenade, the Concrete Donkey and the (exploding!) Old Woman, the original sticks with the basics. Bazookas, grenades, shotguns and dynamite are the main go-to tools of death, although the odd sheep is known to blow up on occasion. Every weapon has a maximum damage limit below a worm's starting health, and the aim is of course to eradicate every enemy worm before your team is nothing but a pile of headstones.

Weapon damage eats away at the mine-strewn landscape, creating craters and caverns to trap worms inside and make it easier to get grenades on target. Wind direction also evolves along with the landscape: the air currents change with every turn, and an ill-judged bazooka shot could very well be blown off course and straight down the gullet of a teammate.

Most levels are surrounded by water and, if you've ever seen a worm work its way to the surface during a rainstorm, you'll know they aren't the biggest fans of the wet stuff. The smartest tactics either involve angling a shot so the worm on the wrong end of an explosion will be propelled into the drink, or blasting a hole in the bottom of a level and creating a drowning pool of your own. Expertly negotiating tricky terrain with ninja ropes before prodding an enemy over a cliff and into the sea with a poke of the index finger (apparently worms have digits) is a kill to gloat about. Expertly negotiating tricky terrain with ninja ropes before *trying* to prod an enemy over a cliff, only to discover they're not close enough to the edge, is as humiliating as it gets – and always ends up with a stick of dynamite to blast you into the ocean in return.

Worms is like that, though. Failures are just as enjoyable as successes. The old saying 'it's not the winning, it's the taking part that counts' really does apply to *Worms*, because every round is a lottery and you could easily get stuck with tricky starting positions on horrible maps. Yet rounds are short and they're uproariously funny regardless of the outcome. If you accidentally bazooka yourself, it's OK – everybody who's ever played *Worms* has done it a hundred times before. You'll shake it off and pray the next misfortune happens to someone else. *Worms* has that carefree effect on its players which is why, five console cycles later, the series is still going strong.

And how to play them all...

Animal Crossing: Wild World
Readily available to buy

Baldur's Gate
Available to buy on PC from GOG.com

Batman: Arkham Asylum
Readily available to buy

Bayonetta
Readily available to buy

Beyond Good & Evil
High definition remake coming to PlayStation 3's PSN service and Xbox 360 Live Marketplace. Original available to buy on PC from GOG.com

Braid
Readily available to buy from Xbox 360 Live Marketplace

Burnout 3: Takedown
Readily available to buy as an Xbox Original from Xbox 360 Live Marketplace

Call of Duty 4: Modern Warfare
Readily available to buy

Civilization
Now 'abandonware' (eBay)

Counter-Strike: Source
Available to buy from Steam website

Dancing Stage
Most local arcades (version varies)

Defender
eBay as part of *Midway Arcade Treasures* (Xbox 360 Live Marketplace
version was pulled due to liquidation of copyright-holder Midway)

Demon's Souls
Readily available to buy

Deus Ex
Available to buy from Steam website

Diablo
Available to buy from select retailers online

Donkey Kong
Available to buy from Wii's Virtual Console service

Doom
Ultimate edition available to buy from idsoftware.com (Xbox 360
version has been de-listed from Xbox 360 Live Marketplace)

The Elder Scrolls IV: Oblivion
Game of the Year Edition readily available to buy

Elite
Available to download from Ian Bell's website

EVE Online
Available to buy from the official website

F-Zero GX
eBay

Final Fantasy VII
Available to buy from PlayStation 3's PSN service

Forza Motorsport 3
Readily available to buy

Geometry Wars: Retro Evolved 2
Readily available to buy from Xbox 360 Live Marketplace

God Hand
Available to buy online

God of War
Remastered version available to buy as part of the PlayStation 3 God of War: Collection

GoldenEye 007
eBay

Grand Theft Auto: Vice City
Available to buy from Steam website

Half-Life 2
Available to buy from Steam website (or part of the Orange Box)

Halo: Combat Evolved
Available to buy as an Xbox Original from Xbox 360 Live Marketplace

Hearts of Iron II
Available to buy online

Hitman: Blood Money
Available to buy online and in some stores

Ico
Remastered version available as part of Ico and Shadow of the Colossus collection on PlayStation 3

Ikaruga
Remastered version available to buy from Xbox 360 Live Marketplace

IL-2 Sturmovik: Birds of Prey
Available to buy online

Katamari Damacy
Not available in the UK – sequels *We Love Katamari* (PlayStation 2)
or *Katamari Forever* (PlayStation 3) available to buy online

Left 4 Dead
Readily available to buy, best bought from Steam website

The Legend of Zelda: Four Swords Adventures
Available to buy online for Game Boy Advance as part of *The Legend
of Zelda: Link to the Past/Four Swords* pack

The Legend of Zelda: Ocarina of Time
Available to buy from Wii's Virtual Console service

Lemmings
Available to buy online for PlayStation Portable or to download
(a slightly inferior port) from PlayStation 3's PSN service

Limbo
Readily available to buy from Xbox 360 Live Marketplace
Little Big Planet

LocoRoco
Readily available to buy

Mega Man 2
Available to buy from Wii's Virtual Console service, PlayStation 3's
PSN service and iPhone

Metal Gear Solid
Available to buy from PlayStation 3's PSN service

Metroid Prime
Modified version available to buy online as part of Wii game *Metroid Prime: Trilogy*

Micro Machines
eBay

Myst
Masterpiece edition available to buy from GOG.com

N
Available to download from official website

NiGHTS into Dreams...
eBay

No More Heroes
Available to buy online

Oddworld: Stranger's Wrath
Remastered version coming for PlayStation 3

Pac-Man Vs.
Available to buy pre-owned (usually on eBay) as part of *Namco Museum DS*

Paperboy
eBay as part of *Midway Arcade Treasures* (as Xbox 360 Live Marketplace version was pulled due to liquidation of copyright holder Midway)

Peggle
Available to buy from Steam website

Phoenix Wright: Ace Attorney
Readily available to buy on Nintendo DS, iPhone and Wii via Nintendo's
WiiWare service

Picross 3D
Readily available to buy

Plants vs. Zombies
Available to buy from Steam website, for iPad or enhanced version
available from Xbox 360 Live Marketplace

Pokémon Red/Blue
eBay

Portal
Available to buy from Steam website (or part of the Orange Box)

Prince of Persia: Sands of Time
Remastered version available on PlayStation 3 as part of Prince
of Persia Trilogy: HD Classics. Original available to buy from
GOG.com

Puzzle Quest: Challenge of the Warlords
Readily available to buy from Xbox 360 Live Marketplace

Resident Evil 2
Available to buy from the American branch of the PlayStation 3
PSN service using an American account

Resident Evil 4
Upgraded Wii version readily available to buy

Rez
Enhanced high-definition version available to buy from Xbox 360
Live Marketplace

Rock Band 3
Readily available to buy

The Secret of Monkey Island
Enhanced version (with classic options) available to buy from
Xbox 360 Live Marketplace, PlayStation 3 PSN service, iPhone
and iPad

Sensible World of Soccer
Available to buy from Xbox 360 Live Marketplace

Shadow of the Colossus
Remastered version available as part of Ico and Shadow of the
Colossus collection on PlayStation 3

Shenmue
eBay

Silent Hill 2
Available pre-owned in many game stores and on eBay

SimCity 2000
Available to buy online

The Sims
Available to buy online

Sonic the Hedgehog CD
Available on eBay as part of *Sonic Gems Collection* for GameCube and
PlayStation 2

Soulcalibur
Readily available to buy from Xbox 360 Live Marketplace

Space Invaders
Available on iPhone

Splinter Cell: Chaos Theory
Remastered version available as part of Splinter Cell Trilogy: HD
Classics on PlayStation 3. Available to buy as an Xbox Original from
Xbox 360 Live Marketplace. PC version (for easy Spies vs. Mercs
greatness) available to buy from Steam website

Starcraft
Available to buy from the official Blizzard website

Star Wars: Knights of the Old Republic
PC version available to buy from Steam website

Super Bomberman
Very tough to track down. However, the similar title *Bomberman '94*
is available to buy from Wii's Virtual Console service

Super Mario Galaxy
Readily available to buy

Super Mario Kart
Available to buy from Wii's Virtual Console service

Super Mario World
Available to buy from Wii's Virtual Console service

Super Metroid
Available to buy from Wii's Virtual Console service

Super Monkey Ball
Available on iPhone and eBay

Super Street Fighter IV
Readily available to buy

System Shock 2
Very tough to track down now. eBay occasionally comes up trumps

Tempest
Available on the PC and Xbox 360 via the Microsoft Game Room arcade service

Tetris
Available on almost every platform in some form or other. Enhanced version Tetris DS available online for Nintendo DS

Time Crisis II
Still exists in some arcades. PlayStation 2 version is available pre-owned and online but is a poor second to the big-screen arcade version...

Tomb Raider Anniversary
Available to buy online

Tony Hawk's Pro Skater 3
eBay

Uplink
Available to buy from the official website

Vib-Ribbon
eBay

WarioWare, Inc: Minigame Mania
eBay – Wii and DS versions are different but much, much easier to find

Way of the Samurai
eBay

Wii Sports
Comes free with every Wii

The World Ends With You
Tough to find new – can be found in some store pre-owned sections and on eBay

World of Warcraft
Readily available to buy

Worms
Enhanced version available to buy on iPad, Xbox 360 Live Marketplace and PlayStation 3's PSN service